WASHINGTON IRVING AND THE HOUSE OF MURRAY

Washington

rving and the House of Murray

GEOFFREY CRAYON CHARMS THE BRITISH, 1817–1856

BEN HARRIS McCLARY, EDITOR

THE UNIVERSITY OF TENNESSEE PRESS : KNOXVILLE

Library of Congress Catalog Card Number 73–77843
Standard Book Number 87049–094–x

For THE GREENS,
Mrs. G. M., Philip, and John, whose classic establishment at 19 West
Hill Place, Brighton, Sussex, is the setting of some
of our fondest English memories

Styled the First Man of American Literature and the Literary Ambassador from the New World to the Old, Washington Irving is still, in spite of his exalted titles, one of the most imperfectly understood figures in his national literature. The antiquarian fact of his historic position is undenied, but his intrinsic value as a writer has been questioned by discerning critics from the beginning of his career. It is likely—I have urged elsewhere[1]—that his ultimate significance is not in his work published for public consumption, but rather in his relationships with individuals within the profession of letters. Because of his acquaintance with most of the interesting literary people of his time, his personal papers sometimes read like a Boswellian notebook. He offers us in his voluminous letters and detailed journals and, indirectly, through the written reactions to him by his contemporaries a guide to the cultural climate in which he lived.

The extant file of the writer's letters to his first official British publisher, presented here, is an entrée for us into the sanctum of the major English-language publisher (rivaled only by Constable in Edinburgh) of the first half of the last century. Fifty-eight of these letters are previously unpublished; portions of four letters and the entire text of five have been used in studies of either Irving or John Murray II. These sixty-eight letters provide the framework for a close look at the relationship of the author and

[1] "Irving's Literary Midwifery: Five Unpublished Letters from British Repositories," *Philological Quarterly*, XLVI (April 1967), 277–83.

vii

his publisher, the result being the most thorough study yet completed of Irving's connections with a single person or firm. Any real understanding of Irving's life after the London publication of *The Sketch Book* in 1820 must begin at 50 Albemarle Street, for—as this work shows—John Murray II (despite the opinions of certain American literature scholars) meant more to Washington Irving's professional life than any other person.

The first American writer to be a notable success in Britain, Irving understood that the very fact of his foreign reputation contributed to the size and worth of his reading public in the United States. Political independence and republicanism notwithstanding, the British could still influence the American public in its reading habits. Adding to Irving's prestige in the United States—as well as in Great Britain—at the start of his transatlantic career was the most valued status symbol to which an author could aspire: the name of John Murray on his published works. This imprint, declared George Haven Putnam of the firm which was Irving's final official American publisher, "was accepted as stamping a book with literary importance." [2] This meant a growing reputation and more money for the author in America, where he was fully protected by national copyright laws.

In addition to these highly desirable indirect results for Irving at home, there were in England direct advantages to being published by Murray, not the least of which was the generous payment he received for copyrights. Putnam estimated that the English payments, at least during the earlier years, had been more important to Irving than those he had secured from American sales.[3] One must remember that any amount Irving could get for a British copyright of his work was, in a sense, extra money, for the absence of international copyright laws left foreign authors (Americans in Britain, British in America), except in unusual cases, at the mercy of pirate publishers, but such publishers in

2 *WI: His Life and Work* [New York: Putnam's, 1903], p. 14.
3 George Haven Putnam, *George Palmer Putnam: A Memoir* (New York: G. P. Putnam's Sons, 1912), p. 126.

England were not so apt to tamper with a title produced under the imprint of an established firm like Murray's. Other American writers (Cooper and Bryant come immediately to mind) tried to make this illustrious connection but failed to secure a workable alliance of any duration. Irving clung tenaciously to Murray until, encouraged by his past successes, he bluffed too hard in 1831 and lost his foothold at 50 Albemarle Street. By that time, however, he was getting ready to return to America, and the advantage of being a part of Murray's coterie, a side benefit for Murray's authors, was no longer an inducement, although fourteen years earlier Irving might have considered this a prime reason for seeking Murray's patronage. Further, Irving could have argued (his mouth betraying the sour grapes) that Richard Bentley, the rising publisher to whom he turned when he broke with Murray, was usurping some of Murray's old publishing magic and that social life at 50 Albemarle Street had lost some of its luster.[4]

To keep things in perspective, then, the reader should remember that when Irving negotiated with Murray he was bargaining for more than immediate financial reward. The British pounds, naturally, were important (a large part of them were spent absorbing the shock of ill-advised speculation in business), but the *ton* which the Murray association gave the climbing American was equally important. This psychological or environmental advantage, extending into Irving's last years, when he was still wont to drop for effect the names of "old Murray" and the drawing-room regulars into his conversations, is the thread of this story. For a full study of Irving or Murray, the reader must consult the standard biographies.[5] This is only a chapter, though it is, as Stanley T. Williams commented, "an interesting chapter in the history of publication by American authors abroad."[6]

[4] Edward Bulwer in *England and the English* identified John Murray's "Authors' *clique* of Albemarle Street" as a thing of the past. His publisher was, significantly, Bentley (1833, I, 147–48).

[5] See Bibliography, Sections II and III.

[6] *WI and the Storrows: Letters from England and the Continent, 1821–1828* (Cambridge: Harvard University Press, 1933), p. 93, n. 1.

I. Transcription of Text

When Washington Irving chose to write with care, his letters could look like examples from a calligrapher's handbook. Unfortunately, however, his carefully penned epistles are the exception rather than the rule—and especially among those which he "dashed off" (the many words which dwindle into wavy lines demand the use of this term) to the John Murrays. If no man is a hero to his valet, surely no author (in those days of valets and handwritten copy) believed he could impress his publisher by the penmanship of his communications. Perhaps this explains why the collection of Irving's manuscript letters at 50 Albemarle Street often leaves much to be desired in readability and unity of style.

Under the best conditions, the job of turning a handwritten character into a mechanical letter of type can be difficult and occasionally arbitrary. A transcriber must attempt to preserve the all-important spirit of the original and, at the same time, seek to achieve complete clarity of meaning. The latter is easy when compared with the near impossibility of the former. For example, how does one show the haste Irving displayed so dramatically by his words which turned into wiggling dashes on the page?

The following rules were used in an effort to provide the best possible printed text from the frequently erratic script of the writer.

1. All sentences and fragments are begun with capital letters and ended with periods or other appropriate punctuation marks. Irving sometimes was deficient in these matters.

2. In general, capitalization is made to conform with standards which produce an easily understandable text.

3. Apostrophes are added to the possessives and contractions, a nicety Irving rarely observed.

4. Most of the abbreviations originally appeared with final superscript letters. No attempt has been made to reproduce them in this extremely artificial fashion. Further, no periods have been inserted editorially after the abbreviations. Some of the irregular ab-

breviations have been standardized, using Irving's most frequent forms.

5. Book titles are given as they appeared in the manuscripts; if there is confusion, they are identified in appropriate footnotes.

6. Material quoted by Irving is enclosed in quotation marks following conventional modern form.

7. Whenever possible, Irving is given the benefit of the doubt in his spelling. When there is no doubt about a misspelled word, the usually preferred spelling is given in brackets on the occasion of the first misspelling. Contemporary spellings, however, such as *controul* and *negociating*, which can be found in newspapers and other writings of the period, are preserved without any notations.

8. All editorial additions within the text are enclosed in brackets and, if necessary, footnoted.

9. Irving's deletions are not recorded. The few which were decipherable seemed to add nothing to the text.

10. The punctuation and arrangement of headings and complimentary closes have been standardized, conforming to Irving's usual practices.

11. Many of the manuscript letters bear the addressee's name in the lower left corner of the first sheet. This is dropped in favor of the editorial practice described in Section II, below.

II. Editorial Contributions

This is a study of the Irving-Murray relationship—not a full biographical look at either of the men. Yet, to preserve a continuity of background, it is often necessary to supply passages covering periods when the author and the heads of the publishing house were not associated in any direct way. The editorial work is designed mainly to identify and explain the position and meaning of individual letters and to evaluate this collection of letters in terms of its significance in the Anglo-American publishing world of its time.

The Introduction and the running commentary provide a background into which the individual letters fit, giving a panoramic view of the relationship of the American author with his English publisher. In form this work is patterned after the nineteenth-century life-and-letters biographies, of which Pierre M. Irving's study of his uncle is a classic example. To the basic text, however, another dimension has been added in the form of seven vignettes, each serving as the introduction to a chapter. These opening sections, although based on facts drawn from the personal writings of Irving and his contemporaries, from newspaper items, and from manuscript records, are sometimes imaginative in minor details; their over-all validity, however, is defended by a source note at the end of each passage.

Each letter has been given an arabic numeral which is followed by the name of the addressee. Although most of the letters were directed to John Murray II (and the others to John Murray III), the repetition provides a uniformity of presentation which seems desirable. Immediately after the name, if circumstances require it, a footnote provides the following information: (*a*) the location of the manuscript, if other than the Murray Archives; (*b*) bibliographical references to any previous publication of the item; (*c*) descriptive comments on the physical appearance of the letter; and (*d*) endorsements made at 50 Albemarle Street, if they are of any interest.

On April 4, 1827, Irving wrote to John Murray II: "I am heartily glad you . . . are once more at your classic establishment in Albemarle Street; which will do more for your fortune and honourable reputation than any other residence or concern" (Letter 20). Irving's reference was to the fact that the Murray family had moved back to their Albemarle Street residence-business house after living for a period of several years near Whitehall. Clearly for the American there was a mystique about the place. Almost one hundred and forty years later, when I completed the research for this volume, 50 Albemarle Street was still that same "classic establishment," and the charm had grown stronger, enhanced by the passage of time and the publication from that address of many epoch-making books ranging from Charles Darwin's *Origin of Species* to C. Northcote Parkinson's *Law*. John Murray was still there too. This gentleman, the great-grandson of Irving's first John Murray, had been knighted in 1932, an honor his father had also earned, for exemplary service to the literary world.

To the House of Murray and especially to the late Sir John Murray V, whose death on October 6, 1967, marked the end of another publishing chapter, I owe many thanks for the pleasant and memorable days I spent at 50 Albemarle Street and for permission to transcribe and publish the Irving manuscript correspondence file preserved there.

A few Irving letters had escaped from the official file, mostly cover letters given by a previous John Murray to a few leading American libraries to use for signature displays. All known copies of these letters have been sought out, and to their present owners, as indicated in the notes, I express my appreciation for permission to use their material.

In the world of American literary scholarship probably no figure of the past has come more dramatically alive in recent months than Washington Irving. Since the completion of the basic research for this edition, a volume has appeared which vividly illustrates this fact. William L. Hedges' *Washington Irving: An American Study, 1802–1832* (Baltimore: The Johns Hopkins Press, 1965) is the first major attempt by the present younger generation to evaluate the writer both in terms of such contemporary frames of critical reference as Freudian implications and social consciousness and with regard to his American milieu.

Further evidence of the vitality of Irving scholarship is the Irving Editorial Board, a group of scholars, headed by Professor Henry A. Pochmann of the University of Wisconsin, working on a "Definitive Edition" of the author's writings to be published by the press of the chairman's university. To the Irving Editorial Board I express my thanks, for such a body of scholars creates a psychical *esprit de corps* which is invigorating and vital to sound scholarship.

Irving had his Navarrete *(Life of Columbus)* and his Forster *(Goldsmith: A Biography);* Irving scholars have their Stanley T. Williams, the seemingly indefatigable biographer, whose *Life of Washington Irving* (New York: Oxford University Press, 1935) probably will remain the basic tool for studying the writer's life. Intended as a "definitive" biography, the work is a storehouse of Irving lore—especially the copious notes at the end of each of the two volumes. Recently, Edward Wagenknecht *(Washington Irving: Moderation Displayed* [New York: Oxford University Press, 1962], p. viii) suggested (more in amusement than in censure) that Williams' judgment was occasionally tempered by a growing not-very-favorable personal opinion of Irving. Indeed, Williams may have wearied of his task, but having committed himself to the project, he saw it through to its conclusion. Whatever his private feelings, Williams prepared a masterly work. Future biographers may surpass his admirable effort, but only because they will have Williams' spadework and scores of recent studies on individual aspects of Irving's life (the present edition being an example) upon which to draw.

Sometime before the death of Sir John Murray IV in 1928, Williams visited 50 Albemarle Street, where he talked with the head of the firm and read most of the letters published here. From certain letters he made notes which he used in the biography of 1935, but the pressure of time and other concerns made it impossible for him to make a careful analysis of the material in London. Consequently, Williams' treatment of the Irving-Murray relationship is, at best, weak. For Irving's general background and for clues to far-flung sources of pertinent material, however, I am heavily indebted to the labors of this great literary historian.

The Murrays have not yet received the biographical coverage which they deserve, though two well-known literary figures have written histories relating to various periods of the firm's past: Samuel Smiles, *A Publisher and His Friends: Memoir and Correspondence of the Late John Murray, 1778–1843* (London: JM, 1891), and George Paston, *At John Murray's: Records of a Literary Circle, 1843–1892* (London: JM, 1932). Smiles, in his *Autobiography* (London: JM, 1905), described the former book as "a sort of drag-horse business" (p. 401) and "a very heavy undertaking" (p. 408). Sifting through the Murrays' vast collection of letters, he seems to have been—not surprisingly—almost overwhelmed by his task, letting several minor errors (some of which will be noted below) slip into his rather perversely organized work. Paston's book, which originally appeared in installments in Murray's *Cornhill Magazine* (N.S. LXIX [Aug.-Oct. 1930], 129–46, 280–97, 436–51), is pleasant reading, but there is still room, in fact a need, for a new look at the role played in nineteenth-century literature by this publishing house. In justice, however, I must say that without the particulars gleaned from the works of Smiles and Paston, this edition would have been virtually impossible within the time allotted for its preparation.

My major financial debt of thanks is to the United States Educational Commission in the United Kingdom (which in the middle of my two-year term became the United States-United Kingdom Educational Commission) whose grant (usually referred to as a "Fulbright") made possible my English years (1964–1966), during which this edition and other related scholarship were completed. The Executive Secretary of the Commission, Dr. D. P. Edgell, and his staff are faithful friends and advisors to United States students in England.

To President W. Earl Strickland and Dean Joseph B. James of Wesleyan College, I am indebted for a research grant which was used during the summer of 1967 to complete my research in this country, specifically for intensive research on elusive American references found in collections from Virginia to New York; the summer culminated in a memorable visit to Sunnyside. Further, the Wesleyan College financial assistance, as a supplement to grants relating to another research project from the American Philosophical Society and the American Council of Learned Societies, made more realistically possible an August 1967 sojourn in England, during which I reviewed once again the Murray manuscripts and had my last visit with Sir John Murray.

Special mention must be made of the encouragment and friendship which, in generous portions, I have had from Professor Marcus Cunliffe, University of Sussex, and Professors Richard Beale Davis and Nathalia Wright, University of Tennessee. These Anglo-American scholars have contributed to the development of this book since it was in the first planning stage. Professor Howell Daniel, Institute of United States Studies, University College, London, read it in the early manuscript version and made pertinent suggestions which are reflected in this text. In Rottingdean, Sussex, Miss Joan Van Wart, the granddaughter of Irving Van Wart, was gracious with her hospitality and generous with her interest in this project. Finally, to my friend Mrs. Edna

Crawford I owe a debt of thanks for the clerical assistance which she so willingly gave in the preparation of the final typescript.

To several libraries I wish to record my appreciation of assistance. In Great Britain: British Museum; Public Record Office; Stationers' Hall; National Library of Scotland; John Rylands Library; university libraries of London, Manchester, and Sussex; public libraries of Brighton, Birmingham, Manchester, and Westminster. In the United States: Library of Congress; Henry E. Huntington Library; Pierpont Morgan Library; The Sleepy Hollow Restorations; university libraries of Columbia, Harvard, Princeton, Rochester (New York), Virginia, and Yale; Scripps College Libraries; public libraries of New York and Philadelphia.

BEN HARRIS MCCLARY

Wesleyan College
Macon, Georgia
October 1968

CONTENTS

ILLUSTRATIONS

Washington Irving to 1817

When Washington Irving[1] stepped over the threshold of 50 Albemarle Street on August 16, 1817, he was not nearly so young as he looked (he was, in fact, thirty-four), and his calm, disturbingly pretty face was a facade concealing—as his private writings show—a mind beset by personal doubts. During the previous months he had been forced to face personal problems which were quite out of his control, and in doing so he had been plunged into a deep mental depression which seemed by this time to be chronic.

The youngest of eleven children,[2] the first of whom had been born and had died before his parents left England for the British colonies in America, Washington Irving, from his earliest memories, was drawn to the country of his ancestry. His parents settled in New York, beginning their family again in 1764 with a son, William, who died within a year. In 1766 another son, also named William, was born. This was the eldest brother who would mean so much to Washington in later years. The next child died in infancy, but the seven brothers and sisters who followed him lived to mature adulthood. As American patriots, the Irvings weathered

[1] Section II of the Bibliography is devoted to autobiographical sources and biographical studies of WI. Information generally available in those references will not be footnoted.

[2] Stanley T. Williams included a fairly complete genealogical table of the Irving brothers and sisters and their descendants in *The Life of Washington Irving* (New York: Oxford University Press, 1935), II, following 254. Hereinafter cited as STW.

the Revolution, and before word reached New York of the sign-
ing of the peace treaty of that war, the family group was made
complete by the birth of Washington on April 3, 1783.

The baby in this family of good-natured older children learned
from birth to depend on his four brothers and three sisters. For
Washington, appearing when brother William was already actively contributing to the financial welfare of the family, life
would always—on the surface at least—be easier than for the other
children. Though the family was decidedly not a part of New
York's smart provincial aristocracy, it had risen to a position of
prominence both professionally and intellectually by the time
Washington reached his teens. Through diligent effort his father,
with the help of the brothers, had succeeded in the mercantile
business, and the older sons had become active in social life,
partly by associating themselves with certain self-styled literary
groups.

Among the family which radiated so much love for its youngest member—the mother whom he revered above all other people
and brothers and sisters who were willing to focus their affections
on him—"Deacon" William Irving, the narrowly religious father,
loomed like a fearful dragon in fairyland. Young Washington,
like the other children, was baptised into the Presbyterian Church
and condemned to Calvinistic Sundays devoted to Bible passages,
Watts' hymns, and *Pilgrim's Progress*. In later years, remembering his earliest lessons of life, he wrote: "When I was young, I was
led to think that somehow or other every thing that was pleasant
was wicked." [3]

The atmosphere of devotion in which the child developed produced, not unnaturally, an individual of extreme sensitivities. He
was undersized and considered, even by his grim father, to be
precocious. Because of his sensibility and because of an innate
pleasantness about his face and personality, Washington began
to work on his family the special magic that he would use
throughout his life.

[3] Pierre M. Irving, *The Life and Letters of Washington Irving* (New York:
G. P. Putnam, 1864), I, 25. Hereinafter cited as PMI.

His formal schooling, which began when he was five, first in a small kindergarten and then for nine long years in the establishment of Benjamin Romaine, was characteristic of the time and his record was as undistinguished as a concerned family might fear for a "precocious" child. College (Columbia College, of course) apparently never entered the family's mind as a possibility for Washington after his tenure with Romaine, even though his brothers John Treat and Peter had been successful students there. The fifteen-year-old lad had no potential as a scholar; on this everyone was in agreement.

"Deacon" Irving had wished that at least one of his sons would enter the ministry. One by one each had failed him. Washington was his last hope—and his least.

In 1799 Washington began his struggle with law, a battle he waged spasmodically for twelve years. After sampling the fare in two law offices, he settled in 1802 under the care of Attorney-General Josiah Ogden Hoffman. In the meantime, brothers William and Ebenezer had established themeselves as figures in New York's commercial world. Peter, while pining after literature, had become a physician, and John Treat had been launched on what would be a distinguished law career.

The significance of Washington's move to the office of Hoffman was not that it furthered his law career but that it brought him into contact with the girl who, except for her premature death, presumably would have been Mrs. Washington Irving. At that time, however, Matilda Hoffman was only ten years old, and in the gay social relationship which Irving shared with the Hoffman family it was his patron's young (second) wife, Maria Fenno Hoffman, who was the focal point of his attention.[4] Even so, these were probably rather monotonous months, broken only in 1803 by his adventures when he accompanied the Hoffmans, including Mrs. Hoffman's two step-daughters Ann and Matilda, on a business trip into Canada.[5]

[4] WI's New York male friends (and WI) jokingly referred to Mrs. Hoffman as his "mistress" for the next decade. See WI's letter to "Quoz" [James K. Paulding or Henry Brevoort], Bordeaux, July 20, 1804, quoted in STW, I, 51.

[5] This trip he described in a notebook edited by Stanley T. Williams and pub-

Peter's medical career was drawing to a close. In 1802 he became proprietor and editor of the New York *Morning Chronicle*, in which on November 15 of that year appeared the first installment of the "Letters of Jonathan Oldstyle, Gent." These amatuerish essays, nine in number, dealing with the theater and New York society and written, no doubt, at the request of Peter, marked the beginning of Washington Irving's literary career.[6]

Early in 1804 Washington was the object of much concern by his family and friends. For almost six years he had been at the law (and seemed no nearer the bar examination than when he started); but, more important, his health was visibly failing. What he needed to stop his hacking cough was a sea voyage; so the four brothers pooled their resources and sent him, for reasons of health, on a tour. He sailed for Europe on May 19, 1804; he was twenty-one years old.

The France into which he disembarked was engaged under Napoleon in the first year of its great struggle with England, but Irving knew little and saw less of the military activities.[7] He was a young adventurer in a strange land; intellectual improvement was not, in his mind, the reason for this trip. His letters back home spoke of "Bordeaux bells" [belles] and the local theater, but they also contained long sections devoted to the friends he left behind him.[8] He fell in naturally with other Americans along his way. On October 20, having reluctantly abandoned Bordeaux after slightly more than a month, Irving arrived in Genoa where he remained until almost Christmas, the attraction there being, not

---

lished as *Journal of Washington Irving, 1803* (New York: Oxford University Press, 1934).

[6] Judged painfully juvenile by modern standards (STW, I, 36–40), these "letters" excited considerable admiration among WI's contemporaries. See Aaron Burr to his daughter Theodosia, January 29, 1804, in M. L. Davis, ed., *Memoirs of Aaron Burr, with Miscellaneous Sections of His Correspondence* (New York: Harper & Bros., 1837), II, 274. These items did not appear in book form until WI's popularity as a writer had been firmly established in the 1820's.

[7] On January 31, 1803, WI reported in his journal the sighting of Nelson's *Victory* and other English ships patroling the Mediterranean. Thus, WI saw the beginning of the battle which would ultimately end at Trafalgar on October 21, 1805. STW, I, 61.

[8] STW quoted a typical letter, I, 48–52.

historical or artistic interests, but the charming British and American colony.

Because his brothers had insisted that he see Sicily, he sailed on December 21 aboard the *Matilda* for Messina. What he had expected to be a quiet Christmas excursion became one of the most exciting episodes of his life when the *Matilda* was captured and ransacked by pirates who, fortunately, chose to spare the lives of all of the people, allowing the ship to proceed to its destination.

On March 7 Irving returned to Italy, to Naples, where he explored the city for two weeks with a new friend, Virginian Joseph C. Cabell, before moving with him to Rome. There Irving began his long friendship with Washington Allston, the American painter. From Rome, Irving and Cabell set their course for Paris, where, once again, they settled into an American colony. Living in the Hôtel d'Angleterre, Irving observed and took part in the activities for which Paris and its women had (he noted) a justified reputation.[9] After four months, on September 20, Irving and two American friends left for Brussels, from whence they moved to Rotterdam, ultimately crossing the channel to see the first of England from Gravesend.

In London, Irving lived off the Strand, attending the theater and making an excursion to Oxford, Bath, and Bristol. He was a tourist unheralded and unknown, his only brief plunge beneath the surface of London life resulting from a letter of introduction written by an American actress to an English actress at whose table he met actor Charles Kemble, years later to be a devoted English friend.[10] On January 17, 1806, Irving sailed from Graves-

---

[9] The Irving–Cabell relationship is discussed by Richard Beale Davis in "Washington Irving and Joseph C. Cabell," *English Studies in Honor of James Southall Wilson* (Charlottesville: University of Virginia Press, 1950), pp. 7–22. For WI's Paris adventures, see Stanley T. Williams, "Washington Irving's First Stay in Paris," *American Literature*, II (March 1930), 15–20.

[10] WI's first visit to London was far less exciting than he had expected it to be; letters of introduction to a variety of interesting people had been promised him by friends in the United States, "but these letters unfortunately miscarried, and the disappointment prevented him from fully enjoying the pleasures of a city . . . ." PMI, I, 162.

end, bound for New York, where he arrived on March 24 to resume his old life. He took back with him not only memories but a stack of notebooks filled with jottings concerning his travels, a practice he had initiated in 1803 on his trip to Canada with the Hoffmans.[11]

The hours in Hoffman's office may have moved slowly, but Irving's experiences outside that place contained enough excitement to keep his life interesting. This was the period when he was a member of the Lads of Kilkenny, a little social and literary group of male New Yorkers.[12] First they met to drink, eat, and talk in select public taverns, but eventually one of their number, Gouverneur Kemble, turned his mansion over to them, this becoming their "Cockloft Hall." Washington, his brother William, and William's brother-in-law James K. Paulding were the satirists, and to a plea from John Howard Payne for a "secret history of the times," [13] these men replied on January 24, 1807, with an anonymously published little pamphlet, *Salmagundi: or, The Whim-Whams and Opinions of Launcelot Langstaff, & Others.*[14] Issues of this tiny imprint continued to appear for the next thirteen months, each satirizing some aspect of contemporary Ameri-

[11] William P. Trent edited the European notebooks as *WI: Notes and Journals of Travel in Europe, 1804–1805* (New York: Grolier Club, 1921), but he did little more than transcribe and introduce the text.

[12] These "Lads" included WI, William, Ebenezer, and Peter Irving, Peter and Gouverneur Kemble, James K. Paulding, Henry Brevoort, Henry Ogden, David Porter, and Richard McCall.

[13] From a letter to Brevoort, quoted in STW, I, 78. The relationship of WI and Payne is one that is far more complex than scholars have previously recognized. Among the WI manuscripts in Columbia University Library are sixty-seven letters from WI to Payne, written between 1809 and the 1830's. Expurgated portions of some of these letters were published by Thatcher T. Payne Luquer ("Correspondence of WI and John Howard Payne," *Scribner's Magazine*, XLVIII [Oct., Nov. 1910], 461–82, 597–616).

In 1807 Payne had already made a name for himself as a critic and playwright; he would soon be a performing star on the American and British stage. He was, however, as Stanley T. Williams pointed out in *DAB*, XIV, 327, "a transient novelty," and by the 1820's, when WI was suffering through his longest intimate period with Payne, all of the successes of his life were already behind him.

[14] New York: David Longworth, 1807–1808. For a discussion of the sources and ideas behind *Salmagundi*, see STW, II, 263–73.

can life and creating more than a ripple on the surface of New York society.

Meanwhile, in November 1806, Washington Irving had passed the New York bar examination. Professionally, Irving seemed satisfied with his position in Hoffman's office. He went to Richmond, Virginia, for the treason trial of Aaron Burr, who had once been Peter's friend. His employer, it seemed, was destined to be his father-in-law. Matilda Hoffman at the beginning of 1809 was seventeen; Washington was twenty-five. That he would marry her and settle permanently into a career in law seemed inevitable. But her death on April 26 of that year of "a swift consumption" [15] precipitated the first real crisis of Irving's life.[16] He never recovered completely from her loss, grieving visibly during the next six years and for the remainder of his life occasionally seeming to lose himself in thoughts of her.

He did not, however, abandon himself to grief but directed his attention to a literary project—a satirical history of New York. On October 24, 1809, Diedrich Knickerbocker's *A History of New York*[17] appeared. It turned Washington into a local literary lion and convinced the Irving brothers, growing more and more wealthy in those prosperous times, that their younger brother should be free to practice his writing more seriously.[18] In 1810 as "A Gentleman of New York," he prepared an American edition of *The Poetical Works of Thomas Campbell*.[19] Though undistinguished in every way, this edition earned for Irving the poet's lifelong friendship and provided an opening wedge into British high life seven years later.

[15] STW, I, 103.

[16] WI's father had died in 1807, an event which, if anything, somewhat relieved the youngest member of the family. The oldest daughter, Ann Sarah, died in 1808 (her children were the Dodge nephews and nieces with whom WI would concern himself in later years) but her death—unlike later deaths in the family—was no personal crisis for him.

[17] Published simultaneously in New York, Boston, and Philadelphia by separate publishers. For discussion of sources and ideas, see STW, II, 273–77.

[18] From this time on, WI was looked upon as a silent partner in P. & E. Irving and Company.

[19] Philadelphia: E. Earle, 1810. For discussion, see STW, I, 120–22.

When the Philadelphia publisher Moses Thomas bought *Select Reviews,* an established periodical, he asked Irving to undertake its editorship, which he did in January 1813, after the name had been changed to *Analectic Magazine.* Depending heavily on reprinting articles from British periodicals such as the *Edinburgh Review* and the *Quarterly Review,* the *Analectic* was also to include original contributions from Americans. Irving himself wrote at least one piece for each number of the magazine, with which he worked for two years.[20] As a critic he was weak; as a biographer he exhibited the ideal he would later develop more fully—his belief that a biographer should present facts but color them with sentiment. The experience taught him that, if he had a future in the literary world, it was in areas other than magazine editorship. When Moses Thomas failed financially at the end of Irving's second year, the editor regretted the misfortune of his friend, but he used this as an excuse for escaping from his editorial thralldom.[21]

Washington was more interested in literary and social matters than in the political and military aspects of the war which was raging between his country and Great Britain, but the burning of the nation's capital (where William was now a member of Congress) inspired thirty-one-year-old Irving to join the fight against the enemy. He was made a colonel on the staff of Daniel D. Tompkins, Governor of New York and commander of its militia, and on September 2, 1814, a General Order appeared from Tompkin's military headquarters under the authority of "Washington Irving, Aide-de-Camp." [22] He saw no fighting, however, for the British had already turned their attention on Andrew Jackson's New Orleans stronghold. By the end of the year Irving was a civilian again.

After a winter of discontent during which he pondered long

[20] The best discussion of WI's editorship is in STW, I, 136–41.
[21] Another publisher salvaged the magazine. No doubt WI's continued editorship would have helped in this effort, but he declined, declaring emphatically that he "would never again undertake the editorship of that or any other periodical work." To G. C. Verplanck, January 17, 1815. Quoted in STW, I, 141.
[22] PMI, I, 312.

over the life behind him and anticipated somewhat fearfully the years before him,[23] he sailed on May 25, 1815, for what he expected to be a short trip abroad. The war over, he was to visit Peter, now director of the British branch of the family business, in Liverpool and their sister Sarah and her family[24] in Birmingham; then he planned to tour England, France, Italy, finally reaching as far as Greece before his return to New York after a year or two to "settle myself down to useful and honourable application." [25]

He landed in Liverpool, unknown except to his brother Peter whom he had not seen for seven years. Peter was not well, and Washington lingered with him for a week before hurrying to Birmingham where he made the Van Wart household his first English home; the nieces and nephews accepted him from the moment he appeared at the door. After this, he visited London, journeying to Sydenham to make a call on the poet Campbell. In London, as in 1806, he was still a routine tourist. True, both *Salmagundi* and *A History of New York* could be purchased from certain London booksellers,[26] but those volumes were just curiosities and the name of Irving was not even associated with them. He did, however, have one real friend in London—Washington Allston, whose Boston wife had recently died. Through Allston he renewed a vague acquaintance with a young Philadelphia painter, C. R. Leslie, who, after Allston's departure for America, became his best friend in England.[27] At 8 Buckingham

23 WI was living at this time in a boarding house. The domestic arrangements in regard to his mother are not clear. He seems to have moved to this place with Henry Brevoort late in 1813. STW, I, 417.

24 Sarah had married (probably in 1804) Henry Van Wart (1783–1873), an American who in 1815 became a naturalized British citizen by special act of Parliament and who was one of the most distinguished citizens that Birmingham, England, produced in the nineteenth century. See STW, I, 418. The Birmingham Public Library has a book of "Newspaper Cuttings" which contains information on Van Wart's long life.

25 From a MS fragment in Yale University Library. Quoted in STW, I, 144.

26 *History of New York* (London: n.p., 1809); *Salmagundi*, Reprinted from American Edition, with Introductory Essay and Explanatory Notes by John Lambert (London: J. M. Richardson, 1811). The latter was favorably reviewed in *The Monthly Review, or, Literary Journal*, LXV (Aug. 1811), 418–24.

27 Born in London in 1794 to American parents, Leslie returned to the city of

Place, Fitzroy Square, where Allston and Leslie lived, he visited and heard stories about the obscure poet-philosopher Coleridge (who regarded Allston with veneration) and other notables of the town.

Then, after a tour of Wales with his Columbia College friend James Renwick,[28] Irving settled in Liverpool into a life centered upon rheumatic Peter. His brother's physical condition was in no way aided by the financial crush in which P. and E. Irving and Company was finding itself. Always the gambler, Peter had bought excessively after the stale war years in luxury goods which had found no market in the United States. When the knowledgeable chief clerk died in the fall of 1815, inexperienced Washington had to take over the giant ledgers of the office in Liverpool. The money intended to carry him to Greece he put into the business in a futile attempt to buoy it up. This was to no avail.

The death of his mother in April 1817 depressed Washington even more deeply. Moreover, he heard rumors from New York that Paulding and even Brevoort were about to abandon bachelorhood for matrimony.[29] Liverpool reverberated with the echoes of his dying dreams; only by breaking away to visit the Van Warts or to go to Allston in London could he find relief.

Such a trip he made at the beginning of August 1817. Antici-

---

his birth from Philadelphia in 1811. He is represented in both the *Dictionary of National Biography* and the *Dictionary of American Biography*. His career was a distinguished one by all accounts, including his portraits of most of the British royal family. His *Autobiographical Recollections*, ed. Tom Taylor (London: JM, 1860), is a mine of WI information, the second volume being made up largely of letters exchanged by the two men. Hereinafter cited as Leslie.

[28] WI's journal, July 21–Aug. 4, 1815, is included in *The Journals of Washington Irving, 1815–1842*, ed. William P. Trent and George S. Hellman (Boston: The Bibliophile Society, 1919), I, 3–18. Hereinafter cited as Trent and Hellman.

[29] When Brevoort finally brought himself to announce officially his marriage plans, WI replied on Oct. 10, 1817: "I am almost ashamed to say that at first the news had rather the effect of making me feel melancholy than glad. It seemed, in a manner, to divorce us forever; for marriage is the grave of bachelor intimacies, and after having lived and grown together for many years, so that our habits, thoughts, and feelings were quite blended and intertwined, a separation of this kind is a serious matter" (PMI, I, 388). After his marriage, Brevoort stopped writing to WI for a time, causing WI to write on July 7, 1818, begging to hear from him: "let me down as easy as possible" (PMI, I, 400).

pating a stay of several weeks, he settled in lodgings of his own on Cockspur Lane.[30] With Allston and Leslie he spent much time, talking at length about the illustrations they had prepared for the new edition of *A History of New York* which Moses Thomas was planning.[31]

Irving made systematic tours of London, carefully taking notes on his adventures, for already he envisioned a series of essays (which would ultimately become *The Sketch Book*) as a means of relieving his financial troubles; two of the sketches, "Little Britain" and "Green Arbor Court," originated during this period. But his more immediate hope was based on a plan by which he would serve, in those times when international copyrights were nonexistent, as the middleman between American and British publishers, providing each with pre-publication copy of the other copyright holder's work. Through him, he believed, the publishers could all but extinguish the pirate book trade.[32]

Irving made an appointment with Longman and Company to discuss his scheme and then took a day off to visit Campbell at Sydenham. The poet was full of concern for himself, still struggling with the multi-volumed *Specimens of British Poets*, on which he had been working since 1813 for publisher John Murray.[33] He did take time to listen to the American's scheme and to offer him letters of introduction to Walter Scott in Scotland and, almost certainly, to publisher John Murray in London.[34]

[30] Now Warwick House Court, off Cockspur Street by Trafalgar Square. Rate Book of 1819 in Archives Department, City of Westminster Libraries.

[31] WI described the two drawings, which eventually served as the frontispieces for the two-volume edition, in a letter to Allston, May 21, 1817. PMI, I, 365–68.

[32] According to manuscript letters from WI to Moses Thomas, Yale University Library (May 8, 1815; April 27, May 18, 19, 1816), WI had been regularly sending choice titles, with the printer's ink hardly dry, to the Philadelphia publisher for unauthorized publication there.

[33] Peter Irving was also a friend of Campbell's. As early as 1813, he had written to WI in New York trying to get him to place Campbell's projected *Specimens* with an American publisher. Efforts to involve WI in an American edition of this work can be traced through PMI, I, 306, 344, and 364.

[34] There is no actual record of such a letter to JMII. Note, however, that Campbell, whom JMII regarded highly, is known to have given at this time to WI a letter of introduction to Scott. PMI, I, 378. WI would never have presented

The House of Murray to 1817

The House of Murray[35] was approaching its forty-ninth year in the book trade when Irving visited 50 Albemarle Street in 1817. The first John Murray, having retired on half-pay from his lieutenancy in the Marines and dropped the Scottish *Mac* from the family name, had settled in 1768 at 32 Fleet Street in a bookselling establishment. For a sum of close to £400 he bought from the previous owner his stock and good will. To a prospective partner, William Falconer, the aspiring book dealer had written: "Many Blockheads in the Trade are making fortunes; and did we not succeed as well as they, I think it must be imputed only to ourselves." [36]

The partnership did not materialize, but with some financial assistance from his father in Edinburgh, John Murray I began in November 1768 his career dealing with books. The first known title which he issued was a new edition of Lord Lyttelton's *Dialogue of the Dead*.[37]

To the young man, only twenty-three in 1768, the new enterprise was not always easy. He wrote to a friend: "I am fatigued from morning till night about penny matters, if any of which is forgotten I am complained of as a man who minds not his business." [38] A legacy in 1775 of over £4,000 from an uncle's estate, however, gave him the necessary capital to extend his efforts to greater things.

In 1777 Murray was responsible for providing Boswell with one of his best-known Johnson witticisms. The Reverend Mr. W. Mason, executor of Thomas Gray's literary remains, began

---

himself socially to JMII, as he clearly did, without a legitimate introduction, which could hardly have come from any of WI's other acquaintances.

[35] The studies of the publishing house and its directors are listed under Section III of the Bibliography. Information generally available in these references will not be footnoted here.

[36] Letter of October 16, 1768. Samuel Smiles, *A Publisher and His Friends: Memoir and Correspondence of the Late John Murray* ... (London: JM, 1891), I, 5. Hereinafter cited as Smiles.

[37] "London: for J. Murray (Successor to Mr. Sandby) at No. 32, opposite St. Dunstan's Church, Fleet Street M.DCC.LXVIII."

[38] Smiles, I, 15.

court action against Murray, who had innocently published several lines of Gray's work in a *Poetical Miscellany* without securing Mason's permission. When Mason refused Murray's offer to settle the matter out of court at any price, the publisher blasted him with a pamphlet entitled "A Letter to W. Mason, A.M., Precentor of York, Concerning his Edition of Gray's Poems, and the Practice of Booksellers." [39] The sale of the *Poetical Miscellany* was stopped by the court, but not without Samuel Johnson's having his say:

> Johnson signified his displeasure at Mr. Mason's conduct very strongly; but added, by way of showing that he was not surprised at it, "Mason's a Whig." Mrs. Knowles (not hearing distinctly): "What! a prig, Sir?" Johnson: "Worse, Madam; a Whig! But he is both!" [40]

While his business was growing, Murray's first wife had died childless and he had married again. In 1778, the baby who would be John Murray II was born; two later sons, born in 1779 and 1781, died in infancy. The elder Murray's life was darkened in June 1782 by a stroke which temporarily paralyzed his left side. The fear of another seizure hung over him for the remainder of his life, but nothing impeded his efforts to improve his lot. In less than a year after his illness he was taking action against the publishers of the *Encyclopædia Britannica* because one of their authors had lifted verbatim great sections from two books on which he held copyrights.

In trade there were good years and bad years. Once, a whole

---

[39] This bit of eighteenth-century bookselling lore was published as "By a Bookseller," with JMI as the publisher. JMI defended the time-honored custom of publishing extracts "in a Magazine, Review, or Newspaper," which really served to publicize the author and his work, and he could see no reason why this should not extend to books. After studying the Rev. Mr. Mason's writings, he found that the divine, in writing his *Memoirs of Gray*, had used a considerable amount of material on which JMI held the copyright—in fact, more than JMI had used of Mason's property. JMI then asked: "What trick, what device, what starting-hole cans't thou now find out, to hide thee from this open and apparent shame?" (p. 47).

[40] *Boswell's Life of Johnson*, ed. George Birkbeck Hill and L. F. Powell (Oxford: Oxford University Press, 1934), III, 294.

xxxiii

cargo of his books was lost in a shipwreck. Authors, good and bad, were forever writing to him or waiting to talk with him. Finally, the end came for this dedicated worker on November 6, 1793. At his death John Murray I was only forty-eight years of age, and though he had worked diligently for a quarter of a century, he had not succeeded in doubling the money he put into the business. He had, however, not lost money, and he left his family financially secure. Samuel Highley, his principal assistant, was appointed to carry on the work until young John would be old enough to assume his duties.

Born on November 27, 1778, John Murray II was only fifteen at his father's death. He had already spent a year at the Royal High School in Edinburgh and had been a student of the school in Gosport kept by Dr. Burney, a friend of his father's. A tragic accident in which the writing master ran the blade of his penknife through the boy's right eyeball cost John the sight of that eye and perhaps was the reason his father transferred him to Dr. Roberts' school, Loughborough House, Kennington, in July 1793. After the death of John Murray I, young John remained at that school until his mother remarried in September 1795.

Although John was still a minor, he and Samuel Highley became partners in this year, the older man controlling the management of the business which he saw as strictly bookselling, not publishing. After almost eight years with Highley's uninspired leadership (but a period during which Murray learned all the facets of the book trade), the partnership was dissolved on March 25, 1804. Murray remained at 32 Fleet Street. As his own master, John Murray II launched off as bookseller *and* publisher. Though he was interested in experimenting with drama and poetry, he preferred to publish "books of a more solid character," [41] including in this category travel accounts and medical and philosophical works.

One of Murray's closest friends was Isaac D'Israeli,[42] and with

[41] Smiles, I, 41.
[42] Smiles printed many letters which reveal their close friendship. See, for example, letters quoted I, 47–55.

few breaks their lives were intertwined until Murray's death. In 1791 the first John Murray had published the original volume of *Curiosities of Literature* for D'Israeli, the twenty-five-year-old scion of a wealthy Jewish family. From that date, if not before, an intimacy existed between the two families. Like all of the John Murrays, Isaac D'Israeli was a bibliophile. Ignoring his family's efforts to turn him into a business man, he entered the world of literature, publishing through Murray in 1803 a collection of poems and in 1804 a curious volume entitled *Flim-Flams! or the Life and Errors of my Uncle, and the Amours of my Aunt, with Illustrations and Obscurities*. This book, in the style of Sterne, went through two editions, mainly because the rumor circulated, falsely, that it contained libellous material.

Isaac and his wife, Maria Basevi, looked upon Murray as being a member of their family circle. To their daughters, especially Sarah, born in 1802, he was like an uncle. When their son Benjamin, many years later to be the illustrious Prime Minister, was born in 1804, Murray rejoiced with them.

By an agreement of June 1803 Murray and the firm of Constable & Co. of Edinburgh became mutual agents for the publications of the other.[43] During the next few years considerable business was transacted between the two houses, and in August 1806 Murray took advantage of the London slack season to go to Edinburgh to confer with Constable. This was the ostensible reason for the trip, but no one—certainly not the D'Israelis—was fooled. Murray's great interest in Edinburgh for several years had been Miss Anne Elliot, whose late father had been an Edinburgh publisher. Murray's business with Constable (whatever it was) successfully concluded, he returned to London—engaged to be married to Miss Elliot on May 6, 1807.

The marriage took place on schedule, and by the last of the month they had settled comfortably into their new life. It was the

---

[43] This early relationship of Constable and Murray is discussed, from the Edinburgh publisher's viewpoint, in Thomas Constable, *Archibald Constable and His Literary Correspondents* (Edinburgh: Edmonston and Douglas, 1873), I, 339–95.

D'Israelis who gave the first dinner party for Mr. and Mrs. John Murray II. Isaac had been one of the marriage trustees, and to him and Maria went the honor of introducing Mrs. Murray to the literary circle of which she would become the First Lady.[44] By 1817 the Murrays had three children; the oldest was a boy, born on April 16, 1808, who would be the John Murray with whom Irving would deal in later years.

The following year, through the good offices of Constable, Murray became the owner of a fourth part of the copyright of Walter Scott's *Marmion* and, as a result, met and became a personal friend of the Scotsman. Then, after months of bickering with Longman and Rees, originally by contract the London agent for the *Edinburgh Review*, Constable switched this magazine into Murray's keeping in London, paying the other firm £1,000 for its claim. But to Murray the *Edinburgh Review* brought nothing but trouble. Constable & Co. became difficult to deal with because of its own financial problems. By the end of 1808 Murray had shed the *Edinburgh Review* and his other official ties with the Scottish firm.

The *Edinburgh Review* had appeared in 1802, the first quarterly publication to devote itself to higher literary criticism. Such leading literary men as Francis Jeffrey, Sydney Smith, Henry Brougham, even Walter Scott contributed to it, creating the major voice on literature in the English-speaking world. Under Jeffrey's editorship, however, its course took an unfortunate direction.[45] The tone of its reviews was often unnecessarily abusive, Wordsworth, Southey, and Coleridge being special targets of its scorn. In addition to this cultish literary bias, the complete devotion it showed the Whig Party was disturbing to Tory readers. Dedicated almost mystically to the cause of literature, Scott, though a loyal Tory, had been willing to overlook the politics of the *Review;* but when Jeffrey turned on him in a

44 Alexander Hunter, of Constable & Co., was visiting in London and attended the dinner with the newlyweds. He described it in some detail. See Smiles, I, 73–74.

45 James A. Greig, *Francis Jeffrey of the "Edinburgh Review"* (Edinburgh: Oliver & Boyd, 1948), *passim.*

bitter review of *Marmion*, accusing Scott of commercialism and neglecting "Scottish feelings and Scottish characters,"[46] the great man of Scottish literature broke with the magazine.[47]

John Murray, in the meantime, was watching the scene with interest. The unchallenged influence of the northern publication with its literary and political prejudices had long troubled him. He had already talked with most of the people who had been associated with the *Anti-Jacobin, or Weekly Examiner*, the short-lived (November 20, 1797–July 9, 1789) but highly lauded (and condemned) Tory publication founded by George Canning and George Ellis. Also interested in Murray's ideas were John Hookham Frere and John Wilson Croker, both significant figures in the Tory camp. They all agreed that there was a desperate need for a more sympathetic periodical to balance the quarterly from Edinburgh.[48] In October 1808 Murray visited Walter Scott, who was more than happy to listen to what he had to say and to give Murray's venture his full support.

Consequently, with John Murray II as founding publisher and William Gifford[49] as editor, the post he had held with the *Anti-Jacobin, or Weekly Examiner*, the first number of the *Quarterly Review* appeared in February 1809, advertised as the voice of Constitutional Toryism. Thus was British literature split into two camps, each with a highly literate vehicle for carrying its messages to the reading public.

The early years of the *Quarterly Review* were not easy ones, especially for the publisher. With his "hopes of fame as a book-

---

[46] XII (April 1808), 12.

[47] See John Gibson Lockhart, *Memoirs of the Life of Sir Walter Scott, Bart.* (Edinburgh: Robert Cadell, 1839), III, 115–76.

[48] True to their promises, these men devoted much time and effort to making the proposed publication a success. Canning, later Prime Minister; Ellis; and Frere were not spectacular in their written contributions, but they were constructive and active advisors. Croker wrote close to 260 articles during his lifetime and was responsible for bringing into the organization Admiralty Secretary John Barrow, one of the more prolific *QR* contributors. Each of these men has been the subject of a biographical study in *DNB*.

[49] Roy Benjamin Clark's standard biography of this man suggests by its title the appropriateness of his selection for the job: *William Gifford: Tory, Satirist, Critic, and Editor* (New York: Columbia University Press, 1930).

seller rest[ing] upon the establishment and celebrity of this journal," [50] he often found it difficult to refrain from attempting to
involve himself in its editorial policy. He appears to have objected
at times to the intellectual war that editor Gifford waged with
the *Edinburgh Review*,[51] but in his mind Gifford's greatest fault
(after all, a good Tory like Murray *could* forgive anti-Whig
anti-Jeffrey slanting of the contents)was his inability to get the
material for the magazine to the publisher on time. Issue after
issue appeared later and later, each losing the advantage of Murray's carefully built publicity for it. By August 1810 the publication was still not paying its way and he had succumbed to
"stomach disorders," [52] but one of the physical afflictions that
would plague him during later financial and publishing difficulties.

During 1811 the *Quarterly Review* began to come into prominence. Murray and Gifford had developed an understanding of
each other. The subscription list was increasing, and literary contributions—from Poet Laureate Robert Southey; Admiralty Secretary John Barrow; the Prince Regent's friend, John Wilson Croker; and other personages—were displaying greater quality. From
1811 on, the *Quarterly Review* grew in strength and in importance. In 1817, discussing privately Murray's business with a
friend, Southey wrote: "The Review is the greatest of all his
works, and it is all his own creation; he prints 10,000, and fifty
times ten thousand read its contents in the East and in the West.
Joy be with him and his journal!" [53]

The most important move of Murray's life came in 1812, when,
during October, he left his rather commonplace Fleet Street address to take up his business residence in the—even then—exclu-
sive Mayfair district of London. From William Miller, a respected
bookseller retiring temporarily from the trade, he purchased the

[50] JMII to William Gifford, September 25, 1810. Smiles, I, 185.
[51] "Publish the best information, the best science, the best literature; and leave
the public to decide for themselves," JMII wrote to Gifford. Smiles, I, 185.
[52] Isaac D'Israeli to JMII, Aug. 2, 1810. Quoted in Smiles, I, 179.
[53] Robert Southey to Grosvenor C. Bedford, Feb. 15, 1817. *The Life and
Correspondence of the Late Robert Southey*, ed. Charles Cuthbert Southey (London: Longman, Brown, Green & Longmans, 1850), IV, 240.

lease, copyrights, and stock of 50 Albemarle Street; the price was £3,822 12s. 6d.

The move to Albemarle Street (soon to be dubbed "John Murray Street" by Charles Lamb) took Murray within easy reach of Gifford's home, the Admiralty, and the more literate nobility and intelligentsia of London. With Samuel Rogers,[54] whose showplace London house was at 22 St. James's Place, Murray divided the day for some of the most important people of the time. Rogers' famous breakfasts were daily social events, and for some fortunate individuals they were the forerunner to an afternoon of political and literary news and gossip at Murray's. By 1815 Murray was presiding daily from two to five o'clock over a drawing room filled with people whose names appeared prominently in *The Royal Blue Books* and who can, with few exceptions, be picked out of the *Dictionary of National Biography* today. The camaraderie of the drawing-room regulars was so satisfactory that in the 1820's the Athenaeum Club grew directly out of 50 Albemarle Street. On evenings when he and Mrs. Murray were not sampling London society, they entertained small select groups of dinner guests in their carefully appointed dining room.

In the meantime, Murray had forever linked his name with that of the English poet who would hold the imagination of the romantics through future generations. Murray had become in 1812 the first publisher of Lord Byron's *Childe Harold's Pilgrimage*, the success of which had left both poet and publisher dazed. There was occasional friction between the two men because, perhaps, they understood each other too well, but from that point on, John Murray meant more than money to the poet. It was Murray, for example, who reconciled Byron and Scott[55] and brought them together for the first time on April 7, 1815, in the Albemarle

---

[54] Two books discuss the social activities of this man: P. W. Clayden, *Rogers and His Contemporaries* (London: Smith, Elder & Co., 1889), and R. Ellis Roberts, *Samuel Rogers and His Circle* (London: Metheun & Co., 1910).

[55] Byron's "unguarded satire" of Scott in *English Bards and Scotch Reviewers* (1809) had caused the disruption of their literary intercourse. JMII reported to Scott (June 27, 1812) Byron's kind words concerning Scott to the Prince Regent and thus healed the breach. Smiles, I, 213–14.

Street drawing room. After Byron's departure from England, it was to Murray that he wrote begging for (and getting) his favorite brand of tooth powder and all the latest literary news and social gossip. And it was to Murray that the great egotist wrote long letters describing his various intrigues, as a contemporary declared, "for the edification of Mr. Murray, and all the visitors of his shop, to whom it is, of course, intended he shall read the gazette of my lord's last Venetian victory." [56]

But John Murray was a bookseller, even though the *Quarterly Review* and socializing were taking large portions of his time. Among his authors of the period who strike an immediate response today were Madame de Staël, Thomas Campbell, Jane Austen, Thomas Moore, and Walter Scott. An item seemingly not in his usual line was Mrs. Maria Eliza Rundell's *Domestic Cookery*, one of the first cookbooks intended for the use of British housewives. First published in 1806, it went through numerous changes and editions, rarely selling less than 10,000 copies per year.[57]

The world of British publications in 1817 was entirely different from that in which John Murray I (and in fact his son) had started in the trade. It is no over-simplification to attribute the vastly improved conditions to two publishers and two authors: Constable and Murray, Scott and Byron.[58] Within the preceding

[56] *Memoirs, Journal, and Correspondence of Thomas Moore*, ed. Lord John Russell (London: Longman, Brown, Green and Longmans, 1853), II, 329. Hereinafter cited as Moore, *Memoirs*.

Byron's lively letters to his publisher illustrate more than any other source a sort of vivaciousness in JMII's character. The poet is presented at his amusing best in three poems concerning JMII: "Epistle from Mr. Murray to Dr. Polideri" (Aug. 1817), in which JMII—rejecting a manuscript by Byron's friend—described the activity going on in his drawing room; "Epistle to Mr. Murray" (January 8, 1818); and "To Mr. Murray" (April 11, 1818). *The Works of Lord Byron: Poetry*, ed. Ernest Hartley Coleridge (London: JM, 1905), VII, respectively 47–50, 51–54, 56–58. Hereinafter cited as *Works of Byron: Poetry*.

[57] The British Museum Library has a copy of the sixty-fourth edition of this book, issued in 1840 by JM.

[58] Perhaps the first person to argue this thesis was A. S. Collins, *The Profession of Letters: A Study of the Relation of Author to Patron, Publisher, and Public, 1780–1832* (London: George Routledge & Sons, 1928), pp. 155–70. A recent scholar discussed it approvingly: Royal A. Gettmann, *A Victorian Publisher: A Study of the Bentley Papers* (Cambridge: Cambridge University Press, 1960), pp. 1–7.

decade these publishers had made cultural history by paying previously unimagined high prices for the copyrights of works by these two authors. Scott and Byron, for their part, had through their contrasting personalities added glamor to the profession (even as Scott had added "glamour" to the language). Breathtaking financial value was attached for the first time to the products of authorship, and professional authors themselves no longer were delegated to the lower levels of society; this occupation took on, in the vernacular of today, a new image: gone was the Grub-Street hack who had been the professional writer of the past; a man could now write for a living and be proud of his vocation. Suddenly, from every Britannic hamlet emerged aspiring authors who imagined they were only a few quill pen strokes from fame and fortune. In a very real sense, authorship was freed from its Renaissance-gentleman fetters. A new era had dawned.

As the status of the author was changing, the book trade was experiencing a slightly less dramatic evolution. "Bookseller" had been an all-inclusive term defined, in the time of John Murray I, as a person whose business was "to purchase original copies from Authors, to employ Printers to print them, and publish and sell them in their Shops; or to purchase Books from such as print them on their own Account, or at Auctions, and sell them at an advanced Price." [59] The infusion of large amounts of money, necessary for the first business transaction listed above, tended to separate the trade into two groups; the sellers (publishers) who could afford to finance the publication of books, and those (factors) who could only purchase from the publisher the finished product which they would market to their customers for a commission. By 1817 the line between the two groups was drawn and the publishing house became a reality.

What better evidence is there of this than Murray's already established practice of giving an annual trade dinner? For over twenty years the Murrays invited booksellers to regular dinners held at the Albion Tavern on Aldgate Street, London. After the civilities of food and drink, a master of ceremonies would describe

[59] R. Campbell, *The London Tradesmen* (London: T. Gardner, 1759), p. 128.

the wares and, offering high discounts for bulk sales, take orders from the trade amounting rarely to less than £20,000.[60] In December 1816 at such a dinner, Murray sold 7,000 copies of the third canto of *Childe Harold's Pilgrimage* and an equal number of *The Prisoner of Chillon*.[61]

"Publisher," however, came slowly into general use. Murray still acknowledged "bookseller" as his profession in London directories as late as 1836, with the difference made clear—he sold only to dealers; not since the Fleet-Street days had the public trafficked in and out of Murray's establishment.[62] Byron had dubbed him in 1813 "the ἄναξ of publishers,"[63] and it was as a "publisher" (in the modern concept of the word) that John Murray had made and would continue to secure his place in literature.

Another change on the literary scene must be noted. The patron system of previous centuries died a quiet death at the end of the eighteenth century, the vacuum being filled by the bookseller-publisher. "The author's customary patron—the bookseller,"[64] Leigh Hunt declared, and Thomas Moore, in a poem entitled "Thoughts on Patrons, Puffs, and Other Matters," commented that fortunate indeed was the author "ta'en by Murray's self in tow."[65] In such a climate authors might well vie for the attention of recognized publishers with as much spirit as their professional ancestors had displayed in pursuit of the patronage of liberal nobility.

John Murray (and his contemporary "publishers") had helped

[60] George Paston, *At John Murray's: Records of a Literary Circle, 1843–1892* (London: JM, 1932), p. 70.

[61] Smiles, I, 369.

[62] Scott clearly made a distinction when he wrote of "the bookshops and publishing Houses" in a letter to his daughter, Sophia Lockhart, Oct. 24, 1828. *The Letters of Sir Walter Scott* [Centenary Edition], ed. H. J. G. Grierson (London: Constable & Co. Ltd., 1934), XI, 21.

[63] In a letter to Thomas Moore, June 22, 1813. *The Works of Lord Byron: Letters and Journals*, ed. Rowland E. Prothero (London: JM, 1904), II, 224. Hereinafter cited as *Works of Byron: Letters and Journals*.

[64] Quoted in Collins, p. 258.

[65] *The Poetical Works of Thomas Moore* [Oxford Edition], ed. A. D. Godfrey (London: Oxford University Press, 1910), p. 683.

to give social acceptance to the "literary urge." Further, they had shown that it could be the pathway to monetary riches. Quite naturally, they soon felt the effect of an unending avalanche of manuscripts and solicitations from authors seeking publication. It was, however, a burden under which Murray rarely flinched, for from these sources came some of his most successful productions. To help pass on the merits of certain manuscripts, from the masses he received, he often availed himself of the talents of his drawing-room friends—Gifford, Croker, Barrow, for example—a practice which would become the standard procedure when paid readers became a part of every large publishing house.[66] "Your corps," [67] Byron contemptuously called Murray's advisors; "Murray's elbow critics," [68] hissed a later author—neither of the writers understanding the nature of the services of these interested readers.

By 1817 John Murray II was an individual of renown. There was a quixotic air about him that matched the time and some of the volatile personalities with whom he dealt. He was, said Lord Greville, a man who "chattered incessantly," [69] sometimes damaging his own causes by talking too freely[70]—a fault perhaps more inherent in his character than resulting from his love of claret and port to which many of his acquaintances attributed it. He preferred to do business in person, avoiding letter writing to the point occasionally of endangering his own interests,[71] but he perfected a smooth reconciliatory technique to use on his authors when they seemed about to reach the end of their endurance with his episto-

[66] See Gettmann's chapter on "The Publisher's Reader," pp. 187-230.

[67] Smiles, I, 209.

[68] See below, p. 120.

[69] Charles C. F. Greville, *The Greville Memoirs: A Journal of the Reigns of King George IV and King William IV*, ed. Henry Reeve (London: Longmans, Green, & Co., 1875), I, 280.

[70] Thomas Moore in his *Memoirs* repeatedly bemoaned JMII's loose talk. See especially III, 280. John Gibson Lockhart went to the extent of referring to "Murray's own leaky lips." Quoted in Myron Franklin Brightfield, *John Wilson Croker* (Berkeley: University of California Press, 1940), 186.

[71] Samuel Smiles found so many instances of this in JMII's career that he found it appropriate to say in his concluding remarks that the publisher "not infrequently caused serious misunderstandings by his neglect to answer letters" (II, 518).

xliii

lary indolence. "Buttered by Murray" [72] might be an apt description of it. As early as 1815 he exercised this charm on Jane Austen, who observed in her wily way: "He is a rogue of course, but a civil one." [73]

William Wordsworth, not yet an exalted figure in English literature, rather bitterly described Murray as "too great a personage for any one but a count, an aristocrat, or most fashionable author to deal with." [74] Another contemporary listed the requirements for being received at 50 Albemarle Street:

> To insure a passport to the table of Mr. Murray, three things are necessary; first, that the party be an author of some celebrity; secondly, that he be an unexceptionable Tory; and, thirdly, that he be, to a greater or less extent, patronised by the aristocracy. [75]

A fourth category might be added: Murray was always eager to entertain foreign visitors, Americans being of special interest to him.

As the publisher of the *Quarterly Review* and of Byron's poetry, John Murray was known throughout the English-speaking world and especially in the United States where—because of Gifford's studied anti-American attitude in the *Quarterly Review*[76] —he was not always seen in a sympathetic light. Still, attending a session in Murray's drawing room was already considered to be an event for visiting Americans. To a literary man, certainly, a visit to the court of "the prince of aristocratic bibliopoles" [77] was an experience to be long remembered. George Ticknor had been

[72] *The Letters of Richard Ford, 1797–1858,* ed. Rowland E. Prothero (New York: E. P. Dutton & Co., 1905), p. 165.

[73] *Jane Austen's Letters to Her Sister Cassandra and Others,* ed. R. W. Chapman (Oxford: The Clarendon Press, 1932), II, 425.

[74] Quoted in Roberts, *Samuel Rogers and His Circle,* p. 168.

[75] James Grant, *Portraits of Public Characters* (London: Saunders and Otley, 1841), II, 8–9.

[76] This anti-Americanism was virtually the only common interest of Jeffrey and Gifford. Clark suggests that Gifford considered it his patriotic duty to belittle the new nation. He adds: "Considering the influence of that periodical [*QR*] during these years, it must have been largely instrumental in keeping alive the animosity of the English Tories toward America. And Gifford had a great share in it" (p. 187).

[77] Grant, *Portraits of Public Characters,* II, 1.

there several times in 1815 and was the first in the lengthy procession of American intellectuals to leave their written impres-
sions of Murray's hospitality.[78] No American, however, took
advantage of it more often than Washington Irving, whose association with the House of Murray, beginning on August 16,
1817, is a major chapter in the history of Anglo-American publishing.

[78] *Life, Letters, and Journals of George Ticknor,* ed. G. S. Hillard (London:
Sampson Low & Co., 1876), I, 58–62, 63, 68.

WASHINGTON IRVING AND THE HOUSE OF MURRAY

CHAPTER ONE

INTRODUCTION TO THE
DRAWING-ROOM CIRCLE

Saturday, August 16, 1817

At the address on the letter of introduction Irving paused on Albemarle Street before the large brass plate announcing:

MR. MURRAY'S
NO. 50

His five-foot, seven-inch height was dwarfed by the towering expanse of the doorway as he presented Campbell's letter, which gained him admittance to the hallway. The servant hurried up the stairway, then quickly down again, to bow him up the steps to the waiting John Murray.

They met on the first floor, in front of the door leading into the drawing room, from which the sounds of quiet male conversation were escaping. For Irving this must have been an event of great excitement as he took the outstretched hand of the smiling gentleman, so cordially welcoming him. For Murray the meeting was of no obvious immediate importance: an unknown American had come to his door with a letter of introduction on a dreary Saturday afternoon, and the publisher had a reputation for always welcoming an opportunity to exercise his celebrated charm on a fresh personality.

This being the off-season—Murray quickly explained—the town was all but deserted; only a few people of importance were still in residence. In fact, it was a bit of luck that Irving had decided to call on this day because the Murrays were leaving for the country on Monday. Earlier in the week, because of the Prince Regent's birthday, there had been an unseasonable amount of social activity in London, but the departure of the Court for Windsor and Brighton yesterday had signaled the close of that social period and the roads to the better places had become clogged with carriages taking society away from murky London. Had the weather and other conditions been better, the Murrays would have themselves departed on Friday—though (the publisher added as an aside) it was fortunate that he had been on hand to take care of some problems in connection with yesterday's scheduled publication of the Earl of Selkirk's Account of the Red River Settlement, *a book which would no doubt interest the young American.*

The two men whose conversation had drifted out of the open drawing-room door stopped talking as Irving and Murray entered. They were strangers to Irving and were introduced as Mr. John Barrow and Mr. George Canning. While appearing to be interested in Murray's introductory remarks concerning the men, Irving allowed his eyes to move along the wall from one portrait to another, looking longest at the Byron study by Phillips hanging over the marble mantle-piece. Two other portraits he could recognize immediately. His friend Thomas Campbell looked approvingly down upon him, and Walter Scott, whom he expected to meet soon, seemed to acknowledge him as a friend. The brief formalities over, Murray drew Irving away from the men to show him "the gallery," which had held the American's attention from the moment he entered the room. Murray pointed to a portrait of Thomas Moore—"Anacreon," he called him, using the Irish poet's popular nickname derived from an early volume of his work; Moore, the publisher declared, was a fine fellow, one whom Irving must certainly meet when the opportunity presented itself. A portrait not yet finished he identified as being a good likeness of Samuel Rogers. Then, taking up a little portrait which Lady Caroline Lamb had given him of herself in a pageboy costume, Murray suggested playfully that he was sure she would like to meet Irving.

Besides the impressive collection of portraits in the main draw-

4

ing room and in a smaller back parlor, there were the books, shelves of volumes so expensively bound and lettered that each was a museum piece and seemed to Irving too precious to handle, though he studied each item carefully as Murray led him around the room, occasionally putting a piece of special interest into his hands.

Returning to Barrow and Canning, the publisher and his American guest settled into a conversation which was dominated by Barrow. He returned to what had obviously been an earlier topic of emotional discussion: how had The Literary Gazette been able to secure a copy of Tuckey's journal of his 1816 exploration of the Congo River? In May, Barrow had given the only known copy to Murray, who had agreed to publish it with an introduction by its discoverer. Now, in the midst of their preparations, installments of the account had begun to appear in Henry Colburn's new weekly, The Literary Gazette, from which it was being reprinted in other papers.

Murray turned the conversation to William Pitt's recent unsuccessful mission to China, explaining to Irving that Barrow had served as comptroller of one of England's first major embassies to China and, in fact, had been an advisor for the present mission in its early stages. The audacity of Robert Owen's plan to reform society, which had filled all the newspapers the previous day, brought a chuckle from Canning, but the other men were inclined to regard it more seriously.

Finally, as Barrow was beginning to explain his ideas on the timeliness of sending expeditions to look for the Northwest Passage (in view of the recent upheavals which had loosened great portions of Arctic icefields), Canning rose as though to leave. But after Irving had made his formal departure (apparently taking his cue from the politician) and was being ushered down the steps, having accepted an invitation to dine with the Murrays that evening, he heard the voices resume in the drawing room. He stepped into a light drizzle as the great door of 50 Albemarle Street closed behind him.

That Evening

The dinner was by candlelight, the curtains of the ground floor dining room shut tightly to keep out the sights and sounds of Albemarle Street. From the moment he arrived, Irving seemed to feel at home. Mrs. Murray's gracious welcome proved that she was a fit hostess companion to her husband. Controlling the servants and the guests from the head of the rectangular table, she was a handsome, authoritative woman. One dinner companion, clearly more a member of the family than a guest, was Isaac D'Israeli, who seemed willing to talk only about his most recent researches in the British Museum. Quickly and busily he ate his food, speaking whenever necessary to Murray or to the man on his left, William Brockedon, an artist just back from Italy with many original sketches of that country, about which he talked constantly to his hostess.

On the other side of the table, Irving sat between John Miller and Walter Hamilton. Miller, who was about to open a bookselling business in the luxurious new Burlington Arcade, only a few yards from Albemarle Street, expressed great interest in American literary productions, even suggesting that he might establish a New York branch of his store, specializing in drama. But with Walter Hamilton, the personable author of several Asiatic studies, Irving was apparently most at ease—not that they spoke of Hamilton's Far Eastern interests. Their conversation, rarely including anyone else, covered in an aimless fashion the weather, last night's reported sighting of a ghost in St. Giles's Churchyard, and finally the London theater.

When a servant announced the arrival of Mrs. and Miss D'Israeli, the hostess retired upstairs with them to the drawing room, leaving the men to enjoy a decanter of what had become known in London as "John Murray's famous port."

As he climbed the stairs, chattering to amiable Walter Hamilton, it appeared that Irving might have had too much of the publisher's nectar, for his usual reserve had disappeared. The crystal

6

chandelier, its drops and strings of prisms sparkling like diamonds, gave life to the portraits on the wall. Sitting on a low divan, Mrs. Murray nodded to the gentlemen as they entered the room. On the divan beside her sat Mrs. D'Israeli, who smiled, acknowledging Irving's introduction. Sarah, the fourteen-year-old D'Israeli daughter, sat on a small chair, as gracefully as her awkward age would allow and appeared painfully ill at ease whenever spoken to.

The dinner group broke into chatting couples, Murray taking Irving aside to inspect some of his Byron items. They read and chuckled over Byron's most recent letters from Venice. The poet promised to deliver the fourth canto of Childe Harold *shortly (Murray bragged that he had already paid £1,600 for it) and raved on in flowing prose about minor events and personalities. The subject of the great poet led Murray finally to lamentations concerning the losses he had suffered through pirated American editions of Byron's work.*

Why, Irving replied, plunging in with his expressed excuse for seeking out Murray, encouraged by the after-dinner port and the genial atmosphere of the room—why did not Murray let him contact his publisher friends in America to arrange an exchange of their wares? Such an arrangement could be advantageous to both sides in the absence of an international copyright agreement. A publisher could furnish pre-publication copies of his work to be dispatched to the co-operating publisher across the sea, thus allowing him to issue the book before pirated editions could be produced from the copies rushed over by ship after the publication of the book.

The idea had possibilities, Murray agreed, smiling pleasantly, the idea did have possibilities; certainly they would want to talk about this matter later; then abruptly changing the subject, he drew D'Israeli to Irving's side, slipping away to talk to Hamilton.

Encouraged by his conversation with Murray, Irving's enthusiasm overflowed with D'Israeli, who beamed and displayed considerable animation as the American congratulated him on his fol-

lowing in the United States. D'Israeli had not known the extent to which he had appeared in unauthorized editions in America, and while paying lip service to the shame of his not being able to profit financially by those editions, he was clearly pleased by the news—and by the young man who outlined his plan for foiling the book pirates. Isaac, his Bourbon nose aquiver and his brown beady eyes sparkling over his spectacles, seemed to be charmed and asked many questions about Irving's country.

At 11:35 the slow drizzle which had been falling since 9 P.M. suddenly erupted into a cloudburst, alerting the visitors to the time and the hazards of the night. When after about ten minutes the torrents changed back to a dependable slow mist, the D'Israelis made ready for a hasty departure before the blustery winds could blow up more mischief. The other guests reluctantly followed them down the winding stairway, John Miller secretively pulling Irving back to promise him a letter of introduction to Archibald Constable for use on his proposed trip to Edinburgh.

At the door the party broke up quickly. After appropriate farewells, the D'Israelis' carriage splashed into Piccadilly. Miller, Brockedon, and Hamilton plunged into the dampness and hurried on their separate ways, but Irving lingered at the door to press his host for a definite date to discuss their publication plans. In the face of the waves of light rain which occasional gusts of wind carried in through the partially opened door, Murray kept his smile and listened as Irving began to outline his plan again. "Ah, now, what you must do," Murray interrupted him, in an unmistakable leave-taking, "is to keep an eye out for my advertisements in the papers and write to me whenever I have anything that might be of interest for republication in America." Irving looked satisfied. He strolled across Piccadilly, down St. James's Street toward his lodgings. Ignoring the rain that was soaking his clothes to the skin, he passed by White's famous bow window, his mind perhaps filled with the portraits on Murray's walls and with his future plans. On Pall Mall, publisher Cawthorne's sign rattled against its chains in the wind but he paid it no attention. In his

*next letter to Peter, ailing in Liverpool, he described the evening's
activities and his host, concluding: "I shall find him a most valuable
acquaintance...."*

Sources for Vignette

WI described this memorable day twice: in *Notes While Preparing
Sketch Book &c 1817*, ed. STW (New Haven: Yale University,
1927), pp. 80–82; and in a letter to Peter Irving, Aug. 19, 1817, printed
in PMI, I, 373–75. Shortly after this, he referred briefly to JM's establishment, comparing it with that of Constable, in *Tour of Scotland
1817*, ed. STW (New Haven: Yale University Press, 1927), p. 28.

A contemporary (June 30, 1817) description of JM's drawing room
is in George Crabbe's diary printed in his son's *The Poetical Works,
with ... his Life* (London: JM, 1847), I, 242–43. F. Espinasse included
good illustrations in a careful reconstruction of early life at 50 Albemarle Street in "The House of Murray," *Harper's Monthly Magazine* [European Edition], X (Sept. 1885), 503–22.

Biographical sketches of all Englishmen (except Walter Hamilton
and John Miller) mentioned by name are in the *DNB*. For additional
information: on John Miller, see T. Constable, *Archibald Constable*,
II, 428; on the D'Israelis, see William Monypenny, *The Life of Benjamin D'Israeli, Earl of Beaconsfield* (London: JM, 1929), I, 21, and
Hesketh Pearson, *Dizzy: The Life and Nature of Benjamin D'Israeli,
Earl of Beaconsfield* (London: Methuen & Co., 1950), pp. 4, 34, 125–
26; on John Barrow, see *An Auto-biographical Memoir of Sir John
Barrow, Bart., Late of the Admiralty* (London: JM, 1847), p. 333.

Weather conditions are from A. Edwin's Weather Diary for 1817
in the Archives of the Royal Meteorological Society, London.

Other items of timely interest are taken from *Morning Chronicle*,
Aug. 13, 15, 16, 18; *Morning Post*, Aug. 15, 16, 18; *Bell's Weekly
Messenger*, Aug. 10; *Times*, Aug. 18; *Courier*, Aug. 18; *Herald*, Aug.
15, 16, 18, 1817.

The Byron letters (July 15, 20, 1817) which JMII read to WI are
printed in *Works of Byron: Letters*, IV, 150–54.

Other material is taken from PMI, I, *passim;* Smiles, I, *passim;* STW,
I, *passim.*

Irving's after-dinner interview with John Murray left him with great hopes for his transatlantic publication scheme.[1] In fact, he was so encouraged by Murray's courteous reception of his ideas that he was hardly concerned when his conference with Mr. Orme of Longman and Company resulted in a rejection of his proposals by that publishing house. His letter instructing Moses Thomas to send Murray "some of the best books published in that country" [2] was dispatched by the next packet ship to Philadelphia. Now, he thought, he needed only to wait for success to catch up with him.

With his letter of introduction from Campbell to Walter Scott (he declined Murray's offer to write one also), Irving left London in better spirits than he had known for several years. By August 26 he was in Edinburgh, where he was received kindly by Jeffrey and, through John Miller's letter, by Archibald Constable, who agreed to avail himself of Irving's agency.[3] From Edinburgh he hurried on to Abbotsford for, perhaps, the most memorable four days of his life. The two men, Scott twelve years older than Irving, were friends from the moment Scott limped, almost running, out to greet his guest on August 30. They talked about literature, folklore, Burns, Byron, and, no doubt, John Murray.[4]

Returning to Liverpool the young American found his menageries of woes had been increased by the addition of twenty-four-

---

[1] JMII could have dampened WI's enthusiasm by telling him about American Theobald Wolfe Tone, who, earlier in the year, had failed completely in an attempt to make workable arrangements such as WI now proposed to undertake. See Smiles, II, 26–27.

[2] Smiles, II, 126.

[3] Miller's letter is published in Thomas Constable, *Archibald Constable and His Literary Correspondence*, II, 428. Through this arrangement Thomas was probably able to get out the first American edition of *Rob Roy*. There seems to be no other record of advantages either to Thomas or Constable. See PMI, I, 384.

[4] STW (I, 116, 159–63, 175–76) discussed this visit, but the most readable secondary account of the friendship is R. B. Van Wart, "WI and Scotland," *Blackwood's Magazine*, CCLXVI (Sept. 1949), 257–63. See also my "WI to Walter Scott: Two Unpublished Letters," *Studies in Scottish Literature*, III (Oct. 1965), 114–18. WI's experiences were, of course, the basis for his lengthy essay "Abbotsford," published in 1835.

year-old William Campbell Preston, who was sick with a high fever. But Irving was too fresh from his successes in London and Edinburgh to be dragged down immediately to his former level of depression. There is an unmistakable air of buoyancy and much-business-to-be-attended-to in his first letter to John Murray. He pressed his watch-fob into the red sealing wax on the edge of the folded sheet, imprinting the outline of the "Irvine" coat of arms, which he had taken as his signet.[5]

1. *To John Murray II*[6]

Liverpool, Octr 16th 1817.

Dear Sir,

I perceive by the papers that the fourth canto of Child[e] Harold[7] is received and understand that Tuckey's narrative[8] is in the press. If it is your wish to secure a participation in the profits of American republication in the way I suggested when I had the pleasure of seeing you in London, I would advise you not to lose time, as ships sometimes loiter in port & days may be lost here even after the work is sent. As the poem cannot be very voluminous it

[5] This signet became as familiar as WI's signature at 50 Albemarle Street, for it appears on virtually all of his letters there. Representing a hand holding three holly leaves, the device refers to an incident in the thirteenth century when Robert the Bruce and William Irvine hid from enemy troops in a holly thicket. See J. F. Leslie, *The Irvines of Drum* (Aberdeen: n.p., 1909), pp. 15–16. This seal is preserved among WI mementos, Sunnyside, Tarrytown, N. Y.

[6] Stamped in Liverpool, Oct. 16 and in London, Oct. 18, 1817.

[7] *The Courier*, Oct. 11, 1817, contained this note: "Lord Byron's fertile muse has again teemed. The lovers of poetry will rejoice to hear the Fourth Canto of 'Childe Harold' has arrived in town from the Continent, and there is no danger of a treasure of this sort being long concealed from the public eye." Actually, the last stanzas of this poem, finally numbering 184, did not leave Venice until Jan. 7, 1818, and JM's first edition did not appear until April 28, 1818. *Works of Byron: Poetry*, II, 315.

[8] After Aug. 16, when WI first visited 50 Albemarle St., John Barrow discovered that the journal of James Tuckey's ill-fated expedition to trace the source of the Congo River had been copied by the purser, whose widow had made it available to the press. Smiles, II, 30–32.

The work was advertised by JMII as "in the press" in the *Courier*, Oct. 15, 1817, but it did not appear until 1818. Two editions of the *Narrative* were published in New York in 1818, neither of them apparently due to WI's efforts. One was brought out by W. B. Gilley, the other by Kirk & Mercein, regular pirate publishers of the American editions of the *ER* and *QR* and of Byron's poetry.

might be worth while to have it transcribed. Tuckey's narrative can be sent in sheets—or the first half of it forwarded as soon as the sheets are printed & the remainder by a subsequent opportunity. I regret I did not see the advertisement of Lord Amherst's embassy[9] in time to forward it to you, as I think something might have been done with it in America.

I wrote to Mr Thomas when I was in London, on the subject—desiring him to send you whatever was interesting from the American press & think it probable you will receive the works in a few weeks. I have no doubt you will find an understanding of the kind a source of considerable and encreasing advantage, & that you will be able to make arrangements for profiting materially by the American market.

It has occurred to me that if you could afford to strike off copies of the Quarterly Review at a cheap rate so as to deliver them in America as low, or lower than the American editions you might authorize Mr Thomas to take subscriptions. They would have the advantage of being put in the hands of the subscribers earlier than the republished copies could be. Should you forward the copies of Childe Harold &c. direct them care of *Messrs. P. Irving & Co., Liverpool,* and they will be transmitted to America by the earliest opportunity.

I have recently returned from a very pleasant time in Scotland.[10] A very few days after I dined with you I was at Constable's table & afterwards at Jeffrey's; and I assure you I found great gratification in thus visiting the advance camps in so short a space of time, and

[9] In the *Morning Post,* Sept. 15, 1817, JM announced the impending publication of Henry Ellis' *Journal of the Proceedings of the Late Embassy to China: Comprising a Narrative of the Public Transactions of the Embassy, of a Voyage to and from China,* popularly known as *Lord Amherst's Mission.* There were pre-publication advertisements by JM in later issues of the *Morning Post, Times,* and *Morning Chronicle;* the book was published on Oct. 6, 1817. The abortive attempt of William Pitt, Earl Amherst, to assert British power in China was a major topic of the day. JM's first edition was so successful that he brought out a second edition in two volumes in 1818. There is no evidence to suggest that an American publisher ever issued this title.

[10] The Scottish trip was described by WI in *Tour of Scotland 1817.* PMI, I, 376–87, quoted several letters that are even more illuminating on WI's activities. WI seems to have dined with Archibald Constable on Sept. 5 (*ibid.,* 384) and with Francis Jeffrey on Aug. 26, 27 (*ibid.,* 378–80) and Sept. 21 (*ibid.,* 386).

having a peep at the two great powers that divide the world of criticism.

When you see Mr Walter Hamilton I beg you will remember me to him; in the mean while if I can be of [any][11] service to you I shall be happy of your commands.

I am dear Sir
Yours faithfully,
Washington Irving.

Shortly after this, Murray received a package from Thomas. Murray's biographer Samuel Smiles reported, without editorializing, that it contained Wirt's *Sketches of the Life and Character of Patrick Henry*, MacClure's *Observations on the Geology of the United States*, McAfee's *History of the Late War in the Western Country*, and Brackenridge's *Views of Louisiana*.[12] On these Murray took a firm stand, declining to publish any of them or to associate himself with Irving's project. Perhaps, though, he did allow Irving to provide Thomas with the fourth canto of *Childe Harold*. An edition was published in 1818 in Philadelphia, presumably by Thomas.[13]

Irving's enthusiasm for his transatlantic publication plan was hardly greater than that shown by Moses Thomas, who agreed to pay him annually one thousand dollars for his services as middleman with the British publishers. Unfortunately, there are no records which throw light on the value of this arrangement to Thomas. Irving's official biographer, however, indicated that after a year "it was terminated by Mr. Irving's request; he finding it not so productive to Thomas as he had anticipated." [14]

After Irving's return from Scotland, he gave the remainder of the year to P. & E. Irving and Company, the effort proving finally to have been put forth on a lost cause. In January 1818 he and Peter met with the bankruptcy commissioners, beginning the long process which saw the final demise of their firm on June 21.

---

11 Paper slightly torn, losing a single small word.
12 II, 126.
13 See *Works of Byron: Poetry*, VIII, 185, n. 2.
14 PMI, I, 396.

The dreadful business in Liverpool behind them, Washington and Peter hurried to Birmingham, where the latter began a translation of Charles Nodier's *Jean Sbogar* (Paris, 1818) which he entitled *Giovanni Sbogarro, A Venetian Tale.* In little more than a month Washington had been lured to London by Allston, who—over his friends' protests—left England before the end of August to return to the United States to live. Ever since Irving's bachelor friends in New York had deserted him for married life, he had clearly fixed upon bereaved Allston as "the man I would have liked to have had always at my side—to have gone through life with." [15] Allston's departure left an even greater void in the life of C. R. Leslie. Quite naturally Irving fell into this vacancy.[16]

To this twosome was added a third American, Stuart Newton, recently arrived from Paris, where he had met Leslie. This nephew-namesake of American portrait painter Gilbert Stuart was already beginning to establish himself as a society painter. The fourth member of the group was sometime artist Peter Powell, a highly animated little man, considerably older than the others. Finally came William Willes, an Irish landscape painter. These five men (plus, occasionally, brother Peter, who came to London when his manuscript was completed) made up the fellowship to which Irving familiarly referred as the "Lads." [17]

[15] *Ibid.*, 405.

[16] A few years later, shortly before Leslie's marriage, he wrote to WI: "You came to London just as I was losing Allston and I stood in need of a friend with similar tastes as my own." PMI, I, 406.

[17] This group needs to be studied as a unit. Such an approach suggests, among other things, that an element of homosexuality was one of the cohesive forces which held the individuals together. Perhaps it was overt, but, in any case, the extreme expressions of need and love which characterized the group's correspondence and a bit of subtle rivalry between the members seem to go beyond foppishness and the customary sensibility of the day.

Like Leslie, Newton was an American-born artist whose appeal to British society proved to be his key to success. His pet group name was "the Childe," after Byron's Harold. See *DNB*, XIV, 368–69. An interesting biographical study and collection of Newton's works is Henry Murray, *The Gems of Stuart Newton* (London: H. Graves and Warmsley, 1842).

Willes, called "Father Luke" by the other "Lads," was a student at the Royal Academy. In 1823 ill health forced him to return to his home in Ireland, and though he recovered and returned to London in 1829, he appears to have

During the fall of 1818 and the winter of 1819 the "Lads" were inseparable: they dined among the actors and painters at the York Chop House on Wardour Street; they visited other Americans in London (George Ticknor, briefly free from his studies; John Howard Payne, often hiding from his creditors; John Allan of Virginia, whose charge Edgar Poe was soaking up English atmosphere for later use; Richard Rush, the United States Minister; and Colonel Thomas Aspinwall, the Consul in London;[18] they rambled about historic London and took excursions into the neighboring countryside; they played blindman's bluff, discussed the condition of the Arts, and consumed gallons of tea prepared by Willes' precise methods.

---

never renewed his intimacies with the others. Walter G. Strickland, *A Dictionary of Irish Artists* (Dublin: Maunsel & Co., 1913), II, 531–32.

Considerably older than the other "Lads," Peter Powell flits in and out of the records of his time, as John Constable said, "meddling with politics, or fighting with windmills or kicking the winds etc etc" (*The Letters of John Constable, R. A. to C. R. Leslie, R. A. 1826–1827*, ed. Peter Leslie [London: Constable & Co., 1931], p. 65). So small in stature that he was virtually a midget, he compensated for his size by animation and humor. See Leslie, *passim* and W. P. Frith, *Autobiography* (London: Bentley, 1887), I, 189–91.

18 See *Life, Letters, and Journals of George Tickner*, ed. G. S. Hillard (London: Sampson Low & Co., 1876), I, 291, 293, for description of the Lord Mayor's Ball and "the damning of a play" which WI and Ticknor witnessed in 1819.

Leslie, I, 219–20, left a vivid picture of Payne during the years after he deserted the American stage to try his luck in England. In 1830 Payne added to his writing and acting the management of Sadler's Wells, which he abandoned a year later. "His finances should have been more secure," a theatrical historian declared. Dennis Arundel, *The Story of Sadler's Wells, 1683–1964* (London: Hamish Hamilton, 1965), pp. 98–99.

John Allan was a cousin of novelist John Galt, a friend of Newton, Leslie, and WI. Hervey Allen, *Israfel: The Life and Times of Edgar Allan Poe* (New York: George H. Doran Co., 1927), I, 63–89.

Richard Rush, the son of Benjamin Rush, was a distinguished figure in English diplomatic circles to the end of his tour in 1825. Of special interest is Beckles Willson, *America's Ambassadors to England (1785–1928): A Narrative of Anglo-American Diplomatic Relations* (London: JM, 1928), pp. 138–59.

Col. Thomas Aspinwall had lost his left arm in the War of 1812. When peace came, he was rewarded by being appointed U. S. Consul in London, a position he held until 1853. Charles C. Smith, "Memoir of Col. Thomas Aspinwall," *Massachusetts Historical Society Proceedings*, 2nd Ser., VII (Nov. 1891), 32–38. Aspinwall gave WI high praise when he addressed the MHS meeting which marked WI's death. See "Remarks of Col. Aspinwall," MHSP, IV (Dec. 1859), 404–408.

Irving's time was not devoted entirely to activity with his four companions. Whenever he could set himself to the task—not always easy for a person of his disposition—he was writing on the essays that would finally compose *The Sketch Book*. By March 3, 1819, he was sending copy to Ebenezer in New York. The first American edition was ultimately published in four parts, the last of which appeared on November 10. The essays received immediate favorable attention in the United States and by the first of September the individual numbers were making their way back across the Atlantic to appear, unauthorized, in *The Literary Gazette*. The rumor that a London publisher—inspired by the popular acclaim in England of the *Gazette's* offerings—planned to issue the sketches in collected form caused Irving, who—as he reported it—had previously considered the work of interest mainly to American readers, to swallow his fear of British literary criticism and seek a publisher.[19]

"Among the admirers [of the typography of the first two sections of *The Sketch Book*] is Murray, the 'prince of booksellers,' so famous for his elegant publications," [20] Irving wrote to Brevoort, September 9, 1819. Brevoort immediately responded with a capital idea: "I wish you would *permit* Murray to publish your work." [21] In fact, the thought had entered Irving's mind; showing no signs of what his biographers called his "characteristic reserve," he had started at the top by first offering this work to Murray when he began his search for a publisher.

Since 1817 Murray's prestige had continued to rise. His purchase of the copyrights of George Crabbe's complete poems for £3,000 revitalized the book world in December 1818. The appearance of Byron's *Don Juan* in 1819 created one of the biggest

19 The first British reprint from *The Sketch Book* was "The Wife" in *The Kaleidoscope* (Liverpool), Aug. 24, 1819, which described WI as "that elegant scholar." *The Literary Gazette*, April 8, 1820, p. 228, stated that during the previous October it had received "a polite letter from the author" indicating his intention of publishing *The Sketch Book* in London. This "induced" it "to desist from further extracts," the original intention having been to reprint in installments all of the essays from the American edition.

20 PMI, I, 432.

21 *Ibid.*, 446.

literary stirs of the decade. The demand for copies of the title was so great that the front door of Murray's establishment had to be barricaded against the clamoring agents of the nation's booksellers; the stock was passed through the dining-room windows to their grasping hands. The completion of Campbell's seven-volume *Specimens of British Poets*, finally achieved in this year, was a less spectacular event, but one which both Peter and Washington witnessed with relief. Also in 1819, after protesting against the personality cult being developed by the contributors to *Blackwood's Edinburgh Magazine*, of which Murray had been half-owner and London publisher, he sold his share of the periodical to devote his full time to the more staid *Quarterly Review* and to the book trade. The pressure of increasing business encouraged the overworked publisher to purchase in that year a country home at Wimbledon, a place to which he could retreat, escaping the problems of London. He was there in May, "unwell with bile and rheumatism . . . for a few days to recruit," [22] but he was back in residence at 50 Albemarle Street to deal with his expanding interests when he heard about *The Sketch Book* from its author.

Years later, Irving recalled his approach to the publisher on this subject.

> I . . . took the printed numbers which I had received from the United States, to Mr. John Murray, the eminent publisher, from whom I had already received friendly attentions, and left them with him for examination, informing him that should he be inclined to bring them before the public, I had materials enough on hand for a second volume.[23]

The material Irving left with Murray included "The Prospectus," "The Voyage," "Roscoe," "The Wife," "Rip Van Winkle," "English Writers on America," "Rural Life in England," "The Broken Heart," and "The Art of Book-Making," in

[22] Smiles, II, 82.
[23] "Preface," *The Sketch Book* [Author's Revised Edition] (New York: G. P. Putnam & Co., 1857), II, vii. This edition hereinafter cited as title, AREd.

all a total of close to one hundred and fifty pages ("of large type and copious margin" [24]) and less than one-fourth the size of the finished work. Still to come were the essays on Shakespeareana, English Christmas, and other aspects of the British scene.

Irving continued his recollections: "Several days having elapsed without any communication from Mr. Murray, I addressed a note to him, in which I construed his silence into a tacit rejection of my work, and begged that the numbers I had left with him might be returned to me." [25] To this, apparently on October 27, Murray replied:

My dear Sir:

I entreat you to believe that I feel truly obliged by your kind intentions toward me, and that I entertain the most unfeigned respect for your most tasteful talents. My House is completely filled with work-people at this time, and I have only an office to transact business in; and yesterday I was wholly occupied, or I should have done myself the pleasure of seeing you.

If it would not suit me to engage in the publication of your present work, it is only because I do not see that scope in the nature of it which would enable me to make those satisfactory accounts between us, without which I really feel no satisfaction in engaging; but I will do all that I can do to promote their circulation, and shall be most ready to attend to any future plan of yours. With much regard, I remain, dear sir,

Your faithful servant,
John Murray.[26]

Humbly and appreciatively Irving responded:

2. *To John Murray II* [27]

Edward Street
Octr 28th 1819.

My dear Sir,

I feel much obliged by your very kind note of yesterday. I am

24 PMI, I, 416.

25 *SB*, AREd., II, vii.

26 Printed *ibid.*, viii. The MS copy of this letter is preserved among the WI Papers in the Berg Collection, New York Public Library.

27 Used by permission of the Berg Collection, The New York Public Library, Astor, Lenox and Tilden Foundations.

"I am astonished at the success
of my writing in England, and can hardly
persuade myself that it is not all a dream," Washington
Irving wrote to John Murray II. Irving was thirty-seven
years old when, in 1820, he sat for an oil portrait
by Gilbert Stuart Newton, of which this is a
romanticized copy. *From Stanley T.
Williams*, The Life of Washington
Irving, *Oxford University Press.*

"I am convinced I did not half know you,
and esteeming you highly as I did, certainly
my esteem is doubled by my better knowledge of you,"
John Murray II told Washington Irving in late 1820,
when *The Sketch Book* was the most popular title
on his list. The original of this portrait,
painted about 1820 by H. W. Pickersgill,
hangs in the offices of his company.
From Samuel Smiles, A Publisher and
His Friends, *John Murray*,
Publishers.

perfectly conscious of the force of your objection to the work I offered, and that my writings have that deficiency of scope and fullness, which results from some degree of self diffidence and a want of practice and experience. I may improve as I proceed and shall feel proud and happy if on some future occasion I may have any thing to offer that may be deemed worthy of your attention.

> With great respect
> Yours truly,
> W. Irving.

Murray could have pointed out the facts of the copyright laws to Irving, certainly in this instance a deterrent to any prospective British publisher. Under the accepted interpretation of the laws, the writings of a person of any nationality could be protected in Britain by a copyright if the work were first published in that country; otherwise, a book was free to any publisher who might choose to hazard the expense of publication. The prior publication of the bulk of *The Sketch Book* in the United States meant that Irving should expect no official protection of his rights to this title in the British Isles.

After Murray's refusal to undertake *The Sketch Book*, Irving appealed to Scott for his intercession with Constable, but though there was much good will on Scott's part, nothing came of this. The author himself then "determined to look to no leading bookseller for a launch, but to throw my work before the public at my own risk, and let it sink or swim according to its merits." [28] On February 24, 1820, Washington wrote to Ebenezer explaining that John Miller, Burlington Arcade, had published, at Irving's expense, the first four numbers as a single volume. "I shall not publish any more, and should not have done this," he declared, "had there not been a likelihood of these works being republished here from incorrect American numbers." [29]

Almost before the volume could get on the shelves, Miller's business failed, but Geoffrey Crayon's *Sketch Book*, already the talk of literate society, was saved by Murray, who purchased the

28 PMI, I, 445.
29 *Ibid.*, 449.

stock at a price which the American thought munificent.[30] Happily, the demand was so great that Murray added a second volume to the series of essays and reprinted the whole under his own imprint.

What of this American graft onto Murray's ever-flowering tree of titles? It represented no innovation for the publisher, who selected each new publication for his own reasons—either because the work personally pleased him, because it was of such timely interest that it could not fail to sell, or because it had been strongly recommended by some of the literary giants who surrounded him. Although John Murray II had early in his career defined his areas of interest, one searches in vain for a genre or a subject to which he did not lend his imprint when the situation merited it. Irving's collection of familiar essays seemed most appropriately placed among the numerous volumes of exotic travels (already becoming a speciality of Murray's), the precise poetry of Crabbe's *Tales of the Hall,* and D'Israeli's antiquarian *Literary Character, Illustrated by the History of Men of Genius.*

In March and April it became clear that Washington Irving, most often answering to the name of Geoffrey Crayon, was a rising figure in London society. Late in March, Scott appeared there to accept his baronetcy from the new king and to pay his respects to the English-speaking world's newest literary noble. This he did in a cozy breakfast chat and among the literati in Murray's drawing room. "Scott for a friend, Murray for his publisher," Stanley T. Williams wrote, "and fame among the civilized readers in England and America":[31] Irving had arrived in Liverpool in 1815 with his stated destinations Rome and Athens; Williams implied, reflecting no doubt Irving's own feelings, that the traveler, now as much at home at 50 Albemarle Street as Gifford, Scott, or even Byron, had overshot his mark and ended on Parnassus.

---

[30] Apparently, the intervention of Walter Scott was largely responsible for Murray's change of mind. See *SB*, AREd., II, xii.

[31] STW, I, 176.

CHAPTER TWO

MURRAY'S MOST VALUED AUTHOR

Saturday, May 27, 1820

The rain outside did not seem to dampen Irving's spirits as he gazed out the window of the second-floor lodgings which he shared with his brother Peter—who sat by his side reading the third thick volume of Anastasius. *Edward Street was deserted and only an occasional carriage moved along Portland Place, spraying dirty water in all directions as it broke through the stream which all but concealed the surface of the thoroughfare. To the east he could see the familiar landmarks of Fitzroy Square where Leslie lived.*

That afternoon Irving had left Murray's drawing room earlier than usual to meet Leslie for an hour or so of rambling about the town, but their excursion had ended where it was scheduled to begin, their meeting place, the York Chop House on Wardour Street. A dark storm with reverberating claps of thunder sent Londoners, unaccustomed to such loud displays of nature, running for home, and as rain began to pour, Leslie remembered his wide-open windows. It was already too late to save the furnishings from a thorough wetting, but nevertheless he left in a dash, followed up Portland Place by his shrieking friend. They ran, splashing and laughing, playing in the rain like two children. In a running stream of vile-looking water Irving lost his right slipper, which Leslie retrieved by finally getting on his knees to search for it with his hands. The treasure found, Leslie ran off waving it in the air, with Irving, still wearing the left mate, in wild pursuit.

Having carefully filled the slipper with water from the over-

*flowing gutter, Leslie left it on the steps of 21 Edward Street and
ran off toward his own lodgings, shouting at Irving, who, panting
for breath and shaking with laughter, stood in the partial shelter
of the doorway and emptied the slipper. He watched Leslie dis-
appear into his building, then stood dripping and laughing for
several minutes before he ventured into the house. His formerly
white stockings were now a dull red-green and his clothes and
curly hair were plastered to his body. Carrying both shoes and
leaving diminishing puddles with each footstep, he made his way
up the stairway.*

*In a matter of minutes Peter had a small fire crackling in the
fireplace. Stripped of his wet clothes, Washington was wrapped in
a bedspread, wriggling his naked toes almost in the dancing
flames.*

*Usually so much interested in everything his younger brother
did, Peter seemed this afternoon more concerned with the book
he had been reading when Washington came dripping and laughing into the room. As soon as he could get the wet clothes stretched
out for drying, he took up the volume again, leaving Washington
to muse by the heat of the fire. Such a slight normally would have
hurt Washington's sensitive feelings, but this special afternoon
nothing seemed to darken his mood. He even expressed aloud his
intention to write a long overdue letter to Paulding and not dis-
turb his brother's reading.*

*He padded across the floor in his bare feet, gathering his writ-
ing materials. To gain full advantage of the dull light, he moved
his chair to the window beside Peter. Once situated, however, he
appeared to find it difficult to write. He stared for several minutes
at the building in the distance, where no doubt Leslie was drying
himself by a fire; then, finally phrasing each sentence in a loud
whisper, he began to put words on the paper before him. After
the customary opening apologies and comments, the composition
moved faster, for he had reached a subject on which he could be
verbose.*

As I am launched upon the literary world here, I find my oppor-

tunities of observation extending. Murray's drawing-room is a great resort of first-rate literary characters; whenever I have a leisure hour I go there, and seldom fail to meet with some interesting personages. The hours of access are from two to five. It is understood to be a matter of privilege, and that you must have a general invitation from Murray. Here I frequently meet with such personages as Gifford, Campbell, Foscolo, Hallam (author of a work on the Middle Ages), Southey, Milman, Scott, Belzoni, &c., &c.

He stopped writing and smiled, undoubtedly remembering Paulding's display of temper when in 1814 he read the vicious review of his The Lay of the Scottish Fiddle in the Quarterly Review; the editor Gifford had carried the burden of his abuse. Irving returned to his letter:

Gifford, of whom, as an old adversary, you may be curious to know something, is a small, shrivelled, deformed man of about sixty, with something of a humped back, eyes that diverge, and a large mouth. He is generally reclining on one of the sofas, and supporting himself by the cushions, being very much debilitated. He is mild and courteous in his manners, without any of the petulance that you would be apt to expect, and is quite simple, unaffected, and unassuming. Murray tells me that Gifford does not write any full articles for the Review, but revises, modifies, prunes, and prepares whatever is offered; and is very apt to extract the sting from articles that are rather virulent.

Then he discussed at some length his friendship with Sir Walter Scott, recently in London to receive his baronetcy, but his face darkened in the last touches of the daylight. He wrote with faltering strokes of more personal matters: the marriages of his bachelor friends in the United States, Stephen Decatur's death, and Paulding's family. For a long time he stared into the wet twilight of the May evening; then with a flourish he signed the page, "Affectionately your friend, W. Irving."

Sources for Vignette

Anastasius: or Memoirs of a Greek, Written at the Close of the

Eighteenth Century, published anonymously in three volumes by JM in 1819, was a picaresque novel presented as a translation. It was the work of one of the London drawing-room dandies, Thomas Hope.

The letter quoted is printed in its entirety in PMI, I, 455–59. Other sources of information are: *Morning Chronicle*, May 25, 1820; Leslie, I, 64 *et passim;* A. Edwin's Weather Diary for 1820.

In view of later developments (see Letter 3, below) it is interesting to notice that when Paulding, who had never been to England, wrote *A Sketch of Old-England, by a New-England Man* (New York: Charles Wiley, 1822), he devoted several paragraphs to a discussion of JM's drawing-room circle, lifting his information mainly from WI's letters. See especially *ibid.*, II, 86, 135–38. Reviewing this work in QR, XXX (Jan. 1824), 519–42, John Wilson Croker and Gifford (Hill Shine, *The "Quarterly Review" under Gifford: Identification of Contributors, 1809–1824* [Chapel Hill: University of North Carolina Press, 1949], p. 88) speculated that Paulding was the anonymous author and made sarcastic remarks about his references to JMII and the QR.

During the summer of 1820 Geoffrey Crayon (Washington Irving) had somehow been lost as an identity) captivated London society. For him there were regular afternoon sessions in Murray's drawing room and dinners among the socially elite. He was, as Leslie later described him, quoting John Miller, "the most fashionable fellow of the day," [1] with precious little time for his friends of recent months. "Since I have published with Murray," Irving wrote Brevoort, August 15, "I have had continual opportunities of seeing something of the literary world, and have formed some very agreeable acquaintances": Lady Caroline Lamb, Giovanni Belzoni, Henry Hallam. . . . But, he added, "it is useless to mention names . . . like entertaining one with a de-

[1] Leslie, II, 105.

scription of a banquet, by merely naming the dishes." [2] Though Irving insisted that the rich diet of his new life was a burden, he remained in London to the end of the social season, relishing every morsel offered to him. Not until August 17 was he able to force himself to leave England for his long-projected continental trip. On that day he and Peter sailed from Southampton for France.

On the previous day Washington had sold to Murray the doubtfully valid British copyright to *The Sketch Book* for two hundred and fifty guineas.[3] The publisher's original suggestion was that he would print a uniform edition of the two volumes at his own expense, the profit to be shared by author and publisher, but Irving declined, insisting that the transaction should be immediate and final. Murray also indicated that he wished to publish *The History of New York*, which had recently been receiving glowing, if belated, notice in the British periodicals.[4] To this idea, Irving agreed heartily. The publisher concluded the business discussion by expressing the hope that Irving would not let his pen stay idle for long and that Crayon's future creative efforts would be issued in London under the Murray imprint. He cautioned, however, the necessity of original publication in England for a legal copyright.

Watching England fade in the distance, Washington Irving must have felt that his finances, like his literary reputation, were serenely secure. Had he been satisfied with his vastly improved financial situation—now as in later years—his story would be a much happier one. Unfortunately, the two brothers had hardly touched French soil when Peter fell prey to a scheme to operate

---

[2] PMI, I, 461–62. To Brevoort's pleas for "more particulars of the interesting characters" WI was meeting, the author replied that he "must save up all his anecdotes and good things for his publishers." PMI, II, 38.

[3] PMI, I, 460, says JMII paid £200 for the copyright; the note still among the WI Papers in the Murray Archives clearly states 250 guineas. See Appendix III, item 1.

As to the validity of the copyright, JMII, capitalizing on the fact that the second volume was an original publication, had registered *SB* and deposited eleven copies at Stationers' Hall. See Appendix V.

[4] One of most laudatory references had been in an article by John Gibson Lockhart in *Blackwood's Edinburgh Magazine*, VI (Feb. 1820), 554–61.

a steamboat on the Seine River between Havre and Rouen. The prospect of reaping a vast profit from the enterprise seemed to be a certainty when Washington poured in his money. The rewards, if there were any, however, were not monetary. The project kept Peter busily occupied in France for several years, but this was psychological medicine for which Washington paid dearly, since it eventually consumed the profit from the American and English editions of *The Sketch Book*.[5]

The reputation of Geoffrey Crayon had gone before him.[6] In Paris the brothers became ornaments in the strong English colony which moved around the British diplomatic corps, Thomas Moore, and Galignani's bookshop and reading room.[7] Visiting with Americans in Paris was in itself a full-time task. Always on the outlook for a family haven, he found the Thomas Wentworth Storrows eager to "adopt" him: the father, with a vocation in financial matters and avocations ranging from linguistics to geology; the mother, cultivated and charming; the five children, lovable and demanding. The United States Minister to France, Albert Gallatin, was always pleased to see the young man who, a decade earlier, had enchanted the ladies in his wife's Washing-

[5] PMI, II, 17, referred to the steamboat venture as a "sordid entanglement." WI welcomed it in 1820, for Peter's recurring hope of a career in literature had been fairly well destroyed by his failure to secure an English publisher for his novel and by the indifference of the public to the American edition, published in this year.

[6] For WI's reputation among the French, 1819-1833, see STW, "The First Versions of the Writings of WI in Spanish," *Modern Philology*, XXVIII (Nov. 1930), 185, n. 2.

[7] In society English influence was at its zenith in Paris, then enjoying a settlement of English dignitaries second only to London. See Roger Boutet de Mouvel, *Eminent English Men and Women In Paris 1800–1850* (London: David Nutt, 1912), pp. 87–164. The vast body of literature left by these visitors in Paris offers excellent sources for studying WI's immediate milieu. There is no better picture of the English-speaking Paris group than is provided through the private journals of Thomas Moore. See Moore, *Memoirs*, III, 139–279. This English society Moore pointedly satirized in *The Fudge Family in Paris* (1818).

The distinguished history of Galignani's, the oldest English bookshop on the Continent, is outlined in *A Famous Bookstore* (Paris: The Galignani Library, 1920) and more recently in Giles Barber, "Galignani's and the Publication of English Books in France from 1800 to 1852," *The Library*, 5th Ser., XVI (Dec. 1961), 267–86.

Since 1812, 50 Albemarle Street
has been the address of the House of Murray.
Here John Murray II entertained the cream of the
literary world, charming prospective authors and placating
those he had published. This sketch appeared
in a commemorative pamphlet, "John Murray,
50 Albemarle Street, 1768–1930."
*Courtesy of John Murray, Publishers,
and the British Museum.*

ton City drawing room. In addition to these residential Americans, there was a steady stream of transients: he met financier John Jacob Astor for the first time, and he was the Parisian guide for a host of young intellectuals such as George Bancroft and Joseph Coolidge. Inevitably, there was John Howard Payne. With few exceptions these friends of 1820–1821 would reappear to play parts in later periods of his life.[8]

Irving's first letter from Paris to John Murray was in tone different from all the later communications. One pictures the American pondering over this unusually (for a letter to Murray) neatly written epistle, remembering the reception which each new Byron letter had created upon its arrival at 50 Albemarle Street and, no doubt, hoping that the publisher might exhibit this product in the drawing room. So he wrote, in a spirited attempt to rival Murray's greatest author, ending with some royal gossip which, if it were news to Irving, was well known to every tosher, climbing boy, and Tory gentleman in London. The carrier of foreign mail along Pickering's Walk delivered his first letter from Washington Irving at Murray's door on October 31.

3. *To John Murray II*[9]

Paris, Octr 26th 1820.

My dear Sir,

On taking up a London paper this morning I found my name giv-

---

[8] WI's relationship with the Storrows can be traced through the next seven years in STW's *WI and the Storrows*.

Gallatin was U. S. Minister to France, 1816–1823. Gallatin's life in France is covered in Raymond Walters, *Albert Gallatin* (New York: The Macmillan Co., 1957), pp. 299–316.

For Bancroft's visit, see M. A. DeWolfe Howe, *The Life and Letters of George Bancroft* (London: Hodder & Stoughton, 1908), I, 106–10. Later, with an introduction from Bancroft, Joseph Coolidge of Boston appeared. See Ellen M. Oldham, "Lord Byron and Mr. Coolidge of Boston," *The Book Collector*, XIII (Summer, 1964), 211–13.

Sometime in 1821 Payne reached Paris, having fled in the night from his British creditors. "The gossip of dining-out gentlemen" in London, he feared, had prejudiced WI against him, but nothing ever accomplished that end. See WI to JHP, London, May 28, 1820, in MS Collection of Columbia University, New York. Hereinafter cited as Columbia.

[9] The first paragraph was printed in a somewhat altered form in Smiles, II,

en at full length in an advertisement of Cawthorn's as author of a poem he has just republished entitled *"The Lay of a Scottish Fiddle."* As I wish to be answerable to no one's sins but my own I would take it as a particular favour if you would contradict it in your next advertisement of the Sketch Book &c. The work in question was written by a Mr Paulding.[10] What particularly annoys me is that this poem was a burlesque on the writings of Sir Walter Scott for whom I have so perfect an esteem & affection, and beside it contained political and national reflections of a different nature from those I have entertained.

I see that you have published The History of N York and understand you hurried it out to prevent a spurious edition from being thrown into circulation: for which I am glad though I should have liked to have read your corrections and alterations.[11]

I see you are all yet occupied with the Queen's pilgrimage to Jerusalem; and have a famous array of Crusaders who have all been

---

131. Marked at the Foreign Post Office in London, Oct. 31, 1820. Distinct impression of design in sealing wax.

10 ". . . a Mr. Paulding" indeed! There is nothing objectionable enough in this little book to justify WI's denial of his close friend of many years. For details concerning the bitter reviews of *The Lay of the Scottish Fiddle* and Paulding's reaction, see: Shine, pp. 40, 41, and Amos L. Herold, *James Kirke Paulding: Versatile American* (New York: Columbia University Press, 1926), pp. 42, 48.

The piece WI read was apparently from the *Morning Chronicle*, Oct. 21, 1820: "WASHINGTON IRVING'S POEMS.—7s. 6d. boards by James Cawthorne, Cockspur-Street, a Second Edition of The Lay of the Scottish Fiddle. A Poem in Five Cantos. By WASHINGTON IRVING Esq, Author of 'The Sketch Book.'" The advertisement appeared only once, suggesting that JMII or other knowledgeable parties may have called attention to the error. In fact, Cawthorne had been the publisher of the original English edition in 1814, and it is unlikely that this was an entirely honest error on his part. At any rate, JMII seems to have not been very disturbed by it, for although he advertised WI's writings frequently in later issues of this paper, he did not trouble to refer to this instance of mistaken identity.

11 JM had just brought out the first authorized English edition of *The History of New York*. Another London publisher, William Wright, issued an unauthorized edition in this year. WI had seen the third American edition through the press in 1819 and no doubt regretted that JMII, in his hurry to get the book to the English public, had used as his text the most easily available copy, one from the second edition (1812). For a precise description of both Murray's and Wright's editions of 1821, consult William R. Langfeld and Philip C. Blackburn, *Washington Irving: A Bibliography* (New York: The New York Public Library, 1933), p. 12.

with her to the Holy Land.[12] I expect Bergamis' effigy will figure cross legged at some future day in Westminster Abbey. By the way I was lately taking care of a young friend who lay very ill of a fever,[13] and was obliged to have a female attendant or *garde* as they are called here to watch with him at nights. She was a very decent French woman. By mere accident I was enquiring one day about her circumstances when she told me that her husband was coachman to Bergamis' daughter—I felt a little surprise, as you may suppose, and on questioning her further I found that Victorine, the child of five years of age, is at a boarding school in the vicinity of Paris, where she has a carriage, and male & female attendants to the number of five for her particular service!—This you may depend on as a fact: for the honest woman told it with the utmost simplicity & frankness. Truly this Bergamis is a fellow of most princely notions!

Present my sincere regards to Mrs Murray & believe me dear Sir,
[Signature cut out][14]

The day before Irving penned this letter to his publisher, John Murray had written his most flattering words to the American. His pen dripping with honey, he wrote: "I am convinced I did not half know you, and esteeming you highly as I did, certainly my esteem is doubled by my better knowledge of you." [15] Murray offered him an additional one hundred guineas because of the con-

---

[12] Caroline, the unhappy consort of the Prince Regent, later George IV, was rumored to have committed adultery with Bergamis, whom the Governor of Lombardy had assigned to her as her guide. His daughter Victorine was a special favorite to whom Caroline eventually gave a luxurious villa in Milan. Victorine was somewhat older than the five years WI attributed to her in 1820. A readable account of this period of Caroline's life is in E. E. P. Tisdall, *The Wanton Queen: The Story of Britain's Strangest Queen* (London: Stanley Paul & Co., 1939), pp. 221–27.

At the time of this letter, the Queen had returned to England and was being tried, at the command of her husband, by the House of Lords on a charge of adultery with Bergamis. The papers were full of the trial testimony, and the market was flooded with pamphlets, street ballads, and broadsides, often bordering on the obscene.

[13] None of WI's available letters or journals offer any suggestions as to the identity of this sick friend.

[14] The complimentary close and signature have been neatly clipped out; no other part of the manuscript is damaged.

[15] PMI, II, 26.

tinued success of *The Sketch Book*, and he reported with pleasure the high praise of Gifford and Byron.[16] In Irving's *History of New York*, which he was about to publish, he found traces of genius. "It is the Don Quixote or Hudibras of your country," Murray declared.[17] Finally, indicating that he was trying to establish the extent of his legal copyright coverage of *The Sketch Book*, the publisher asked for a listing of the essays that had been published first in England. He concluded with a warm remembrance from the D'Israelis for Irving.

4. *To John Murray II*[18]

Paris, Octr 31st 1820.

My dear Sir,

I have just received your letter of the 25th which has almost overpowered me with the encomiums it contains. I am astonished at the success of my writings in England, and can hardly persuade myself that it is not all a dream. Had any one told me a few years since in America, that any thing I could write would interest such men as Gifford and Byron I should have as readily believed a fairy tale. If Mr Gifford will be so good as to suggest what parts of Knickerbocker might be curtailed with advantage I shall endeavour to mod-

---

16 Unfortunately, there is no record of exactly what Gifford had to say about *SB*, though it is clear that he was highly pleased with it. In an undated letter at JM's, he wrote: "If our friend [Henry] Matthews does not give us a much better review of the Sketch-book than theirs [*Edinburgh Review*], I will, without ceremony, fling it in the fire." See below, n. 35.

Gifford's comments on *The History of New York* were perhaps similar to Leslie's: the artist (Dec. 3, 1820), in referring to proposed illustrations, hoped that WI would omit certain unrefined jokes in future editions. Leslie, II, 99. In fact, WI did cut later editions. See C. M. Webster, "WI's Expurgation of 1809 *History of New York*," *American Literature*, IV (Nov. 1932), 293–95.

JMII was reporting on Byron's comment in his letter of October 12, 1820. (See *Works of Byron: Letters and Journals*, V, 94). Yet PMI, II, 25–26, with the now-missing manuscript of JMII's letter before him, wrote: "In another part of his [JMII's] letter he says: 'By the way, Lord Byron says in his pithy manner, in a letter received to-day, of date October 8th, "Crayon is [very] good," interlined as I have written it.'" It was an interesting but not important mistake of JMII's part, this quotation being in the letter of Oct. 12. Worth noting is the fact that the editor of the previously cited definitive edition of Byron's works did not enclose the *very* in brackets.

17 PMI, II, 25.

18 The first five sentences were printed in Smiles, II, 131–32.

ify the work accordingly. I am sensible that it is full of faults, and would almost require rewriting, to make it what it should be, but I find it very difficult to touch it now; it is so stale with me. I shall write to Mr Leslie on the subject of the Sketches.[19] I am very glad you have seen him and have taken an interest in him. He is deserving of the highest encouragement and patronage; he is full of talent, and full of merit. You can be of great service to him, and I think with advantage to yourself. It is one of the enviable circumstances of your lot, that you are enabled to do so much good to a variety of the most interesting and valuable people and to surround yourself with agreeable talent of every kind.

The specimen you have sent me of the new edition of the Sketch Book is very handsome. I like the size.[20] I will look over the work and send you any corrections that may occur, and when I have a spare copy, will underline the passages first published in England. The *articles* that were first published there were "Westminster Abbey—Stratford-on-Avon—Little Britain—The Angler—& L'Envoy." Galignani says that you can send any parcel for me to their correspondent Baldwin & Co.[21] but that it must be mentioned to the Baldwins that it is with Galignani's permission—otherwise the

[19] On this date, WI wrote to Leslie: "I have just received a very long and friendly letter from Mr. Murray, who in fact overwhelmed me with eulogiums. It appears that my writings are selling well, and he is multiplying editions. I am very glad to find that he had made your acquaintance, and still more that he has taken a liking to you. He speaks of you in the most gratifying terms. He has it in his power to be of service to you, and I trust he will be. He tells me he has requested you to look over Knickerbocker for subjects for eight or ten sketches, and the Sketch Book for a couple, and he wishes me to assist you with my opinion on the subject. I will look over the books and write to you in a day or two. Murray is going to make me so fine in print that I shall hardly know myself." Leslie, II, 90.

By degrees the "Lads" were being introduced into JM's drawing room. A month later (Nov. 30) WI wrote to Leslie: "I hear that you have taken the 'Childe' Newton to Murray's; you have only to make his acquainted with Willes and Peter Powell, and he will then be able to make one at your tea-kettle debauches." Leslie, II, 93. WI's reference is to a letter from Newton telling of his introduction to JMII and a gathering of the "Lads" at Willes', from which they departed at 4 A.M. "reeling with Bohea." PMI, II, 30.

[20] JMII's original edition of *SB* had been demy octavo (8¾ x 5⅛); the new edition in untrimmed form was crown octavo (7½ x 5). Based on copies in the British Museum. JMII sold the volumes at 12*s* each.

[21] Most likely Baldwyn & Co., Booksellers, 122 Newgate Street, Cheapside. *Johnstone's London Commercial Guide and Street Directory* (London: Barnard and Farley, 1817), col. 351.

parcel may be refused. They have a parcel sent from London the first of every month, but it is likely they will have one the middle of November. I am much obliged to you for what you say about my drawing on you; as in the state of my finances it will be a matter of some convenience.

I have been rather an idle man since my arrival in Paris; and indeed have been so flattered by the circumstance of republishing in England, and the attention that has been so liberally shewn to my writings and myself there, that I must take a little time to let my mind get calm and collected. I feel a little too anxious just now.

I have just received a letter from a Bookseller in New York who is publishing a poem written by a son of his, lately deceased; a young clergyman of great promise. The subject of the poem is taken from the story of King Philip the celebrated Indian chief— (on which by the way Southey is writing a poem).[22] It is in six cantos & forms about 300pp. 12 mo. It is entitled "Gamoyden: a tale of the Wars of King Philip, with notes and preface by *the late Rev. James Wallis Eastman M. A. and his friend.*" [23] The friend is a young gentleman who at the age of 18 produced a poem entitled

[22] WI had also written on the subject—"Philip of Pokanoket" in *SB*, where this footnote appeared: "While correcting the proofsheets of this article, the author is informed that a celebrated English poet has nearly finished a heroic poem on the story of Philip of Pokanoket." (In *American Literature*, XVIII [Nov. 1946], 247–49, J. L. Wilson identified "WI's 'Celebrated English Poet'" as Robert Southey.)

Southey himself made an interesting comment on the subject: "Murray has sent me the 'Sketch Book,' the author of which I met in his room. It is a very pleasing clever book. What the writer says concerning the Indians is more creditable to his humanity than to his judgement. It is quite an *ex parte* view of the case. Philip of Pokanoket, with whom I shall make you better acquainted than Irving seems to be, had all the treachery of a true savage, as well as some of a savage's virtues. His Indian name was Massosoit (not Kawnacom); and the historical grounds of my poem are, as Irving supposes, to be found in the main events of what is called Philip's war." Southey to C. W. W. Wynn, Nov. 13, 1820, in *Selections from the Letters of Robert Southey*, ed. John Wood Warter (London: Longman, Brown, Green, Longman, & Roberts, 1856), III, 218.

Southey never completed this poem, though fragments of it were published posthumously as "Oliver Newman: A New-England Tale" in 1845. It is included in *The Poetical Works of Robert Southey* (London: Longmans, Green & Co., 1873), pp. 788–809.

[23] New York: James Eastman, 1820. Young Eastman's collaborator was the poet Robert Charles Sands (1799–1832), whose *The Bridal of Vaumond; a Metrical Romance* had been published in 1817 by James Eastman & Co. There is no evidence to indicate that JMII or any English publisher brought out *Gamoyden.*

"The Bridal of Vaumond," which shewed great poetical promise.[24] These young gentlemen had visited all the scenes of King Philip's exploits: noted the scenery & collected all the historical and traditional facts that were extant. The poem is very highly spoken of, by various persons of cultivated taste that have seen it—and the novelty of an Indian poem, written on the spot and by persons familiar with Indian manners may give it additional interest. The object of all this, is to recommend the work to your attention. I am requested by the author's father to do so. He writes that he will send the sheets as they are printed to my correspondents in Liverpool and a complete copy when finished. I will write to have them submitted to you for your perusal, and you will determine whether the work will be desirable for republication, and what terms you can afford to offer. I have not seen the work, and only speak from the representations of others, which are very strong in its favour.

Present my best regards to Mrs Murray, and likewise to my friends the D'Israelis; by whose kind enquiries I am very much obliged.

I am my dear Sir
With very great regard
Yours faithfully,
Washington Irving.

P.S.   As you are printing the Sketch Book I just recollect an error I observed this morning Vol. II, P. 50, line 6 for "*grazing*" read "*dozing.*" [25]

With the passing of time *The Sketch Book* was even more popular. "Its success, considering all things, is unparalleled," [26] Murray told Newton as the artist completed Irving's portrait for the publisher's gallery.[27] By December Murray's edition was out of print,[28] and he was busily trying to fill the booksellers' orders for more copies. Peter Powell, writing to Irving at this time, summed up the critical reaction to *The Sketch Book:*

[24] For Sands, see *DAB*, XVI, 344. *The Bridal of Vaumond* had been dedicated to WI.

[25] This insignificant change was finally made by JMII in "A New Edition," 1821. See II, 20, line 3.

[26] PMI, II, 48.

[27] This portrait now hangs in the back drawing room of 50 Albemarle Street.

[28] Leslie, II, 226.

34

in regard to your debut amongst us in this critical age, . . . I have not heard of your having so much as a nose or a member of any kind cut up by the anatomists of literature; on the contrary, there seems to be almost a *conspiracy* to hoist you over the heads of your contemporaries.[29]

Certainly John Murray had rarely—if ever—published a work which pleased more and offended fewer people. He scanned the reviews, which delighted in reprinting generous extracts from the polished essays, unable to find any adverse criticism stronger than the feeble assertion of the *Monthly Review* that the author was too free with his epithets and apostrophes.[30] One wonders if the experienced publisher did not recognize the delicate position in which *The Sketch Book*'s almost-too-favorable reception placed Irving. Would his future writings be anticlimactic? Whether or not it troubled Murray, it was a problem which was starting to weigh heavily on Irving's mind. Coupled with this growing anxiety, as early as December 19, 1820, the writer was beginning to imagine intended slights on the part of the publisher. "I had hoped to hear from Mr. Murray before this . . . , but I presume he has been too much hurried to attend to it," he wrote Leslie.[31]

For the moment, however, Irving was enjoying Paris society as he had reveled in London high life the previous year—though he was beginning to be pursued by the expectations of his publisher and public. It was Thomas Moore, physically small but a giant in personality and ideas, who suggested the subject of his next book: why not make "a slight thread of a story" of the Christmas essays and Master Simon Bracebridge from *The Sketch Book* "on which to string remarks and sketches of human manners?"[32] Within ten days (on May 19, 1821) Irving had written one hundred and thirty pages of the volume eventually to be

[29] PMI, II, 32.
[30] XCII (Oct. 1820), 207.
[31] Leslie, II, 101.
[32] Moore, *Memoirs*, III, 211.

called *Bracebridge Hall; or, The Humourists.* The father of the
idea, Moore was to witness its somewhat painful growth throughout the later spring months.[33] Having heard Irving read the bulk
of the manuscript, Moore concluded in his diary on June 21: "It
is amusing, but will, I fear, much disappoint the expectations his
Sketches have raised." [34]

Perhaps the news of the developing manuscript had reached
London, for on June 29 John Murray wrote to Irving: "Draw
upon me for a hundred pounds, of which I beg thy acceptance,
and pray tell me how you are and what you are about; and above
all, pardon my short letter." As an afterthought he added at the
bottom of the page, "There is a review of the Sketch Book in the
Quarterly,[35] which you will like." [36]

5. To John Murray II[37]

Paris, July 6th, 1821.

My dear Sir,

I write in great haste, to acknowledge the receipt of your Letter
of the 29th ult. I am extremely happy to hear that the Sketch Book
has been favourably noticed in the Quarterly. I have not seen the
review, but I doubt whether any criticism in it can be so emphatic
as that in your letter. You were certainly intended for a critick. I
never knew any one convey so much meaning in so concise and
agreeable a manner.[38] In compliance with your request I have drawn
on you for an hundred pounds—in favour of Mr Sam Williams on
London.[39] The supply came opportunely. I am at the point of

[33] *Ibid.*, III, 211–53, *et passim.*
[34] *Ibid.*, III, 244.
[35] Henry Matthew's review (Hill Shine, *The "Quarterly Review" under Gifford 1809-1824* [Chapel Hill: University of North Carolina Press, 1949], p. 83)
began: "The author before us is the best writer of English, in our estimation of
that term, that America has published since the era of her independence." *QR*,
XXV (April 1821), 50–67.
[36] PMI, II, 48.
[37] Printed with minor corrections in PMI, II, 48–49; fifth sentence quoted in
Smiles, II, 130. Marked at Foreign Post Office in London, July 10, 1821.
[38] Even at this stage money spoke more forcefully than words to the American who coined the phrase "the Almighty Dollar!"
[39] Samuel Williams was an American merchant and banker in London who

leaving Paris for Bruxelles, and where I shall go from thence is at present undetermined; but I shall write to you from the Netherlands, should I make any stop there. I have been leading a "miscellaneous" kind of life in Paris—if I may use a literary phrase. I have been rather distracted by engagements, in spite of all my efforts to keep out of society.

Anacreon Moore is living here, and has made me a gayer fellow that I could have wished; but I found it impossible to resist the charms of his society. Paris is like an English watering place, with the advantage of the best kind of amusements, and excellent society.

I have scribbled at intervals, and have a mass of writings by me; rather desultory, as must be the case when one is so much interrupted; but I hope, in the fulness of time, to get them in some order.

I write in extreme haste, having to pack up and make other preparations for departure.

With my best regards to Mrs Murray and the rest of your family

I am my dear Sir

Very faithfully yours,

Washington Irving.

The projected tour of Belgium and the Netherlands was canceled, Irving returning to London in time to watch the coronation procession of George IV with Leslie and Newton. Sir Walter Scott later chided him for not taking an active part in the ceremony, declaring that his distinction in literature had already earned for him a place in British tradition. Irving settled into Newton's lodgings, where he remained until late summer trying to get his new work in shape for autumn publication. He toyed with one idea concerning the adventures of a young man named Buckthorne, finally putting it aside to use in a later work. This story, at that point, was a combination of his observations and the experiences of Moore and Payne. The scenes resulting from the ad-

---

specialized in helping Americans. His home was a sort of American Express where visitors from the United States received mail and credit. See Edgar P. Richardson, *Washington Allston: A Study of the Romantic Artist in America* (Chicago: The University of Chicago Press, 1948), p. 116.

"Murray's drawing-room," Washington
Irving wrote to an American friend, "is a great
resort of first-rate literary characters; whenever I have a
leisure hour I go there, and seldom fail to meet with
some interesting personages." *Courtesy of John
Murray, Publishers, and the British Museum.*

venturer's encounters with London publishers and literary figures, apparently written during this period, came directly from the strongholds of Murray and the Longmans.[40]

On September 9, in company with Leslie, Irving left London for a tour of Oxfordshire,[41] ending at the home of the Van Warts in Birmingham. From there, the humble author wrote to Ebenezer: "Murray is . . . extremely desirous [to get a new manuscript into print]; and indeed the success of my former writings would insure a run to any thing I should now bring forward." [42] To Leslie, back in London, he issued this directive: "When you see him [Murray] you need not say where I am. I want the quiet, and not to be bothered in any way." [43] Did Irving imagine that the eager publisher would take horse and ride posthaste in pursuit of him? Perhaps he would have done exactly that. John Murray II did not shrink from literary endeavors which were assured of financial success. He had the pride of a Scotsman, but in business matters of prime importance he had learned to temper it with humility. Lord Byron had heaped verbal abuse upon him, making it clear that no matter how helpful or necessary Murray was to him, the publisher was still a tradesman. For so long as Byron's writings registered enough profit and excited enough interest in the drawing room, the publisher persevered, but when Byron's decline came as Irving's public reputation was in the ascendancy, even Murray cooled to the romantic poet. The later John Murrays could have calmly waited for the American's manuscript, but the second John with his quick temper, flamboyant nature, and restless energy must have been in a state of high agitation, for in 1822 Geoffrey Crayon seemed to have more potential than any other name on the British literary scene.

Securing Crayon's next manuscript, however, was only one of Murray's problems. At home, life had been darkened by the death of his son William in May. Shortly after this, Mrs. Murray's

---

[40] Cf. Moore, *Memoirs*, III, 252–53.

[41] For an account of this tour, during which "The Stout Gentleman" originated, see Leslie, I, 63–66.

[42] PMI, II, 58.

[43] *Ibid.*, 60.

health failed, causing the family to remove to Cheltenham. The publisher had been in London for the coronation, which he attended with Sir Walter Scott, but even that had failed to brighten the summer. His relationship with Byron had become impossible. The poet's immoralities had raised doubts that were strengthened by the quality of the works he was producing. "Nobody would read them," Murray moaned.[44] Byron, for his part, retorted to Murray's obvious displeasure with him by citing Washington Irving's approval of his recent work.[45] The publisher and the poet began to bicker, finally breaking off all intercourse for a while.

Murray was keen, nevertheless, to the value of Byron's name—at least to posterity. In a contract signed in Newton's flat, the publisher readily agreed to buy for two thousand guineas from Tom Moore a manuscript autobiography (for posthumous publication) which Byron had given Moore in 1820.[46] With the money Moore was able to return to England, settle his debts, and resume his society larking there.

In Birmingham trouble—if not his publisher—caught up with Irving. The news of the death of his brother William and a painful inflammation of the skin about his ankles depressed him, increasing the difficulty of his struggle to perfect his manuscript. His spirits still low, on December 26 he returned to London, this time staying with an American family at Hanover Square. He continued to work on his manuscript, leaving his "sick chamber" only once—to confer with John Murray on behalf of James Fenimore Cooper's *The Spy*.[47]

Murray did not take Cooper's novel, which, already printed in the United States, had no copyright value in Britain. On March

---

[44] Moore, *Memoirs*, III, 280. One wonders if WI's statement of Dec. 28, 1820, as reported by Moore, was original, or if JMII's comments had prompted it: "Mr. Irving complains grievously of the last thing Lord Byron has sent, as unworthy of himself, and likely to injure Murray's property in the former works." *Ibid.*, 185.

[45] Byron to JMII, Nov. 3, 1821, in *Works of Byron: Letters and Journals*, V, 471–72.

[46] Moore, *Memoirs*, III, 260.

[47] PMI, II, 73–74.

6, 1822, Irving wrote to Cooper's friend, Charles Wiley, in New York concerning the matter. Henry Colburn

> is a fashionable publisher, liberal in his prices and anxious to get American works of merit, whereas Murray is precisely the worst man that an American work can be sent to. He has the offer of almost everything that is choice, and is extremely fastidious, and he is surrounded by literary advisers who are prejudiced against anything American. . . . The best course for American authors to take would be to send manuscript copies of their work to Mr. John Miller, Bookseller, Fleet Street, and request him to dispose of them to the best advantage.[48]

This letter grows more interesting in the light of future events in Irving's life.

Sometime during the last of February or the first of March Irving received two visits which proved to him that he had not over-estimated his value on a publisher's list. The first was from Henry Colburn, the same "fashionable publisher" referred to above, who offered him one thousand guineas for the new manuscript, sight unseen. In the face of this, Irving remained cool, declaring his allegiance to Murray. "He should have my second [work] even at a less price than the one offered to me by himself (Colburn)."[49]

The second visit, on March 12, was from John Murray. "This interview," wrote Stanley T. Williams, "was the meridian of Murray's favor."[50] Basing his description on presently unobtainable Autobiographical Notes, Williams re-created the scene:

> "Experience," Irving thought, as Murray bowed, "has taught me a lesson." When Murray inquired urbanely what the manuscript might be expected to fetch, the author replied: "Fifteen hundred guineas." Murray's astonishment was visible. "Have you not," he said, "overvalued your performance? I have come prepared to offer a thousand." So the venerable ruse was successful. Irving ac-

[48] WI to Charles Wiley, in *Correspondence of James Fenimore Cooper*, ed. James Fenimore Cooper (New Haven: Yale University Press, 1922), I, 89.
[49] From Autobiographical Notes, quoted in STW, I, 206.
[50] I, 207.

41

cepted the honorarium, and watched Murray sign the check. Now, as Murray handed it to him, was his own turn to be astonished—and embarrassed. It was a draft for twelve hundred guineas, to be paid before the book was published.[51]

Pierre M. Irving gave a somewhat different version of this business transaction:

> Mr. Irving went to him [Murray], at the instance of his friends, who probably knew his too easy acquiescence in any sum that might be offered[.] he [Irving] was induced to name his own price, which was fifteen hundred guineas. This staggered Murray, who, after a moment's hesitation, began: "If you had said a thousand guineas;"—"you shall have it for a thousand guineas," said Irving, breaking in. Murray was taken aback by this. He had probably been prepared to divide the difference, and go to the length of twelve hundred and fifty guineas. When he found Mr. Irving respond so promptly to the lesser sum, he sat down at once, and drew out the notes for the amount, and gave them to him, although he did not receive the manuscript until nearly two weeks afterwards.[52]

On May 17 Murray registered *Bracebridge Hall; or, The Humourists* in Stationers' Hall.[53] Shortly after this, it was published from manuscript copy in the United States, but the prior appearance in England had made valid Murray's sole right to the title and Irving's revisions as the book went to press gave Murray a much more polished version than the American edition. Gifford told Irving it was "superior to the Sketch Book, as to composition, and calculated to increase [your] reputation." [54]

It was a success, but it suffered in comparison with *The Sketch Book*. The reviewer in *The New Monthly Magazine and Literary Journal*, under the editorship of Thomas Campbell, echoed other critics with his suggestion that if he had not read *The Sketch Book* first, he would have thought twice as highly of *Bracebridge*

---

[51] I, 207. A good story—but the draft still on file at 50 Albemarle Street was made out for 1,000 guineas. See Appendix III, item 3.

[52] II, 76–77.

[53] See Appendix V.

[54] PMI, II, 77. JM's two-volume octavo edition sold for £1 4s. 0d.

42

"The Author of *The Sketch Book*," a
lithograph offered for sale at the height of
Irving's literary acclaim, shows the author holding wax
and, perhaps, his seal bearing the Irvine coat of arms.
Courtesy of the University of Virginia Library.

Hall.[55] Unable to find any reasons for disapproving of the meek and mellow picture of British country life, other reviewers picked at little things such as the subtitle.[56] *The London Magazine*'s commentator noticed a commercialism not present in Irving's earlier writing, but it absolved the author of the blame: "Mr. Murray and Mr. Davison [the printer] have had their influence over Mr. Crayon." [57] Such carping, however, was minor. Francis Jeffrey of the *Edinburgh Review*, visiting in London, saw Irving at Murray's and reported: "he is a good deal in fashion, and has done something to deserve it." [58] The publisher had no reason to regret his purchase of Geoffrey Crayon's second book.

John Murray owned Irving's British copyrights and his drawing room was still Irving's favorite place in London, but the American suavely accepted the tribute of the other London publishers. The Longmans entertained him; plump bibliophile and gourmand John Andrews of Bond Street launched an enticing campaign to get him into the editorship of a proposed quarterly, *The Albion*; Taylor and Hessey, proprietors of *The London Magazine*, listened attentively to his suggestions; and in spite of Irving's rejection of his liberal offer for *Bracebridge Hall*, Colburn courted his views on literary matters.[59]

With British society *Bracebridge Hall* made Irving even more of a lion. At Lady Spencer's Wimbledon seat he finally met Sam-

[55] V (July 1822), 65–68.

[56] The reviewer for *The European Magazine, and London Review*, LXXXII (July 1822), 55, found nothing humorous in the work.

[57] VI, (Nov. 1822), 438. Thomas Davison did a great deal of JMII's printing, including most of Byron's work. He printed *Bracebridge Hall, Tales of A Traveller*, the first impression of *Life of Columbus, Conquest of Granada*, and—just before his death—the first issue of the abridgment of the *Life of Columbus*. For an appreciation of Davison's work and personality, see C. H. Timperley, comp., *Dictionary of Printers and Printing* (London: H. Johnson, 1839), pp. 919–20.

[58] Lord Henry Cockburn, *Life of Lord Jeffrey* (Edinburgh: A. & C. Black, 1852), II, 206. In a very favorable review in *ER* Jeffrey declared that he thought *BH* as good as *SB* even though "the common buz among the idle and impatient critics of the drawing-room is, that, in comparison with the Sketch Book, it is rather monotonous and languid." XXXVII (Nov. 1822), 338.

[59] PMI, II, 50; WI described his "acquaintance with some of the Booksellers" in a letter to Payne, March 17, 1822. MS in Barrett Collection, Alderman Library, University of Virginia.

uel Rogers (whose extended travels in Europe had deprived London of one of its most accomplished hosts during Irving's previous periods there), and Rogers' showplace home overlooking Green Park became one of Irving's haunts.[60] *Bracebridge Hall*, with its idealized picture of manor house experiences, established the author as a chronicler of that type of life. During the remainder of his years in England he moved freely from one stately home to another, reveling in the charms of each.[61] Further evidence of how completely he was being absorbed into British life was his selection to sit on a committee proposed to erect a monument to the memory of Shakespeare in Stratford-upon-Avon.[62]

But he had, as he reported it, become too popular. To Peter, still in France barely treading financial water on the Seine, he wrote on June 30:

> I have been leading a sad life lately, burning the candle at both ends, and seeing the fashionable world through one of its seasons. The success of my writings gave me an opportunity, and I thought it worth while to embrace it if it were only for curiosity's sake. I have therefore been tossed about "hither and thither and whither I would not;" have been at the levee and the drawing-room, been at routs, and balls, and dinners, and country-seats; been hand-in-glove with nobility and mobility, until like Trim I have satisfied the sentiment, and am now preparing to make my escape from all this splendid confusion.[63]

Since his ankles were still giving him trouble, he decided to try the baths at Aix-la-Chapelle, which was his destination when he left London on July 6, 1822. The water treatment did seem to help his skin trouble; in fact, he was soon almost well. Suddenly

---

[60] With the poet-banker WI's friendship would be enriched by the passing of time. To his death at the age of ninety-three in 1855, Rogers regarded WI as one of his warmest friends.

[61] Visiting the Deepdene estate of Thomas Hope, June 21, 1822, WI left one of his best personal pictures of this life in a letter to his sister Catherine. MS in Yale University Library; portion printed in PMI, II, 83–85.

[62] Mrs. Charles Mathews, *Memoirs of Charles Mathews, Comedian* (London: Bentley, 1839), II, 300.

[63] PMI, II, 88–89.

he was a young wanderer again, traveling about Germany with chance companions until finally, in the last days of November, he arrived in Dresden.[64]

Literary reputation had preceded him. Even before the British Minister John Philip Morier (whom he had met in 1812) presented him to the Court of Frederick Augustus, his name had been known there—carried in "by Saxony's eager interest at this time in British literature." [65] In this tight-knit society of royalty and diplomats, he repeated his conquests of London and English-speaking Paris, here an even more complete success because of the stable nature of the microcosm. Occasionally he thought that he would write a book concerning Germany or German legends (Walter Scott had planted the germ in his mind in 1817), but his efforts rarely got beyond a thought on the matter.

At the center of much of his activity was the John Foster family, in many ways a replica of the earlier Hoffman circle he had enjoyed so much. There was a fairly young attractive mother and two daughters, one, Emily, to whom, legend says, Irving proposed marriage.[66] When finally he was able to tear himself away from the provincial grandeur of Dresden on July 12, 1823, he traveled with Mrs. Foster and her England-bound retinue as far as Rotterdam, there bidding them a temporary goodbye and turning his course toward Paris.

The Storrows welcomed him back, and he found the colony was much as it had been in 1821 when he left—excepting only the absence of Moore. News from England came regularly: from Miller, now established as an "American Bookseller" in Covent Garden, and from the "Lads," each individually successful. Mur-

---

[64] WI's German period has been fully treated in Walter A. Reichart, *WI and Germany* (Ann Arbor: University of Michigan, 1957). Fortunately, most of the research on this volume was completed before World War II, during which many of the original references were destroyed or since which they have been lost behind the Iron Curtain. These months of adventure (Aug. 1, 1822–July 11, 1823) were recorded by WI himself in his journals. See Trent and Hellman, I, 49–225.

[65] STW, I, 229.

[66] See *ibid.*, 237–42, 243–54, 448–52.

ray had moved his family residence to 14 Whitehall Place, someone reported, adding that the drawing room was, however, unchanged. Another correspondent commented on the bother
caused Murray by the friendship of Lady Caroline Lamb, a former paramour of Byron's, whose society novels were rocking
high places.

Payne was there. In the first months after Irving's arrival, his
inclinations to write were either hampered by Payne's many personal and financial problems or, under Payne's influence, they
were channeled into dramatic efforts for which Irving had little
flair.[67] Finally—a happy day—leaving Irving to scribble in Paris,
Payne went to London in November to try to sort out some of
his financial troubles.

Irving fretted about Paris for a few days, shuffling through his
notes in the seclusion of his chamber, wondering what his next
move should be. On November 13, from Galignani's Library he
"took out Arab[ian] nights" [68] and the next day wrote to Murray and Newton.

6. To John Murray II

Paris, Rue Richelieu No. 89
Novr 14th 1823.

My dear Sir,

After rambling about Germany for upwards of a year, part of
the time in rather indifferent health, I have settled myself down
for some time in Paris, with an intention of applying myself to
the pen. Among other things I feel an inclination to take hold of

---

[67] Of little interest as literary items, WI's plays reflect his compulsive interest
in the theater. Stanley T. Williams declared that "his stage lore surpassed, it is
safe to say, that of any American layman" (I, 266). Well acquainted with all of
the important actors and actresses of his middle years, he might have written a
contemporary history of the theater which would have outlived anything else he
wrote. WI obviously realized his weakness as a dramatist and insisted that Payne
and his other intimates not publicize his ventures into playwriting.

[68] *Journal of Washington Irving (1823–1824)*, ed. Stanley T. Williams (Cambridge: Harvard University Press, 1931). Hereinafter cited as STW, *Journal
(1823–1824)*.

the MS. Arabian tales which you once put into my hands.[69] I think I could work at them when I could not employ my mind more originally. I have always felt an inclination towards these MSS. and a persuasion that I could make something out of them worth your publishing. If you should feel inclined to hand them over to me Mr Newton will take charge of them & forward them. *I should not wish it to be known, however, that I was employed upon them—until they were ready for publication.*

I hope Mrs Murray and your family are all well. Will you present Mrs M. my sincerest regards and likewise remember me kindly to the D'Israelis.

> I am my dear Sir
> With great regard
> Yours truly,
> Washington Irving.

P.S. Should you think of sending the MSS. I would thank you to let Mr Newton have them immediately, as there will be an opportunity of sending them to me by a sure private hand.[70]

Having mailed Murray's letter, Irving returned to his lodgings to find a letter waiting there from the publisher. Payne had called at 50 Albemarle Street on November 8 (no doubt hawking his plays from publisher to publisher trying to make a few shillings) and had agreed to carry a note back to Irving. Deciding to prolong his stay in London, he had slipped it into the mail. Murray wrote:

[69] In 1802 William Miller, whose business and materials JMII had purchased at 50 Albemarle Street, published a five-volume edition of *The Arabian Nights*, translated by the Rev. Mr. Edward Forster. It is pure conjecture but not unreasonable to suggest that JMII may have found Forster's MS among his papers and considered the possibility of a new version from a celebrated pen such as WI's.

[70] Certainly a reference to John Howard Payne. Writing to Payne Nov. 12, WI said: "Bring with you any thing you can lay your hands on that will be interesting and amusing in new publications &c. &c.—and that you can beg borrow or steal." Further on, he added: "I wish a copy of the last edition of Knickerbocker—Murray will no doubt furnish it free of cost." On Nov. 29, when Payne had given no signs of returning to Paris directly, WI wrote him: "If you see Newton tell him should Mr. Murray deliver to him the parcel I wrote about—I would thank him to forward it to me by coach—unless you are coming off immediately and will bring it with you. I want it as soon as possible." Columbia.

Mr. H. Payne tells me he is a fellow-lodger with you in Paris, and as he is expected quickly to return, I cannot refrain from sending compliments to you, and of adding an inquiry as to your literary occupations, and what your publisher may be allowed to expect from you in the course of the winter. I am perfectly ready for you, and the sooner you take the field the better.[71]

There is no record of a reply to Irving's letter of November 14. Irving addressed a note on December 22 to Murray telling him that he should "probably have 2 vols. of the Sketch Book ready for him in ye Spring." [72] Murray made no reply, and Irving wrote again.

7. To John Murray II [73]

[Paris, Jan. 27, 1824]

. . . .

I wrote you above a month ago on the subject of a couple of volumes of the "Sketch Book" which I hope to have ready in time for the spring season. I wished also, if they are not otherwise disposed of, to have the MSS. of the Arabian tales you once put into my hands, as I had, and have, an idea that I could make something very taking out of them. . . . I requested in a former letter,[74] the new series of the Curiosities of Literature,[75] but as I have been furnished with a pt. by a friend in Parish [Paris] they need not be sent. . . .

Finally, in March a letter arrived from the publisher. To begin with, Murray lamented at great length about his biggest problem of the moment—that of finding a successor for Gifford who, because of declining health, had to resign the editorship of the *Quarterly Review*. Then, turning to business matters with Irving,

[71] PMI, II, 177.

[72] STW, *Journal (1823–1824)*, p. 91.

[73] The present location of this MS is unknown. The excerpt quoted here is from the 1935 catalogue of Thomas F. Madigan, Inc., New York City. Item 197 on page 56, this was listed as A.L.S., 2 pp., 4 to. and priced at $50.00.

[74] Apparently the lost letter of Dec. 22, 1823.

[75] Isaac D'Israeli, *Curiosities of Literature* (5 vols.; [7th ed.]; London: JM, 1823).

Murray bluntly offered the writer twelve hundred guineas for the manuscript of his next production.[76]

8. *To John Murray II* [77]

Paris, March 18th[78] 1824.

My dear Sir,

Your letter of the 18th was a very gratifying one, as it so satisfactorily accounted for a silence which much perplexed me. I do not regret having turned aside from my idea of preparing two more volumes of the Sketch Book as I think I have run into a plan & thrown off writings which will be more novel & attractive. I have the materials for two volumes nearly prepared, but there will yet be a little rewriting & filling up necessary. I hope however to lay the work before you in the course of six weeks. I think the title will be "Tales of a Traveller, by Geoffrey Crayon Gent." Your offer of twelve hundred guineas without seeing the MSS. is I confess a liberal one and made in your own gentlemanlike manner, but I would rather you would see the MSS. and make it *fifteen hundred*. Don't think me greedy after money, but in fact I have need of all I can get just now—as I can do five pounds worth of good with every pound I can spare—and since the world won't let me live as I please, I find it very expensive to live with the world.

Those who have seen various parts of what I have prepared think the work will be the best thing I have written and that it will be very successful with the public. An author is not perhaps the best judge of his productions otherwise I might throw my own opinion into the scale.

I shall go on to finish the work as soon as possible, and shall bring it over to England before long; as I can write upon it while there and indeed while it is printing.

I write in excessive haste to gain the mail which is nearly closing.

[76] Although a copy of JMII's letter is not available, its contents can be determined from WI's journal entry (STW, *Journal [1823–1824]*, pp. 151–52) and from his reply.

[77] Printed in its entirety, with slight alterations, in PMI, II, 191–92; sentences six and seven printed in Smiles, II, 133.

[78] The holograph letter was dated thus by WI, but the actual date was the 26th—the error no doubt the result of the author's "feverish head."

Present my most kind remembrances to Mrs Murray and believe me dear Sir

> Very sincerely
> Your friend,
> Washington Irving.

—I am writing with a bewildered head and feverish hand, having returned at almost daylight from a fancy Ball at the British Ambassador's. The most magnificent thing I have ever seen & which must dazzle all Paris.[79]

Only silence from 50 Albemarle Street. Irving continued to work on his manuscript of *Tales of a Traveller* and to enjoy the Parisian spring.

The news of Byron's death on April 19 reached London on May 14, throwing his circle of friends and especially the Murray establishment into confusion. High on the list of factors now to be considered was the manuscript autobiography deposited at 50 Albemarle Street. On May 17 a meeting of the concerned parties was held in the famous drawing room. Representatives of Byron's relatives protested; Moore's generosity overflowed; and Murray magnanimously (having never read the manuscript) acquiesced: the pages written in Byron's unmistakable scrawl were fed one by one into the fire burning in the grate beneath the poet's portrait.[80]

By the last of May, Irving could stand the suspense of Murray's silence no longer: he prepared to go to London to see what the situation was regarding his publisher's plans for the *Tales*. Arriving on Friday, May 28, took temporary housing on Cavendish Square[81] and prepared to seek out John Murray the next day.

[79] *The Morning Post*, March 29, 1824, offered Londoners a full report of the ball.

[80] WI read the manuscript while Moore had it in Paris. "There was exquisite humour, though it could not all have been published," he told Leslie. *Autobiography of Benjamin R. Haydon*, ed. Tom Taylor (London: Peter Davies, 1926), II, 514. A recent scholar has argued that the reason for the destruction of the memoirs may have been that they contained evidence of Byron's homosexuality. See G. Wilson Knight, *Lord Byron's Marriage: The Evidence of Asterisks* (London: Routledge and Kegal Paul, 1957), pp. 225–27.

[81] He was staying with his traveling companion, Frank Mills, an amiable aspirant dramatist. See STW, *Journal (1823–1824)*, pp. 187–90, 198–206.

CHAPTER THREE

THE RETURN OF A PRODIGAL

Saturday, May 29, 1824

Breakfast with Leslie, tea with Sir Samuel Edgerton Brydges, a visit to the Royal Academy to see Newton's and Leslie's latest paintings, a round of calls with Moore on Lady Lansdowne and other society notables—finally, Irving arrived rather late at 50 Albemarle Street on this gray Saturday afternoon, a day not unlike the first day he visited John Murray.

But only the weather outside bore a similarity to the atmosphere of that first visit. Murray's exuberant welcome clearly took Irving aback. On the landing before they had reached the drawing room, Murray poured out his apologies for not writing, explaining that he had daily anticipated Irving's arrival in London, and offered him fifteen hundred guineas for Tales of a Traveller *without even hearing more about the manuscript. Irving was visibly stunned.*

The social season was at its peak; the drawing-room assemblage hummed pleasantly before him. But the first thing he noticed in the room was his portrait by Newton, painted in 1820, now hanging just to the right of Lord Byron.

Gifford, looking frailer and more deathly than ever, sat on the low couch beside the fireplace and held out his hand in a beckoning motion. His pleasure in seeing the younger man was clear, but after a brief greeting, gasped out between asthmatic heaves, he fell back among the pillows, exhausted by the slight exertion of his lungs, and began fumbling for his snuff box, the contents of which had already been sprinkled liberally on his cravat and waistcoat.

Murray and his other visitors, however, were capable of much talk. With frequent dramatic gestures of hands toward the offending fireplace, they discussed the destruction of the Byron memoirs —this and the plans, now being made, for the poet's last rites. Even in the presence of this timely topic, however, all the people seemed properly interested in Geoffrey Crayon's activities since he departed from their midst in July 1822. Was a "German Sketch Book" in the making? Or perhaps it would concern France, where it was evident from the gossip of the British colony that the author was a great favorite? Irving was reticent, occasionally exchanging knowing smiles with his publisher, who stayed at his elbow, guiding him about the room.

Between sips of strong coffee, Irving learned from Murray of the edition of the Oldstyle Letters *just off the press in London. Murray offered to publish a corrected or revised edition, but Irving's obvious embarrassment over the subject and his serious protests describing the* Letters *as "juvenile writings" caused the host to abandon at once the idea.*

A chronic play-goer tried to draw Irving aside, asking in a carefully modulated stage whisper about the rumors lately circulating around town concerning his ventures into playwriting. In the background, beneath the hard oily gaze of Crabbe, a young man with a monocle noted dryly to his companion, young Benjamin Disraeli (who had thus assumed the anglicized spelling of his name), that Irving's claret-colored coat was rather more pigeon-tailed than one expected to see in a London drawing room. "But," objected Disraeli, eyeing Irving's highly polished shoes, his ribbed flesh-colored silk stocking, and his revealing tights, "Paris sets the style these days."

The questions of the thespian-minded gentleman were proving to be a discomfiture to the American, who took the occasion of the arrival of Francis Cohen to plead an early dinner engagement and make his departure, bowing slightly to the gathering, which respectfully watched his movement through the doorway.

To Murray who accompanied him down the stairway, repeating his original apology and offer, Irving gave assurance that the manuscript of Tales of a Traveller, *in need of only a little*

53

"touching-up," would be his and in his hands within a matter of days.

Sources for Vignette

Sources used in writing this section include: STW, *Journal (1823–1824)*, pp. 190–91; WI's letter to Peter, May 31, 1824, in PMI, II, 193–95, *Morning Chronicle*, May 27, 1824; S. G. Goodrich, *Recollections of a Lifetime* (New York: Miller, Orton, and Milligan, 1857), II, 198; A. Edwin, Weather Diary, 1824.

Sunday began with breakfast at Rogers', in in the company of Leslie and Newton; the main topic of conversation was the destruction of Byron's memoirs. Toward midnight Irving left a dinner party at Samuel Williams'. Monday,[1] Tuesday, Wednesday: every day fell into the same pattern—with the addition of Payne, who kept reappearing with plays for Irving to work on. Thursday he attended the Epsom Races; Friday he was at White's in the company of Lady Morgan and Lord and Lady James Stewart, after which he retired to an intimate private party where he met the Duke of Sussex and heard his Paris acquaintance Madame Giuditta Pasta sing. Saturday he attended a performance of Charles Mathews' *Trip to America*, with its soon-to-be famous caricatures of American characters.[2] Sunday night, returning by coach through a thick London fog from a dinner party at Paddington, Irving realized that *Tales of a Traveller* was no nearer completion than when he had spoken so confidently of it to Murray. Only if he could get away from the demands and temptations of social London could he finish the job.

[1] On May 31, WI moved his quarters to the lodgings of William R. Spencer, society wit and poet. He remained here until he returned to France in August. See STW, *Journal (1823–1824)*, p. 192 *et passim*.

[2] See Francis Hodge, "Charles Mathews Reports on America 1824," *Quarterly Journal of Speech*, XXXVI (Dec. 1950), 429–99, and PMI, II, 484.

TALES

OF

A TRAVELLER.

BY GEOFFREY CRAYON, Gent.

I am neither your minotaure, nor your centaure, nor your satyr, nor your hyæna, nor your babion, but your meer traveller, believe me.

BEN JONSON.

IN TWO VOLUMES.
VOL. I.

LONDON:
JOHN MURRAY, ALBEMARLE-STREET.
1824.

Murray's edition of *Tales of a Traveller* was printed by Thomas Davison, who did most of Murray's high-quality work. This title page is a typical performance of a time when mechanical exactitude and "modern" type faces of extreme contrast were the prevaling typographical fashions. *Courtesy of the University of Virginia Library.*

At 8 A.M., on Monday, Whit Monday, he left for Southampton. He was traveling with Frank Mills; their destination was the New Forest, specifically the Manor House home of Mills' brother-in-law, where the American was able, among the legends of the New Forest and in the excellent family library, to return to his pen.[3]

After a week he moved on to Salisbury and Bath, where he was met by Thomas Moore, fresh from London. After a taste of Bath's rich watering society, they hurried on to Moore's home in Devizes,[4] from whence Irving dispatched this missive to Murray.

9. *To John Murray II*[5]

Sloperton Cottage, Devizes
June 18th 1824.

My dear Sir,

I send you a portion of my manuscript, and shall furnish you with more in a day or two, and indeed as fast as you want it. It will be in four parts making two volumes about the size of the Sketch Book.[6] The title page that accompanies this MSS. is the title page of the first part merely. The general title page will be "Tales of a Traveller, by Geoffrey Crayon Gent." with a motto which I have not at present at hand.

I have been passing a week in the New Forest, and three or four days at Bath and Moore's cottage, where I now am. I leave them tomorrow morning, but shall continue visiting about in different parts of the country. Proof sheets, letter, &c. directed to me at Birmingham will be looked after & forwarded to me wherever I may happen to be. If they could be franked it would save me a good deal of expense.

Moore has read a considerable part of my manuscript and gives me great encouragement by the opinion he expresses of it.[7] I think

---

[3] See STW, *Journal (1823–1824)*, pp. 198–207.

[4] Moore's "cottage" is briefly described in Mr. and Mrs. S. C. Hall, "Memories of Authors: A Series of Portraits from Personal Acquaintance, Tom Moore," *Atlantic Monthly*, XV (Jan. 1865), 103. It is pictured on the title page of Moore, *Memoirs*, VI. WI's visit is described in STW, *Journal (1823–1824)*, pp. 210–11.

[5] Paper watermarked "Bath 1824."

[6] The four parts were "Strange Stories, by a Nervous Gentleman," "Buckthorne and his Friends," "The Italian Banditti," and "The Money-Diggers."

[7] Moore's opinion in his private journal was a bit more critical than his kind

the style & plan of it will be a little peculiar.

Present my best regards to Mrs Murray and believe me dear Sir

Very faithfully yours,

Washington Irving.

From Moore's he journeyed on to the Van Warts' Edgbaston home, where he finished the first full version of the work.

10. *To John Murray II*

Edgbaston, June 25th 1824.

My dear Sir,

I inclose you more MS. making the whole of Part 1, or the Suite of Strange Stories.

You will find a little tale, which I have just scribbled from an anecdote picked up the other day and which I think will add to the effect of the Strange Stories. It is to be inserted after "the Adventure of My Grandfather or the Bold Dragoon" & just following the words.

"Did your grandfather walk in his sleep?"

"Not that I knew of"——[8]

Should there be any proof ready for me I will thank you to send it directed to me at Birmingham post office. It will be forwarded to me wherever I may happen to be.

I will send you more copy in a day or two, tho' as the printers are not fully underway I presume they are not in want, and I do not like my manuscripts to be about before publication.

With best regards to Mrs Murray I am my dear Sir

Very faithfully yours,

Washington Irving.

When, after due time had elapsed, no proof sheets arrived, Irving went to London to find that the publisher had planned to hold *Tales of a Traveller* until November. But, since the American edi-

---

words to WI might have indicated. WI "read me some parts of his new work 'Tales of a Traveller.' Rather tremble for its fate." Moore, *Memoirs*, IV, 208.

[8] This story, "The Adventures of the German Student," became pp. 71–83 of the JM edition. Of course, it did not appear in the first American edition. It is followed by this note: "The latter part of the above story is founded on an anecdote related to me, and said to exist in print in French. I have not met with it in print."

tion was expected before that date, this delay would have invalidated Murray's British copyright. "On finding the danger of being anticipated by an American edition, he [Murray] changed his plan and has advertised it for the first of August and set the press hard at work." [9] During this period Murray asked him for a corrected copy of *Salmagundi*, with an eye for producing a complete and uniform edition of Irving's work. The project was later dropped.[10]

At the beginning of August, Irving was in London, involved again in society but also busily correcting the proofs which came regularly from the press of Thomas Davison. But the excitement of the social season faded when Irving received a letter from Murray explaining in some detail criticism given by a "friend" who had been allowed to read the proofs of the new work.[11]

[9] PMI, II, 202.

[10] *Ibid.*, 203. WI even wrote to Paulding suggesting that he contribute his ideas to the planned JM edition of *Salmagundi*.

[11] As WI quickly surmised, the "friend" was William Gifford. Still in the Murray Archives is Gifford's letter to JMII, dated August 1, 1824, from Ramsgate: "I return by the Coach, Mr. Irving's papers which I have run slightly over. It is well it was sent for there are some mistakes which would have done him no credit. He talks of little Cathedral towns. Cathedrals make cities; in short he is [all abroad on?] this subject. It is worse when he talks of Prebends—There are no such persons as Prebend is an office—The holder of it is Prebendary. I am sorry he has taken it into his mind to ridicule our provincial clergy, an exemplary body of men of whom he is completely ignorant. Most of what he says resembles Paulding whom he has apparently read. [See above, p. 24] The [ladies stuff?] about Cathedral circles must be abridged or omitted. It is not a picture of the present times, but of those of Queen Anne. [three sentences mainly concerning the Fantadlins are not decipherable] There is much to praise. All that Buckthorne says of his mother is beautiful—all that he says of his father, his uncle, his cousin is also very good indeed. This picture of Oxford is false & slanderous, & could only have been there about half a century ago. That page should be altered. "Why does our young friend [WI was 41] give so revolting a picture of an English nobleman at Terracina? Our travelling city & county squires are rude & ignorant enough, but vulgarity & impudence are not the characteristics of an English peer—& then to contrast him with the politeness of a Venetian or [Albenian?]. Alas alas! it was not thus that Mr. Irving obtained his deserved reputation."

After some further comments about Paulding's *A Sketch of Old-England, by a New-England Man*, the weather, and his own failing health, Gifford concluded with a postscript: "Do not tell Mr. I what I have written in terms—but make your own use of it. If my name be mentioned let it be tenderly, for he is a real favourite of mine. There is another thing that struck me—He takes Crabbe's descriptions and applies them to a different rank of people. Now the delineations of this admirable man will only serve those for whom it was [formed?]. This

11. *To John Murray II*

[August 5, 1824.] [12]

My dear Sir,

I am always thankful for criticism when in season, and am always eager to prosper by it to the most of my abilities. I feel the value of the suggestions of your friend, and only regret that he had not read my work in manuscript that I might have had more fully the benefit of his good plan & good taste and been more completely able to modify my writings accordingly. If it is Mr Gifford to whom I am indebted I beg you will assure him that I feel honoured by his censorship, as I have heretofore felt flattered and stimulated by his approbation.

I have been at work half the night to make additions & alterations which might obviate the impression some parts of the story have made upon your friend.[13] I have no idea of ridiculing the provincial clergy; the mentions I have casually made have been individual sketches from originals which happen to present themselves to me, but I was not aware that I had sketched in such a way as to incur a suspicion of this kind. There could be nothing more humiliating to me than to be mistaken for one of that loose rabble of writers who are ready to decry every thing orderly & established—my feelings go the contrary way. I have thrown in a sketch therefore of a country clergyman, as one of a valuable class, which I hope may meet with the approbation of your friend.[14] It shall

---

great poet never confused his classes." [Smiles, who seemed to also have trouble reading Gifford's handwriting, gave a condensed and considerably altered version of this letter. (II, 158–59)] How much of the letter JMII quoted can be seen through WI's reply.

12 This letter is marked "September 1824" by a hand other than WI's, but it can be more closely dated by WI's journal entries recorded in STW, *Journal (1823–1824)*, pp. 242–43. Walter Reichart, however, kindly pointed out to me that the entry dates as published by STW are incorrect and that the actual date of composition is Aug. 5.

13 WI's revisions are of more than passing interest. Since the first American edition of *Tales* went to press without any of these changes, it is easy enough to see what they were by a comparison of the English with the American. The modern reader would be able to appreciate few changes which WI made under pressure from his English publisher, for the general effect is one of watering down and sweetening. See below for specific references.

14 The saccharine picture of the parson and his family is in the JM ed., I, 316–25.

be my care in any future writings, more effectually to do justice to this body of men, & in so doing to do justice to my own way of thinking of them.

The picture of the cathedral city[15] I will modify, & obliterate every thing that might be considered satirical on the clergy. The picture of the cathedral circle, however, which your friend thinks is "of the tune of the Spectator" was drawn from actual observation, and the lamentations of the young ladies about the dullness of their own & the gaiety of the inferior circle, &c. &c. were really made to me to greater extent than I have set them down.[16] However, I shall be cautious not to venture too far even when I have fact on my side, lest I should be considered as levelling impertinences at reverend persons & reverend establishments.

The affixed anecdotes are founded on real characters & circumstances, & the picture of a student's room drawn from observation; but I am aware of the general description of college life being applicable only to the tune of "town & gown" and had meant to alter it; but in the hurry of various subjects & of printing, it had escaped me. I will attend to it.[17]

The picture of an Englishman at Terracina is not meant for that

[15] In "Buckthorne and His Friends" WI had referred to "little cathedral town" (Amer. ed., II, 145); Gifford said that cathedrals made cities; consequently this, and other later references, became "little cathedral city" (JM ed., I, 346).

[16] WI's description of life in a cathedral town is well done (Amer. ed., II, 147–53). One of his points is that the young ladies of the provincial society were dying of boredom, longing for an exciting man to appear on the scene. A typical sentence from the male narrator: "I was quite a brilliant acquisition to the young ladies of the cathedral circle, who were glad to have a beau that was not in a black coat and clerical wig" (148–49). This sentence and other such references were cut from the English edition with no attempt at replacement (JM ed., I, 348–55).

[17] This section having to do with Buckthorne's days at Oxford university were changed little in content—though the style is improved in the JM ed. (Cf. Amer. ed., II, 128–29, and JM ed., I, 325–36). "The affixed anecdotes" were apparently not added to the printed copy, for none appear in JM's edition which were not already in the American edition. There was only one change worth noting in the American edition, II, 127: "I found that study was not the fashion at college, and that a lad of spirit only ate his terms; and grew wise by dint of knife and fork, I was always prone to follow the fashions of the company into which I fell." These sentences were cut from the Murray edition, the following replacing them: "The chances were in my favour, for the riotous times of the University were past. The days of hard drinking were at an end. The old feuds of 'Town and Gown,' like the civil wars of the White and Red Rose, had died away, and students and citizens slept in peace and whole skins, without risk of

of an English *nobleman* specifically; but as one of the general run of
English travelling gentlemen; also appears in the light I have presented this one, in the eyes of foreigners. I have drawn him with
the coldness, reserve & abruptness with which English are characterized abroad; but it will be seen that I have done it with a proper
motive; as I make him, in the end, when a real call is made upon
his better feelings, come out generous, disinterested, brave, and
truly gallant. I have drawn the character to exhibit for foreigners
what are the real qualities of an Englishman; and how little he is
to be judged by this external crust which is to them so revolting.
For this purpose I must make my contrast a little strong between
his character at rest & his character in action. I shall look over the
scenes however, with an eye to the objections made; but if I were
to make the Englishman a fine polished fellow in the first instance,
his chivalry would follow as a matter of course & I should lose my
object, viz that of indicating the generosity of John Bull, with all
his apparent phlegm & that peculiar reserve & testiness which he
has when travelling.[18]

The Fantadlins were drawn from life; they may be over charged.
I will do the best I can with them, but to dismiss them entirely

---

being summoned in the night to bloody brawl. It had become the fashion to study
at the University and the odds were always in favour of my following the
fashion. Unluckily, however, I fell in company . . ." (I, 327).

A novel entitled *Reginald Dalton* (London: T. Cadell, 1823) created a popular
stir with its description of the life of the townspeople and the university students in Oxford. It was so true to life that in 1824 Oxford printers Munday and
Slatter published a little booklet proving, with graphic illustrations, its validity.
The anonymous novel, from the pen of John Gibson Lockhart, contained sly
references to the Whiggery of Holland House and Samuel Rogers and mentioned several of WI's English acquaintances, such as Isaac D'Israeli and Henry
Hallam. An account of a visit to Stratford-upon-Avon could have come from
WI's essay in *SB*. The "Town and Gown" conflict is depicted in B. II, Chap. IV,
259–82. WI's natural interest in reading had, no doubt, introduced him to the
novel before this time.

18 The greatest indignity suffered by the English nobleman who moved
through "The Italian Banditti" was the censorship of his language. In the American edition he exhibited a habit of using "d——n," but this disappeared in the JM
edition. For example: "d——n country" (Amer. ed., III, 127) became "vile country" (JM ed., II, 221), and "D——n the purse" (Amer. ed., III, 128) became
"Curse the purse" (JM ed., II, 221). To help account for some of his "testiness,"
WI added (JM ed., II, 71): "Perhaps too he was a little sore from having been
fleeced at every stage of his journey."

would make a chasm in my story which I could not readily supply.[19]

I am not aware of making any use of Crabbe's descriptions.[20] I read several tales of Crabbe's Parish Register (I think it was so called) about twelve years since, with great interest. I was not in health nor spirits at the time & the gloomy nature of his pictures affected me unpleasantly. One of his stories I could not finish & what I had read disturbed me for a day or two. I may have looked into the volume once or twice since, but merely casually. The painful effect on me has deterred me from reading them again. Of his Tales of the Hall I merely read one story, that of "the Sisters." I did so at your request. I therefore have no distinct recollection of any of Mr Crabbe's characters & scenes, as my memory is so bad that it never retains things long. I do not know of any one character or description in any of my writings, that has been suggested by any thing of Crabbe's. If there is any coincidence it must be accidental. My sketches are drawn in general from actual observation and so are Mr Crabbe's: as the scenes lay in the same country & among the same kind of people it is natural to suppose there will be casual resemblances; Mr Crabbe having had more experience, and better opportunity of observing, is of course more accurate and discriminating than I.

I have made these observations both to satisfy you, and to be communicated to the friend who has thought my writings worthy of his critical perusal. I beg you will make him my acknowledgments, and assure him that if I do not purify my page as thoroughly as he could wish, it will not be from a want of diffidence to his opinion or diffidence of my own, but heavier circumstances may prevent my being able, at this state of the publication, thoroughly to rewrite whole portions of this work. I will, however, work diligently to prune & retouch.

Excuse the long scrawl, which is written out of anxiety to give satisfaction for I should feel no comfort even in success if I thought

[19] The portrait of the Fantadlins, Buckthorne's patrons during his days in the strolling theater, was untouched. Amer. ed., II, 200–204; JM ed., II, 38–42.

[20] George Crabbe's verse tale-sketches bear a kinship in subject with WI's writings—though with *SB* and *BH* perhaps more so than *TT*. *The Parish Register* (1807) has been Crabbe's first success. Smiles, II, 71–72.

I had in any way [word omitted] the feelings or judgement of those whose good opinion is dear to me.

Believe me my dear Sir,

Ever very sincerely & gratefully
Your friend,
Washington Irving.

Mount St
Thursday morng
P.S. I beg you will not refrain from looking over the remaining sheets as they are struck off. While I am on the spot I am ready to do every thing in my power to improve the work, and I shall always feel obliged to you for this frank communication of any ideas that may arise in your mind. By the suggestions of last evening you saved me, just in time, from suffering pages to pass through the press which I could not afterwards have recalled & might have forever regretted.

On August 13 Irving received Murray's draft for fifteen hundred guineas and left London on the 2 P.M. Brighton coach. The last sheets of *Tales of a Traveller* he proofed in a Brighton inn before sailing for Dieppe the next day.[21]

12. *To John Murray II*[22]

Brighton, Aug. 14th 1824

My dear Sir,

Among the commissions that I have requested Mr Miller the bookseller[23] to execute for me, was that of presenting a few copies of my work to some half dozen friends in this country & America, the names of which I have furnished him. Will you have the kindness to let me have a few volumes for that purpose?

I return the slips corrected, and also some MS. send by Mr

21 WI's stay in Brighton is described in my "WI in Brighton, 1824," *Sussex Life*, II (July 1966), 35–36.
22 Embossed "Extra Bath" with Crown, in upper left corner.
23 WI received a copy of *TT* from Miller, Sept. 25, 1824. Trent and Hellman, II, 28. PMI, II, 212, said that JMII's price for *TT* "occasioned some murmurs," but there seems to be no reason for this objection since it was the same as for *Bracebridge Hall*—£1 4s. 0d.

Davidson [Davison] for me to render a few words more intelligible.

I am my dear Sir

In prime haste
Truly yours,
WI.

P.S. I would be much obliged if you would forward me a copy or two to Paris by the earliest opportunity—perhaps you can by the ambassador's bag. I should like to revise a copy & return it to you for the second edition.

Irving was anxious to get to Paris because he was excited by the prospect of a project in which the Galignanis had sought his assistance. It was to be a collection of English literature, amounting to one hundred and ninety-seven specified volumes, all edited by Irving.[24] While in London he had collected information for his planned biographical editions of the works of Campbell and Rogers. In *Galignani's Messenger*, October 20, 1824, the prospectus of the Library of English Literature was published, and on October 26 Irving's edition of Goldsmith was announced as for sale. At this time, *Tales of a Traveller* had gone into two French translations,[25] and Irving's reputation was at its peak in France. Copies of Irving's portrait were having a brisk sale at ten francs each from Galignani's,[26] where the American's works were available at one-third of the cost of the English editions.[27]

This success, however, did little to encourage Irving. Back at 89 Rue Richelieu, he sank into a depression. The Goldsmith volume was the only title from the proposed Galignani collection to appear, the venture fading from the public eye with the last printing of the prospectus on November 12. Gifford's supposed pre-publication attack had hurt Irving's feelings; now the reviews of *Tales of a Traveller* left him crushed. The British re-

[24] The contract with Galignani's and W. Didot, dated March 14, 1824, agreed to pay WI 250 francs for each volume. MS in Alderman Library, University of Virginia.

[25] Trent and Hellman, II, 77.

[26] *Galignani's Messenger*, Nov. 13, 1824.

[27] *Ibid.*, Oct. 26, 1824.

viewers suggested that his stories were occasionally indecent (in "The Bold Dragoon" a pair of "amorous [fire] tongs" set physically upon the task of seducing a shovel, and a character cracked a joke about the maid making "grandfather's" bed "too hot to hold him"; in "The Young Robber" a "spotless virgin" was captured, repeatedly raped, and finally killed by Italian bandits);[28] further they charged him with political timidity and tufthunting: he "would strike out his best passage, dilute his best argument, or recant his sincerest opinion, in the fear of losing the next invitation to dinner he may expect from Grosvenor-Square." [29] The critic for the *London Magazine*, previously Geoffrey Crayon's devoted follower, shuddered as he expressed his belief that the American's latest production was—as Stanley T. Williams summarized this interesting review—"offensive to the chastity of the Georgian home." [30]

Aside from the moral issue, the tales were attacked as being too derivative. *Blackwood's Edinburgh Magazine*, in a review attributed to Lockhart, suggested that Isaac D'Israeli could show Crayon at least three-fourths of the stories already in print in the British Museum. The critic went on to predict that unless the American author turned to fresh subjects his high reputation would be lost: "He may go on publishing pretty octavos for John Murray for several years to come; and he may maintain a very pretty rank among the Mayfair blue-stockings, and their half-emasculated hangers-on; but he must infallibly sink in the eyes of really intelligent and manly readers." [31] Quite naturally,

28 *Tales*, JM ed., I, 66, 64; II, 198–208.

29 *Westminster Review*, II (Oct. 1824), 346.

30 I, 276. The reviewer took many slashing jabs at WI. One of the more colorful images created follows: "The Tales of a Traveller seem to tell one more tale than the author would wish to make public,—viz: that Geoffrey Crayon knows something of 'The Art of Bookmaking' beyond the mere theory. They bear unequivocal marks of having been composed for Mr. Murray, and not for the public. Whilst reading them, I was perpetually haunted by a singular vision; I fancied that I saw the author at his writing desk, armed with a goose-quill and other implements of literary husbandry, whilst the afore-said eminent bibliopolist stood at his elbow, jingling a purse of sovereigns, from which a couple descended into the author's pouch according as he finished every page of foolscap." X (Oct. 1824), 404.

31 XVI (Sept. 1824), 295–96.

American critics did not allow the British to outdo them; the more chauvinistic Democratic spread-eagles accused him of being downright un-American.[32]

It is not surprising then, to find Irving at one of his lowest ebbs in several years. In December he wrote to Leslie:

> I am isolated in English literature, without any of the usual aids and influences by which an author's popularity is maintained and promoted. I have no literary coterie to cry me up; no partial reviewer to pat me on the back; and the very review of my publisher is hostile to everything American. I have nothing to depend on but the justice and courtesy of the public, and how long the public will continue to favour the writings of a stranger, or how soon it may be prejudiced by the scribblers of the press, is with me a matter of extreme uncertainty.[33]

Doggedly—trying to push his unappreciative public from his mind —he began to study Spanish and to think about a "project of an American work." [34] Off and on Irving worked on his "American Essays" for the next twelve months, recording his progress in his journal.

At 50 Albemarle Street the scene was being affected by two factors: the backwash produced by Byron's death and the final definite resignation of Gifford as editor of the *Quarterly Review*. Still holding the copyrights to Byron's writings and possessing the most valuable and extensive collection of Byron letters, John Murray was the object of great interest and considerable controversy. Typical was Thomas Medwin's *Conversations of Lord Byron*,[35] which was filled, Smiles declared, with "many false as well as libellous statements against Mr. Murray." [36] To this, the publisher responded with a pamphlet, under his own imprint, "*Conversations of Lord Byron*, as Related by Thomas Medwin, Esq., Compared with a Portion of his Lordship's Correspondence."

[32] STW discussed at length this hostile reception by critics on both sides of the Atlantic. I, 275–78; II, 294–96.
[33] PMI, II, 224.
[34] Journal entry on Feb. 5. Trent and Hellman, II, 89.
[35] London: Colburn, 1824.
[36] I, 449.

Even Thomas Moore, whose collection of Byron letters was it-self second only to Murray's, watched Murray with dark green eyes, for Moore's hope of writing a life of Byron for Longmans, to repay the two thousand pounds they had loaned him, was hampered by Murray's possession of some of the most informative source materials.

December 1824 witnessed the official departure of the long-suffering Gifford from the editor's chair. He was replaced by John Taylor Coleridge, a promising young barrister and frequent contributor to the *Quarterly Review*, who had been considered for the post since 1823. The change-over was effected with com-parative ease, but it was the end of an era, and melancholia hung heavily over the men who had worked with the periodical since its beginning under Gifford.[37] Among the papers which the re-tiring editor left for his successor was a review of *Tales of a Traveller*. Originally the work of Canon Thomas Hughes of St. Paul's Cathedral, the critique had been drastically revised by Gifford, emerging as a survey of Irving's British reputation from the time of the publication of *The Sketch Book*.[38]

In Paris, Irving was being led by Peter into another scheme for getting rich quickly. The freeing by Spain of its South American colonies had opened that general area up as the new Eldorado. A "Bolivar copper mine" [39] took the fancy of the Irving brothers and, like the ill-fated Seine steamboat line, helped rid Washington of his recent financial harvest and to speed him to the edge of poverty.

With John Murray, Irving had no direct communication. The reviews of *Tales of a Traveller* inspired the publisher to offer no congratulations to the author, and that author was smarting too sharply from criticism to seek intercourse with anyone who reminded him of the recent unpleasantness. Murray appears, however, to have broken the silence, asking of Irving a service

[37] See the affectionate letters concerning Gifford in Smiles, II, 166–70.
[38] Roy Benjamin Clark, *William Gifford: Tory, Satirist, Critic, and Editor* (New York: Columbia University Press, 1930), p. 181; Smiles, II, 158.
[39] PMI, II, 240.

(for which the American had likely volunteered the previous summer) in Paris.

13. *To John Murray II* [40]

Paris, Jany 26th 1825
Rue Richelieu No. 89.

My dear Sir,

I have disposed of the copy of Count Gamba's memoirs [41] to the Galignanis, though I fear you will think the terms quite inconsiderable; but there is no competition here in English publishing, to cause any anxiety in securing early copies. Baudry[42] is their only rival publisher & he will not buy works. They are to give a guinea a sheet, calculated on their own edition, which they suppose will contain about twelve sheets. There was no doing any thing better; they even made a merit of giving any thing; as it was but paying for the start of four or five days, which in the sale of English works in Paris is not a matter of great importance. They would have received the work through their ordinary channel in four or five days, and would have put it to press immediately, even though another house were publishing it: as they feel their ascendancy in the market.

The terms they give in this instance is what they give by standing agreement to one of the principal Booksellers in London,[43] for early sheets of new-publications of first rate merit.

I have nothing of my own in any state of forwardness; though my brain is teeming. Whenever I have any thing worth offering I

[40] Marked at the Foreign Post Office in London, Feb. 1, 1825.

[41] Count Pietro Gamba, *Lord Byron's Last Journey to Greece. Extracted from the Journal of Count P. Gamba who attended his Lordship on that Expedition* (London: JM, 1825). *Galignani's Messenger* advertised this title from Galignani's press on Feb. 26, March 23, and May 3, 1825. In 1821 Galignani's had written to JMII concerning his desire to be Byron's official publisher in France. Smiles, II, 116–17.

The copyright situation in France was similar to that in Britain. Original publication was the only way to secure a copyright. See Stephen P. Ladas, *The International Protection of Literary and Artistic Property* (New York: The Macmillan Co., 1938), II, 1017–26.

[42] Louis Claude Baudry (1794–1852) was a publisher-bookseller of Paris, occasionally engaging in English editions. See Barber, "Galignani's and the Publication of English Books in France," 271. In 1836 Baudry published the complete works of WI in one volume.

[43] Probably Baldwyn & Co. See above, p. 32.

shall be happy to lay it before you. Give my sincere regards to Mrs Murray & the family and believe me my dear Sir,

Very faithfully yours,
Washington Irving.

14. To John Murray II

Paris, Feb. 2d 1825.
Rue de Richelieu No. 89.

My dear Sir,

I wrote to you some days since stating the terms on which I had disposed of the copy of Count Gamba's work to the Galignanis—viz a guinea a page,[44] calculated on their edition. It is an inconsiderable sum; but the most that I could procure. I am in want of occupation for my leisure hours. I have been amusing myself for some time in reading Spanish authors and have an idea of making a translation of the novels of Cervantes. Would such a work be desireable [desirable] to you? It would be preceded by a Biography of Cervantes, a dissertation on his dramas, romances & other writings, with such extracts as might seem interesting. The whole would make three volumes about the size of Bracebridge Hall; or might be comprized in two stout volumes. Don Quixote of course would not be included in this work. I could have it ready about midsummer, provided I get about it immediately.

Have you ever heard any thing about the MSS. of the Arabian tales?

With best regards to Mrs Murray & the family,

I am dear Sir
Very faithfully yours,
Washington Irving.

P.S. A letter sent by the Ambassador's bag will always reach me safely.

To the query about the work on Cervantes, Murray appears to have made no reply,[45] and the elusive manuscript of the "Arab-

---

[44] A printer's sheet.

[45] In annotating WI's journal entry of Feb. 6—"talked with Peter about Cervantes' life—" PMI declared rather sourly: "a theme for his pen which had been suggested by Murray and which was afterwards adopted by Lockhart." II, 320. For Lockhart's work on Cervantes, see below, Chap. IV.

ian tales," about which Irving and Murray had perhaps talked during the summer of 1824, is heard of no more. On February 18 Irving received from Galignani's "fourteen sovereigns for Murray," [46] which he made available to Murray through Samuel Williams in a letter to the publisher dated March 3. This missing letter probably contained little more than another apology for the size of the payments from Galignani's and a repetition of his inquiry about Murray's interest in a study of Cervantes, for Irving's main activity continued to be his effort to master Spanish.[47]

From 50 Albemarle Street—silence.

In March, however, the *Quarterly Review* containing the Hughes-Gifford summation of Irving's British editions was published.[48] This discussion, because it must have been close to the views of the proprietor of the periodical, might be read as the official evaluation of Irving's work from 50 Albemarle Street.

The first paragraph expressed the idea that the time had come

> for forming a real estimate of his [Irving's] merits, when the first glowing sunshine of success has been sobered down by some clouds of neglect; and it is also probable, that friendly criticism may find in him now a more patient and tractable hearer, than he might have proved at the brilliant commencement of his career.[49]

Beginning chronologically with *Salmagundi*, the review insisted that this collection owed "its principal pretensions to his exertions." [50] Knickerbocker's *History of New York* was

> a tantalizing book, of which all that we understand is so good, and affords us so much pleasure, even though an imperfect acquaintance

46 Trent and Hellman, II, 93.

47 See Feb. 2–March 3, 1825, Trent and Hellman, II, 87–98. A biographical sketch of WI written in Paris indicates that he was actively trying to stir up a demand for his work on Cervantes. "It is whispered that at a late convivial meeting of literati, some one hinted to Mr. Irving his fitness to undertake a translation of the minor tales of the author of Don Quixote. Such a version must of necessity be an improvement on the original; and what a high treat might we not expect from the united talents of Irving and Cervantes!" *The European Magazine, and London Review*, LXXXVII (March 1825), 201.

48 XXXI (March 1825), 473–87.

49 *Ibid.*, 474.

50 *Ibid.*, 475.

with its [American] history, that we cannot but conclude that a thorough knowledge of the whole point in every part would be a treat indeed.[51]

The Sketch Book was so highly thought of that words were not wasted repeating praise of it. *Bracebridge Hall*, with its pictures of "Every Man in his Humour," was a pleasing work, though it should have been condensed into one volume; to add to the size, the author had clearly pulled scraps from his literary store to use as "make-weights." [52]

Of *Tales of a Traveller*, Irving's latest "scrap-book" (here used as a derogatory term), the first part, "Strange Stories, by a Nervous Gentleman," was "indeed a most amusing specimen of that piquant cookery which makes something out of nothing"—the main merit of the stale stories resting in the "minute and rueful caricature" used in describing the scenes.[53] "Buckthorne and his Friends" was judged as being "excellent" because the author had "been driven to tax his own invention in good earnest." [54] "The scenes in the cathedral town[55] form a strong contrast to the broad farce of the strolling company"—every extreme of character and scene being balanced by a counterpart "in as different a taste from each other, as the broad flowing freedom of Rowlandson, and the dark, worm-eaten, characteristic touches of Quintin Matsys." [56] On Buckthorne's "moral tendency" too much praise could not be heaped, and "the portrait of the good clergyman, Buckthorne's private tutor, is drawn with a flow of persuasive moral eloquence, which would be broken by quoting any particular part." [57] "The Italian Banditti" read too much like an authentic journal of an English traveler in Italy, but the story of the multirape was a false note: "it ought not to have been written—it ought not to be read . . . and if the book should ever reach a second

[51] *Ibid.*
[52] *Ibid.*, 481.
[53] *Ibid.*, 482.
[54] *Ibid.*, 483.
[55] See above, n. 15.
[56] QR, XXXI, 484.
[57] *Ibid.*, 485.

edition, we trust Mr. Irving will expunge it." [58] "The Money-Diggers," "the parings and shreds" of Irving's previous Knickerbocker stories, was "puny degenerate bantling." [59] In general, the review concluded, the book failed to rise to the author's previous level of merit because of his "habits of indolence," [60] that is, his insistence on using the dregs of past successes when exertion on his part might produce original work that could surpass previous efforts. Summing up Irving's standing in England in 1825, the *Quarterly Review* concluded:

> The indulgence which he so fairly deserved at his outset, as an ingenious stranger . . . must now cease, and he must be considered in the future as not only admitted to the full freedom and privileges of the English guild of authorship, but amenable also at the same time, as an experienced craftsman, to its most rigorous statutes.[61]

Such was the message to Irving in the periodical which bore John Murray's imprint. How much of the review was Gifford's and how much was Hughes' we have no way of knowing, but the last sentence must be Gifford's fond farewell to a "real favourite" from Murray's drawing-room circle: he congratulated Irving "on the rank, which he has already gained, of which the momentary caprice of the public cannot long deprive him; and with hearty good will, playfully, but we hope not profanely, we exclaim as we part from him, 'Very pleasant hast thou been to me, my brother Jonathan.' " [62]

Throughout the spring and summer Irving continued to work on Spanish, to write on various little projects which never seemed to materialize, and to enjoy (as much as his depression would allow) the society of Paris.[63] Leslie's marriage in April widened

---

58 *Ibid.*, 483.
59 *Ibid.*, 483.
60 *Ibid.*, 486.
61 *Ibid.*, 486–87.
62 *Ibid.*, 487.
63 See WI's journal covering this period. Trent and Hellman, II, 99–157. Also of interest is Part IX of *Wolfert's Roost*, "Sketches in Paris in 1825," nine essays he wrote late in life based on notes of this stay in the city.

the gap between Irving and London,[64] and the British and Americans in Paris were anxious to keep his amiable personality among them.

On June 1 he addressed young John Murray.

15. *To John Murray III* [65]

June 1st [1825].

My dear John,

I will thank you for a copy of the "Tales of a Traveller—"—a neat copy, *bound*, if you have one, as it is to present to a lady.

Very truly yours,
Washington Irving.

The identity of the lady is not known, Irving's journal and other letters offering no clue. That he was anxious to present her with a copy of his most recent book is indicated by the next communication to 50 Albemarle Street, this one addressed to the senior John Murray and couched in stiffly formal language.

16. *To John Murray II* [66]

Mr Irving will thank Mr Murray for a copy (in boards) of the "Tales of a Traveller."

Monday morng
June 13. [1825]

It seems likely that Murray sent the book and with it a personal letter in which he accounted for his long silence. It was the same story of "stomach disorder" brought on—though he rarely admitted it—by the strain of his old business responsibilities and the new ones he was thinking up. The big project at hand was a daily newspaper, eventually to be named *The Representative*, which he was financing, to be operated in partnership with young Ben-

[64] With "Harry" (as her husband called her) Leslie, WI maintained cordial public relations, but privately he referred to her as the "creaking door." STW, II, 334.

[65] Used by permission of the Clifton Waller Barrett Library of the University of Virginia Library.

[66] Used by permission of The Sleepy Hollow Restorations, Tarrytown, N. Y.

jamin Disraeli. The agreement was signed on August 5, and Murray was soon in the process of establishing offices and printing facilities on Great George Street, Westminster. This news Murray surely gave Irving before he concluded, adding that he "hoped seriously that he [Irving] had not been idle, and that he [Irving] would allow him [Murray] to look for a communication from him 'on the subject of an original work,' which he was 'happy to say the public would be much delighted to receive.' " [67]

17. *To John Murray II* [68]

Paris, Aug. 19th 1825.

My dear Sir,

    I am extremely sorry to hear that you have been severely ill; but I hope and trust that you are again in your usual good health.

    In consequence of receiving no reply from you on the subject of Cervantes's life and writings I concluded that the proposition was no[t] sufficiently interesting and I abandoned all idea of the subject. I have nothing ready for the press, nor do I know at present when I shall have, my mind having been rather diverted from composition of late, and occupied by a course of study.

    Mr Newton is with me at present and has been confined to the house for some time by indisposition but is getting about again. Wilkie is likewise in Paris, and appears to be slowly recovering from the malady that has for several months disabled him from all application to his art. [69]

    With kind remembrances to Mrs Murray and the family

Believe me dear Sir
Very truly yours,
Washington Irving.

The last of September, forsaking Galignani's and Paris society, Washington and Peter moved to Bordeaux, where they enjoyed

[67] PMI had this letter in his possession, II, 238.

[68] Used by permission of The Pierpont Morgan Library, New York. Marked in London Aug. 26, 1825.

[69] For details concerning Wilkie's illness and his and Newton's relations with WI at this time, see Allan Cunningham, *The Life of Sir David Wilkie* (London: JM, 1843), II, 144–45; Trent and Hellman, II, 142–47. Wilkie, to whom WI would dedicate *The Alhambra*, later became close friends with WI in Spain.

74

the hospitality of the Guestier family, whom they had first met in Paris. Washington was in a feverish state: not only did he see his literary star in the decline and fear that he had written himself out; he had to accept the consequence of the bankruptcy in October of Samuel Williams in London,[70] by which he may have lost two thousand pounds in one fell swoop. The novelist G. P. R. James, later a protégé of Irving's, had his first glimpse of the American about this time: Irving was calming a cat he had startled in a passageway with these words, "Ah! pussy! pussy! If you had seen as much trouble as I have, you would not be surprised at anything." [71]

As 1825 came to a close with Irving on the Continent bemoaning his fare in life, John Murray in London was conscious that his world of book publishing was changing, and with remarkable tenacity he prepared to adjust to the situation.

The most recent scholar to review English publishing of this period suggests that, first of all, the glamor was dimmed, if not very nearly extinguished.[72] Byron was dead and Scott, still active in every way, had, nevertheless, become more of a fixture than an ornament. Within the profession, a blighting mold had been spreading in the form of publishers, notably Henry Colburn, with neither literary taste nor scruples. Willing to pay enormous prices for works, Colburn contrived by elaborate "puffing" campaigns to foist off all types of inferior books on the public.[73] The result had been a general reaction in which the book industry had suffered from a disappointed and sometimes indignant clientele. Colburn was "the butt of the trade" and was considered by many of his fellow publishers "a disgrace to the profession." [74] We have already had Washington Irving's evaluation of him.

70 Under bankruptcies, "SAMUEL WILLIAMS, of Finsbury-Square, merchant" in *The London Gazette*, Oct. 29, 1825.

71 Stewart M. Ellis, *The Solitary Horseman; or, the Life and Adventures of G. P. R. James* (London: Cayme Press, 1927), p. 38.

72 Gettmann, *A Victorian Publisher: A Study of the Bentley Papers*, p. 7. Gettmann's "Introduction," pp. 1–14, is a brief but knowledgeable discussion of British book publishing in the 1820's.

73 See Gettmann's chapter on "Puffing," pp. 55–75.

74 *Ibid.*, p. 9.

John Murray could do nothing about Colburn's effect on publishing. His attention—concerning book publishing—was focused on the idea of "cheap literature," making the best titles and information available at a reasonable price to the ever-increasing reading public from the middle class. In 1825 Murray proposed to offer a series of voyages and travels in pocket editions.[75] From Archibald Constable, with whom after fifteen years he resumed his close personal friendship, Murray received encouragement, for the "Czar of the North" was making plans for such a series under his imprint to be known as *Constable's Miscellanies*. Murray would still be the Great Bibliophile, the publisher's publisher, but he would also, of necessity, be the people's publisher.

The *Quarterly Review*, on which he had based his hopes in years previously, continued to hold its honored place. In December 1825, the former editor having resigned to devote his full time to law, John Gibson Lockhart, Scott's son-in-law, became the editor, a post he held for the remainder of his life, long after John Murray II had died. Lockhart's distinguished work as editor and contributor to the periodical caused it to be Murray's greatest single asset.

But for Irving, back in Bordeaux, the future looked dark. Dipping his pen in bile, he turned in earnest to the "American Essays," perhaps working out his personal frustrations and bitterness in them. His American subjects included character, union, public prosperity, the navy, education, rural life, manners, national prejudices, treatment of strangers, and patriots and demagogues.[76] His collection seemed to be fairly well completed at the end of January 1826, but Irving tempted no publisher with the prospect of this manuscript as a future imprint. Yet he needed money and, with his financial reversals, he and Peter could ill afford the luxury of four months spent in scribbling for his self-enrichment. Such had been the case, however, and at the end

[75] Smiles, II, 246.
[76] Topics gleaned from Trent and Hellman, *passim*.

Washington appears to have consigned the labored-over pages to the flames.[77]

Had Alexander Hill Everett, Minister Plenipotentiary of the United States to Spain, not come to his rescue, Irving might well have been forced by reasons of pecuniary distress to throw his essays before the public rather than into the fire, and though it is mere conjecture, the world might today have from Irving's pen a volume of essays vastly different in tone, at least, from anything else he ever wrote for public consumption. It is not unreasonable to suppose that Irving's recent experiences had caused him to shed —for the time being—the smooth pale skin of sentimentality in which he chose to enclose his writings. His country viewed through his critical eyes at this juncture of his life would have been an interesting sight, and the resultant study would have, no doubt, given Irving a prominent place among the social critics of the United States.

Irving had met Everett the previous summer in Paris, where they had talked much of the writer's interest in Spain. Consequently, the ambassador was not greatly surprised to receive a letter from Irving in January 1826 asking that he be attached to the United States Embassy in Madrid. "It would be perhaps an advantage and protection to me in the present state of the country," Irving wrote, "to be able at anytime to announce myself as attached to the embassy." [78] Everett replied favorably, suggesting that Irving consider translating Navarrete's study of Columbus' voyages, the first volume of which was soon to appear in Madrid.[79]

This was not the "original work" Murray had longed for from Irving, but the idea appealed to the desperate American. He wrote

[77] See STW, I, 292–93; 464, n. 101.

[78] PMI, II, 246.

[79] Martin Fernandez de Navarrete's *Coleccion de los Viages y Descubrimiento* was printed by the government, having been specifically commissioned by the king. Vols. I and II appeared in 1825, III in 1829 (with introductory section discussing WI's writings on Columbus), IV and V in 1837.

immediately (February 3) to Leslie about this Spanish work he intended to translate:

> I wish you to make an arrangement with Murray at once for the purchase of the translation, or, if he will not buy it, with Longman or Colburn. . . . Mr. Everett thinks I ought to get 1,500 or 1,000 guineas for it. I shall be content with the last sum. I should have written to Murray on the subject, but I have had such repeated instances of his inattention to letters, and have been put so much back thereby, that I won't trust to correspondence any more, either with him or any other bookseller.[80]

Irving made ready to depart, with Peter in tow, for Madrid; then, as he nervously considered his situation, he decided he couldn't let the matter rest in Leslie's hands.

18. *To John Murray II* [81]

Bordeaux, Feby 6th, 1826.

My dear Sir,

I have desired my friend Mr Leslie to wait upon you with a literary proposition on my part. There is a very interesting work printing at Madrid of which you have no doubt heard, The Voyage of Columbus, compiled from his own papers, and composed in part of extracts from his Journal, by the Bishop Las Casas.[82] Mr Everett our minister at Madrid has written to me wishing me to undertake the translating of it into English, and I have agreed to do so. It will make, I am told, about two volumes octavo. As I shall have some assistance in the rough labour of the translation I shall be able to finish it pretty speedily, & can forward the manuscript as fast as it is ready for the press. I hope it will be a work to tempt you.

I leave this place in a day or two for Madrid, where I shall pass some time, with Mr Everett, who has attached me to the Embassy.

[80] Leslie, II, 169.

[81] Marked at the Foreign Post Office in London, Feb. 13, 1826. Watermarked "JN CLAVAUD 1823."

[82] The original journal kept by Columbus was presented to Ferdinand and Isabella, after which it was lost. There was, fortunately, at least one copy preserved by Bishop Las Casas, still in the National Library, Madrid. See Samuel E. Morison, "Texts and Transcriptions of the Journal of Columbus's First Voyage," *Hispanic-American Historical Review*, XIX (Aug. 1939), 235–61.

I shall make excursions to some of the more interesting parts of Spain. If I can be of any service to you command me; a letter addressed to me at the American Legation Madrid will be sure to find me. The British Ambassador's bag will perhaps be the surest conveyance. I have been writing a little of late but nothing in forwardness for the press nor shall I have any thing this spring, except the translation.

You seem to be making a great noise with your Representative;[83] for his voice reaches even here, echoed from one French paper to another. As to an English paper there is no such thing to be seen in Bordeaux. I hope to meet with a file of it at Madrid.

Present my kind remembrances to Mrs Murray and the family and believe me my dear Sir

Very faithfully yours,
Washington Irving.

On February 23, in Madrid, having heard nothing from Leslie or Murray, Irving addressed the artist, explaining again what he should tell the publisher: the proposed work would not (he had expanded the concept of the project since his previous letter) be just a translation of Las Casas' manuscript such as he had "offered to him [Murray] a year or two since"; it would not even be limited to merely a translation of Navarrete's work.[84] Irving could not be more specific because he knew little about the project he was intending to undertake.

If Irving was vague in Madrid, Murray was definite in London.

---

[83] The first issue of *The Representative* appeared on Jan. 25, 1826, priced 7*d*. The paper included all the usual sections: news involving shipping, sports, fashion, markets, etc. It was hoped by the backer that foreign news would be an important department, and to this end, special correspondents were engaged throughout Europe.

[84] Leslie, II, 173.

Friday, February 17, 1826

The trip all the way from Lisson Grove had been through freezing drizzle, and Leslie nervously hit the palm of his gloved hand with the rolled-up copy of the Times *to stimulate the circulation in his fingers. Fortunately, John Murray arrived at 50 Albemarle Street even before Leslie had time to lift the heavy knocker. Leslie explained that he had stopped by on his way to view the Poecilorama in Egyptian Hall, Piccadilly. Together they climbed the broad stairway to the first floor, Murray inquiring about Mrs. Leslie's accouchement, approaching its conclusion, and Leslie unfolding the* Times *to show him the article on the nearby popular sensation, which had just opened.*

The fire burning in the drawing-room fireplace had only recently been lit, but it gave a cheery glow to the dark corners— though it had not had time to take the sharp edge off the painful cold. Leslie loosened his greatcoat and settled into a chair offered by his host. Murray seemed to sink deeper into the fur collar of his coat, his face appearing in the firelight more drawn and haggard than his recent illness or his financial worries should have been able to produce in such a short period of time.

Laying the paper aside, Murray pulled a chair closer to Leslie's. The pressure of business and his unstable health, he began to apologize, had caused him to be uncertain as to a definite time when he could talk with Leslie and, frankly, since he could surmise the purpose of Leslie's visit, he had felt no real sense of urgency in the matter. In the process of pulling Irving's letters from an inner pocket, Leslie opened his mouth to speak, but Murray hurried on: he too had received a letter from Irving which he supposed had stated the situation as fully as the one which Leslie now held in his hand, and he wished it to be clear that it would be impossible for him to consider the value of Irving's proposed work on Columbus until he could have the opportunity of seeing the finished manuscript. Murray said further that he hoped Leslie would remind Irving of the slump in business activities and especially in those of bookselling at the present time. Constable's failure, he added, laying his hand on his chest, was a heavy burden and a warning to all book dealers. And The Representative! *His eyes twinkled; even in such a time, he chuckled, a good anecdote is worth telling.*

The previous night, he began, headed for Whitehall Place and trying to think of a suitable editor for his newspaper, he motioned a greeting to an acquaintance who happened to be passing. Mistaking the gesture for a beckon, the friend approached. "What is it, Mr. Murray? What do you want?" Seizing the question and the moment, the publisher cried to the flabbergasted pedestrian: "I want an editor! I want an editor!"

Leslie and the publisher talked for some time about the newspaper; Murray freely admitted for Leslie's private knowledge that it was fast becoming a painful burden. Then, returning to the reason for Leslie's visit (though the painter through the kindness of Murray had never found it necessary to mention Irving's name), Murray adopted a somewhat more affectionate tone as he pointed to Irving's portrait. "Thy friend is a remarkable person, but why will he not trust his own genius? I would gladly receive anything from him of original matter, but I fear a translation does not do him justice."

Leslie shuffled in his chair. Murray returned to the Times, *reading aloud from the article Leslie had pointed out to him: "The exhibition . . . attempts to combine the advantages of Cosmorama with some of those previously belonging to the Diorama." In silence he read on; then returning the paper to Leslie, he observed with a more friendly smile than he had yet displayed during the*

81

morning visit that he would accompany Leslie if he did not have pressing appointments all morning. He certainly wished to see the two scenes depicting the location of Byron's Prisoner of Chillon. *They talked briefly of young Clarkson Stanfield, the artist of the exhibition, and of the dioramic technique which seemed to give action to paintings by reflecting moving lights off them.*

Finally, movement in the hallway indicated the arrival of the publisher's first appointment. Leslie fastened his greatcoat again and prepared to return to the freezing winds, displaying a distinct sense of relief that the interview was over. Conducting this sort of business with John Murray, whose family had become social friends of his and his wife's, was clearly distasteful to him—a fact which the publisher had recognized. Probably only the urgent appeal from such a friend as Irving could have prompted the painter to put himself out in this way.

Sources for Vignette

This section is based on: Smiles, II, *passim*; Leslie, II, 173 *et passim*; PMI, II, 25; *Times*, Feb. 17, 1826; A. Edwin, Weather Diary, 1826.

Leslie could do no more than report what Murray had said. Irving read the letter[1] with a heavy heart, abandoned any plan to secure a publisher for the elusive proposal at that point, and turned to the task of producing his work on Columbus. His biographers suggest that he never worked harder than in the following months—yet one must not imagine that he was a recluse.[2] In Madrid, as in London, Paris, and Dresden, he

---

[1] The letter is quoted in PMI, II, 251.
[2] Cf. Trent and Hellman, III, 1–63. Claude Bowers, *The Spanish Adventures of Washington Irving* (Boston: Houghton Mifflin, 1940), pp. 1–126, provides an informative and entertaining picture of the entire length of Irving's stay in Spain, 1826–1829.

was a familiar figure in society, his friends including an ever-widening circle of Spanish nobles and diplomats. Presented to King Ferdinand VII in March, Irving mingled occasionally with some members of the native aristocracy, even winning the approval of the Duchess of Benavente, arch-rival hostess of the Duchess of Alva. On February 21 the aspiring biographer called on Martín Fernández de Navarrete, who warmed heartily to the newcomer and showed him his coveted store of Columbus material.[3] Among Americans in Madrid, the Everetts and the Obadiah Riches (officially he was the consul in Valencia, but they lived in Madrid) offered him friendship and encouragement. The British Embassy sported the well-known name of Stanhope, George Joseph, the younger brother of Philip Henry Stanhope, Viscount Mahon, who—twenty-three years old and fresh from Oxford—arrived for an extended stay and formed a close friendship based on common interests with the forty-three-year-old American.[4] The French and Czarist Russians, however, offered more than the other nationalities. The domestic circle of the French Minister, M. D'Oubril, was Irving's favorite home in Madrid. There was the charming wife, a bevy of lively children and comely governesses, a beautiful niece named Antoinette Bolviller, and—a regular member of the household—Prince Demetri Ivanovitch Dolgorouki, the twenty-nine-year-old attaché of the Russian Embassy. Already a published poet in his homeland, Dolgorouki was avidly interested in art and literature and became fast friends with Irving.[5]

---

[3] Trent and Hellman, III, 10.

[4] By the time WI returned to England, Lord Mahon had become a Member of Parliament and JMII had published his *History of the War of the Succession in Spain*. George Joseph Stanhope served as an attaché in Madrid from May 4, 1825, to April 21, 1828, when he returned home because of ill health. His activities can be traced through random remarks in the official dispatches to the Foreign Office, now preserved in the Public Record Office (F.O. 72/300, 301, 329, 349). *Burke's Geneological and Heraldic History of the Peerage, Baronetage and Knightage* (London: Burke's Peerage, Ltd., 1963), p. 2295, indicates that he died on Nov. 25, 1828, at the age of twenty-two.

[5] See WI's description of the D'Oubrils in PMI, II, 273–78. Dolgorouki had previously served in the Russian embassies in Rome and Constantinople; in 1828 he became Secretary of the embassy in Madrid. See STW, I, 326–27, 481–82, *et passim*.

Then, of course, there were transient Americans to be welcomed and guided about Spain. Among the nephews who appeared was William's son, Pierre Monro Irving, twenty-three years old and eager to know his famous uncle better. A young American named Henry Wadsworth Longfellow also dropped by to gain inspiration from the great man of his native literature.[6] One American friend of 1826 appeared prominently in Irving's dealings with Murray in later years—Alexander Slidell. The young naval adventurer was on leave in Spain, recording his activities in journals from which would come a two-volume book entitled *A Year in Spain.*[7]

The almost unsurpassed private library of Rich[8] became Irving's home; he and Peter actually took rooms on the first floor of the Rich house and Washington opened his trunks—already something of a literary joke[9]—to begin packing in notes that would keep him in writing matter for the remainder of his life. Since 1816 Rich had been devoting most of his time to the hobby which would eventually become his profession and make his name known to future generations of bibliographers. From the unexplored Spanish storehouses he had been collecting manuscripts and early printed books relating to America. He had no competitors in Spain; the field was his to command, and he let few opportunities escape him.

Irving's project had not been defined in any clear fashion. Everett had suggested a translation of Navarrete's work. Irving knew enough about publishers and public taste to fear the reaction to a work so unoriginal and dull. Somewhere along the way he began to visualize a full biography of Columbus, some-

---

[6] See PMI, II, 253, 265–66.

[7] See below, Letters 40–42, 45, 48. Slidell, who later (1838) changed his name to Mackenzie, was the brother of John Slidell, the Confederate diplomat. *DAB*, XII, 90–91.

[8] See *DAB*, XII, 549. For later references to Rich, see below, Letters 22 and 26. Bowers, pp. 5–11, draws a good character sketch of this bibliophile.

[9] Reviewers of *Tales of a Traveller* had been amused to imagine Crayon pausing in his journey to pull the bits and pieces which went into the work from his dusty traveling trunks. See especially *The European Magazine, and London Review*, LXXXVII (March 1825), 199.

thing Rich's library made possible. One must never discount the value of this private collection in Irving's work, for in those troubled times all people, and especially foreigners digging into official papers, were suspect in Spain. In later months Irving would gain access to the Archives of the Indies only after the intercession of the king himself.[10]

In the midst of his intense work on Columbus' life (August 1826), Irving's unstable interest shifted to the expulsion of the Moors from Spain, and not until two months later was he to return to his original subject.[11] Ultimately the interlude proved to be a valuable one, since it provided him with the basic material for his next work, *A Chronicle of the Conquest of Granada*, but at the time it seemed to smack of madness. His finances were in ruin. With all of his British capital apparently lost, he and Peter lived for several months by way of an involved system of drawing upon their brother-in-law Van Wart, who received reimbursements from Washington's funds in the United States; but even that source was dwindling.

In December, working once again on his far-from-finished biography of Columbus, Irving wrote to Murray. Though his tone was firm and unbending, Irving was hoping, even begging, for reassurance from the publisher that the proposed work had his approval.

19. *To John Murray II*[12]

Madrid, Decr 21st 1826.

My dear Sir,

I have heard from various quarters that you have threatened hard

10 For a discussion of the situation, unchanged in 1843, see Pascual de Gayangos to William Hickling Prescott, Feb. 2, 1843, in *The Correspondence of William Hickling Prescott, 1833–1847*, ed. Roger Wolcott (Boston: Houghton Mifflin Co., 1925), p. 335.

11 During this summer WI apparently received a letter from the Storrows suggesting that he should make definite arrangements at once with JM for the publication of his next work. He replied: "I do not wish to communicate with Murray on the subject until my work is compleat. He is a capricious man and sometimes neglectful; and has two or three times given me complete checks to my undertakings, either by his silence, or his discouraging replies." STW, *WI and the Storrows*, p. 93.

12 Parts of three sentences quoted in garbled form in Smiles, II, 256. JM's Note:

for some time past to write me a letter and I have been waiting for you to put your threats in execution but in vain. I have now a word or two to say on business. I have a work nearly ready for the press, "The Life and Voyages of Columbus." I have availed myself of the work of Navarrete as far as it was valuable, also all the other historians in print and some in manuscript, and various documents which I have met with here. The work will make a couple of volumes quarto of respectable size, including illustrations and documents. The documents will comprise all those of real importance which have appeared relative to Columbus, rejecting only the trivial & superfluous. I have worked excessively hard to make this work full, particular and exact as to facts, and at the same time to make it interesting to the general reader. Having been for nearly a year past living in the midst of a library of old Spanish works I have had the materials immediately under my hand. If you think the work will be desireable [desirable] for you I will forward you specimens of the life, the voyages & illustrations as soon I hear from you. I will either sell the copy right or you may print an edition and we will share the profits.

I have also another work in hand, more in my own way, and which I could soon get ready for the press but I do not intend to publish it until after Columbus.

I beg you will let me hear from you soon on this subject as I want to make all my arrangements as soon as possible that I may make a tour to the South of Spain.

Present my kind remembrances to Mrs Murray and the rest of your family & believe me my dear Sir

Very faithfully yours,
Washington Irving.

P.S. Address to me at the Legation Americaine à Madrid.

This letter reached John Murray at the end of the most traumatic year of his business career. With the other British publishing houses tottering or falling, he had managed to stand straight and to give assistance to some of his weakening colleagues.[13]

"ansd Jan. 4th 1827." Marked in Foreign Post Office in London, Jan. 4, 1827.

[13] See Smiles, II, 213. Reading in the British papers of the failure of Constable

Henry Colburn, in his sensational way, had even increased his wealth and list, publishing, among other titillating novels, *Vivian Grey*, the work of an anonymous author, of interest here because one of the principal characters was a thinly veiled picture of John Murray II and one of the marginal characters was Washington Irving, described through the eyes of an English dandy.[14] And tradesmen other than Colburn had managed to make advantageous book dealings in 1826; remainders men such as Thomas Tegg, looking like vultures to publishers trying to hold on to their businesses, circled London loading carts and wagons with stock from the financially distressed sellers.[15] Unwilling to engage in Colburn's tactics, only by sharply curtailing his book publication activities had Murray been able to remain the bulwark of the profession.

In the publication of his daily newspaper, *The Representative*, he had been less successful. The desertion of his fair-weather partner young Disraeli[16] (who was later identified as the author of *Vivian Grey*), his failure to secure a suitable editor, and the confused conditions of the times combined to cause Murray to abandon the project, the last issue appearing on July 29. His losses amounted to over twenty-six thousand pounds.

Murray's reply to Irving on this occasion was immediate. The letter, written and mailed on January 4, was received by Irving on January 16, when he joyfully recorded in his journal: "letter

---

and of the publishing firm of Hurst, Robinson and Co., WI wrote to A. H. Everett, Jan. 31, 1826: "These are severe shocks in the trading world of literature. Pray Heaven Murray may stand unmoved and not go into the Gazette [his reference to the *London Gazette*, the official announcer of bankruptcies], instead of publishing one." PMI, II, 249.

14 John Murray II was the Marquis of Carabas. For WI, see Benjamin Disraeli, *Vivian Grey* [Collected Edition, X] (London: Longmans, Green and Co., 1871), p. 50.

15 Gettman, p. 23.

16 After this, the relationship of the D'Israeli and Murray families was strained for several months, though it was eventually restored to its original high vein. In fact, in the 1830's JMII would publish some of Benjamin Disraeli's best writings. Smiles, II, 208–18.

from Murray's agreeing to publish 'Columbus.' " [17] This is a curiously unreserved statement in view of the later bargaining that transpired between Irving and his publisher. Lacking a full copy of Murray's letter, we can only guess at its contents by piecing together a published fragment and clues from Irving's belated reply. Murray began:

> One cause of my not writing to you during one whole year was my "entanglement," as Lady G—— says, with a newspaper, which absorbed my money, and distracted and depressed my mind; but I have cut the knot of evil, which I could not untie, and am now, by the blessing of God, again returned to reason and the shop.[18]

He must have gone on to explain that in the tightening up necessitated by the financial disasters of the previous year, the family had settled once again into 50 Albemarle Street. Young John Murray, now eighteen years of age, had gone to Edinburgh to continue his formal education at the Royal High School there. Gifford's death on December 31 had occasioned great sadness among the Murrays; now the publisher looked forward to seeing Irving's new work. Beyond that, Murray likely did no more than generate his customary charm. Irving's later letters and action indicate, the journal notation notwithstanding, that Murray did not offer him a blank check for a contract.

20. *To John Murray II*[19]

Madrid, April 4th 1827.

My dear Sir,

I have suffered a long time to elapse without answering your very kind letter, but in fact I have been deferring my reply from time to

[17] Trent and Hellman, III, 51. In a letter to PMI, Jan. 18, 1827, WI wrote: "I received a letter from Murray the day before yesterday on the subject of Columbus. He is extremely anxious to receive it as soon as possible, that he may put it immediately to press" (PMI, II, 255–56). JMII meant perhaps that he was anxious to put the MS to press if he bought it.

[18] Smiles, II, 215.

[19] Marked in Foreign Post Office in London, April 19, 1827.

time in hopes of being able to forward some part of my work for publication. After writing to you so long since in terms as if the manuscript was nearly ready for the press you will smile perhaps when I tell you that it is yet incomplete. You must be accustomed however to the miscalculations of literary men, and aware how many circumstances may occur to delay a work of the kind. One of the principal [reasons] is the delay in the receipt of the manuscript history of Las Casas, which had been promised me, but with held until a recent period,[20] and on consulting which I was induced to make many alterations and additions throughout my work. The history will however be greatly improved by this delay, and I am bestowing incessant labour upon it to make it as worthy as my abilities will permit of public approbation. I will make no promise about when it shall be forwarded, lest I should disappoint both you and myself, but above one half of it is corrected and copied and I will finish off the remainder as fast as possible.

I am heartily glad you have extricated yourself from the toils and troubles and vexations of a news paper concern and are once more at your classic establishment in Albemarle Street; which will do more for your fortune and honourable reputation than any other residence or concern.

What news is there from Timbuctoo and when are we to have the travels of Laing? [21] I presume you are to be his publisher. I am extremely interested in the African travels. I am anxious to know whether the description of Timbuctoo as given by Laing agrees with that of Giovan[ni] Leone Africano in Ramusio,[22] and whether the temple and the palace built of stone by an architect of Gra-

[20] WI had seen this manuscript on Feb. 12. Trent and Hellman, III, 54.

[21] Alexander Gordon Laing (1793–1826), an African explorer, left England February 5, 1825, on an expedition by way of Timbuctoo to find the source of the Niger River. He reached Timbuctoo, but was murdered by natives on Sept. 26, 1826. These facts were not known for some time. *DNB*, XI, 399–401. In 1825 JMII had published Laing's *Travels in the Timannee, Koorank, and Soolima Countries of Western Africa*.

[22] Giovanni Leone Africano (*ca.* 1485–*ca.* 1554) was an Arab scholar and traveler whose *Decrittione del 'Africa*, completed in 1526, was the principal source of Europe's knowledge of Islam until the nineteenth century. It was first published by Giovanni Battista Ramusio, as volume one of his *Navigazioni e viaggi* (1550).

nada still remain.[23] I should suppose the fashions of these African cities vary but little, though the materials of their private buildings must be very perishable.

I shall probably be detained here for some time longer until I complete my work. Any letter or parcel sent for me by the courier to the British Legation will come safe, and if sent to the Hon. Frederich Byng[24] at the Foreign Office he will take care to forward it.

I will thank you to present my kind remembrances to Mrs Murray and the family, and to my friend John at the High School when you write to him, and believe me my dear Sir

With very sincere regard
Your assured friend,
Washington Irving.

If the publisher smiled over Irving's deception, there is no record. In fact, the absence of any further communication might suggest that he was far from being amused. Finally, seven months after Irving had announced the manuscript was "nearly ready," he had sufficiently covered his subject to make concrete offers to a publisher. To strengthen his bargaining power he appointed as his literary agent in London the American Consul, Colonel Aspinwall.[25] On July 29, 1827, Irving wrote three letters which he dispatched to the Colonel. One was a personal letter to Aspinwall requesting his services. For Aspinwall's eyes alone he wrote:

I am extremely anxious about the success of this work, on which all my future prospects depend. Its pecuniary success is not the least important to me, my purse being at a low ebb, if in reality it

[23] In Timbuctoo "there is a most stately temple to be seene, the walls whereof are made of stone and lime; and a princely palace also built by a most excellent workeman of Granada." *A Geographical Historie of Africa*, trans., John Pory (London: n.p., 1600), p. 287.

[24] The Honorable Gerald Frederick Byng (1785–1871), son of the Fifth Viscount Torrington, was a clerk in the Foreign Office. Clare Jerrold, *The Beaux and the Dandies: Nash, Brummell and D'Orsay and their Court* (London: Stanley Paul & Co., 1910), pp. 229, 276, 305. WI had met Byng through Frank Mills in 1824. STW, *Journal (1823–1824)*, p. 244.

[25] In this capacity WI addressed numerous letters to Aspinwall.

90

be not worse than empty. I have had munificent overtures[26] from other quarters, but I wish to keep with Murray, whom I have found prompt and free in pecuniary arrangements. . . . I do not wish my manuscript to be shown to any other person than Mr Murray, or such as he may hand it to for consultation. . . .

P.S. I know nothing of the standing of Mr Murray since the late convulsions in the business world, but trust though he may have lost considerably, he is sound and safe. I have left the letter to Murray open that you may read it. Put a wafer on it and either throw it in the twopenny post or deliver it personally as you please.[27]

The second letter[28] was, as Irving described it, "a business letter written in a business manner, in case you think proper to show it to Murray." [29] In this attempt at psychological manipulation Irving coolly instructed Aspinwall to offer Murray the possibility of publishing the Columbus manuscript. The third letter, directed to Murray, Aspinwall appears to have delivered himself, for the folded sheet is neither stamped nor wafered.

21. *To John Murray II*[30]

Madrid, July 29th 1827.

My dear Sir,
    I have at length concluded my history of Columbus. As I cannot come to London to make arrangements for its publication, and as time might be lost in negociating at this distance I have transmitted a portion of the manuscript to my friend Col. Aspinwall, American Consul at London, who will arrange the matter with you in my name. I have sent as much of MSS. as I will venture to intrude

---

[26] No record exists of the nature of these "munificent overtures," yet there should be no doubt that WI, with his reputation, could have secured a publisher in London.
[27] WI to Aspinwall, Madrid, July 29, 1827. From the MS Collection of the Henry E. Huntington Library, San Marino, Cal. Hereinafter cited as Huntington.
[28] Now in the Berg Collection, New York Public Library.
[29] WI to Aspinwall, July 29, 1827. Huntington.
[30] Printed in full in PMI, II, 262–64.

upon the civility of an English courier.[31] The rest will be forwarded by the first opportunity. The first volume will end with the last chapter of the tenth book, forming 756 manuscript pages, besides a preface of a few pages. The second volume may possibly be a little larger, containing, beside the remaining eight books, a number of illustrations which I have endeavoured to make as interesting and entertaining as possible and a few important documents. The latter eight books contain the third voyage of Columbus: the troubles of himself and his brothers in the island of Hispaniola with the natives and the rebels. His being sent to Spain in chains. His fourth voyage, in the course of which I have brought forward many particulars of his singular and disastrous voyage along the coast of Veraguas or Isthmus of Panama. The transactions in the island of Jamaica, where he lived for a year in the wrecks of his stranded ships &c.&c. so that the latter part of the work is full of incident and interest. I have woven into my work many curious particulars not hitherto known concerning Columbus and I think I have thrown lights upon some parts of his character which have not been brought out by his former biographers. I have laboured hard to make the work complete and accurate as to all the information extant relative to the subject, while I have sought to execute it in such a manner as would render it agreeable to the general reader. Considering its magnitude and the toil it has cost me I should not be willing to part with the copy right under three thousand guineas. As I mentioned in one of my letters, however, I am willing to publish it on shares. The mode of doing so,[32] as I once understood from Sir Walter Scott, is to agree about the number of copies in an edition and the retail price to be placed upon them. To multiply the number of copies by the price of each, and divide the gross amount by six. For this sixth part the publisher to give his notes to the author. If this meets with your approbation, all the incidental arrange-

[31] "Mr. Newman the British Courier departs this day and takes part of my Ms. to Lond and Paris," WI wrote in his journal on August 9. The parcel had been prepared for shipping on July 30. "WI's Madrid Journal 1827–1828 and Related Letters," ed. Andrew Breen Myers, *Bulletin of the New York Public Library*, LXII (June 1958), 303.

[32] "The mode of doing so" which he laborously outlined came from Scott's letter to him, dated Dec. 4, 1819, and concerned possibilities for getting the *SB* into print in Britain. The Scott letter was first printed in PMI, I, 442–44, from which it was taken for *The Letters of Sir Walter Scott*, ed. Grierson, VI, 44–47.

ments can be made with Col. Aspinwall. I should like, however, to have an advance of two or three hundred guineas on the work as a matter of private accommodation, my funds being all in America, from whence I find both loss and trouble in procuring them.

Should you undertake the present work the sooner it is put to press the better as I have other writings in preparation which I should soon be able to furnish. I hope you will let me hear from you as soon as possible. With kindest remembrance to Mrs Murray and the family,

I am my dear Sir
Very truly your friend,
Washington Irving.

On August 19, having heard nothing from London, Irving wrote to Aspinwall, sending the remainder of the manuscript text. "I hope you have been able to agree with Mr Murray about the publication in which case hand him the MS. and the enclosed letter.... I am waiting with great anxiety to hear of the fate of my manuscript, and until I hear I shall be good for nothing." Then, in a postscript, he added: "If you have not made any arrangt with Mr Murray you need not hand him the enclosed." [33] Aspinwall gave the material and the letter, sealed with a wafer, to Murray, though the transaction was not closed until late in September.

22. To John Murray II[34]

Madrid, August 19th 1827.

My dear Sir,

I send you the residue of the manuscript of the main body of my history.[35] The first volume will end with the last chapter of Book 10. By the next opportunity which presents I will send you the illustrations which will make between one and two hundred pages and the documents, which will complete the volume and will prob-

---

[33] This letter is in the MS Collection of Sunnyside, The Sleepy Hollow Restorations.

[34] Text printed in full in PMI, II, 264–65. MS endorsed "With the compliments of T. Aspinwall."

[35] WI noted in his journal: "pack up the Second volume for London to go by Mr. Dedel the Dutch Minister who goes tomorrow morng early." Myers, "Madrid Journal 1827–1828," 305. Cf. STW, I, 479, n. 127.

ably make it a little larger than the first.[36] The illustrations are to be printed in the same type with the body of the work. The documents may be printed smaller. I am writing with great anxiety to hear from you. Any corrections or alterations that may be suggested in my work, by competent persons, if transmitted to me by post, I shall be able immediately to attend to, as I retain a copy of the work to serve in case of accidents. I am unable to find any satisfactory portrait of Columbus. All that I see are either portraits of his son Don Diego, or vary essentially from the description given of his countenance. I shall send a chart by the next opportunity in which his route in his first voyage is marked; Navarrete has given him a different landing place in the New World from that hitherto assigned, but I am in favour of the old landing place and I trust I shall give satisfactory reasons for the opinion.[37]

With kindest regard to Mrs Murray and the rest of your family I am my dear Sir

Very faithfully yours,
Washington Irving.

The biographer's anxiety would have been considerably heightened had he known of the reception his manuscript had received at 50 Albemarle Street. The publisher had been far from certain that he would avail himself of Irving's offer. Murray turned to his "elbow critic" Southey, who wrote a critical appraisal containing a comment that piqued his interest:

I return the MS. of Columbus' Life by this day's coach. It appears to me to have been compiled with great industry and to be well received, presenting a most remarkable portion of history in a popular form, and therefore likely to succeed; not for the ability displayed in it, but because the book is interesting and useful. There is neither much power of mind nor much knowledge indicated in

---

[36] See below, n. 44.

[37] Samuel Morison found both Navarrete and WI to be wrong. "Navarrete . . . selected the Grand Turk, which threw off all his subsequent identifications until Columbus reached Cuba. Washington Irving (1828) and Alexander von Humboldt (1837) lent their weighty authority to Cat Island." Modern scholarship, however, recognizes the landfall as Watlings, first chosen by J. B. Munoz, *Historia del Nuevo Mundo* (1793). *Admiral of the Ocean Sea: The Life of Christopher Columbus* (Boston: Little, Brown and Co., 1942), I, 309.

it, but a great deal of diligence employed upon the subject which the author has undertaken.[38]

Though this estimate contains only weak compliments for the author, "popular form," "likely to succeed," and "interesting and useful" were the magic words Murray was anxious to hear.[39] On September 24 the publisher accepted the manuscript for publication, agreeing to give three thousand guineas for the copyright—the payment to be made in eight installments over a period of two years. By extending the payments in this way, Murray hoped that steady sales from the book would keep pace with the recurring notes.[40]

The long-anticipated news reached Madrid on October 8 in a letter from Aspinwall. As he reported the situation to Irving, the publisher had high hopes for the new work: "Murray says of the work, it is beautiful, beautiful—the best thing he has ever written." [41] The fact was that John Murray liked the amiable American who had so frequently ornamented his drawing room and whose writings were always polished compositions. Murray knew, too, that Irving was popular enough with the public to expect at least a moderate sale of anything he might produce.

Irving's immediate reply to Aspinwall was a victory cry. "I am heartily glad that Murray has acceded so handsomely to my terms. I shall not feel satisfied in dealing with any other publisher. I am accustomed to him. I have a friendship for him, and I like the truly gentlemanlike manner in which he publishes; destitute of all the petty puffing arts that others practice." [42] He casually allowed a week to pass before addressing himself to his publisher. His letter, which contained certain corrections to be made on the Columbus manuscript, must have been a study of admiration for himself and his publisher. Unfortunately, this epistle is no longer

[38] MS in Murray Archives. Printed in Smiles, II, 256–57.
[39] STW, II, 322, presents a chronologically confused account of JMII's purchase of this book.
[40] See Appendix III, item 5.
[41] PMI, II, 268.
[42] Oct. 8, 1827. Alderman Library, University of Virginia.

known to exist.[43] On October 18 he sent the packet of illustrations, promised in his letter of August 19, which Rich, who was going to London, agreed to deliver to Murray.[44]

From Murray only silence.

Between his social engagements with David Wilkie, who had suddenly appeared on tour, and the diplomats and nobility of Madrid, Irving continued to work on manuscripts relating to Spanish history and to grow bitter about his publisher's inattention and about the lack of information from Aspinwall. To the latter he wrote on November 27 begging for at least "a word or two of intelligence as to the work." He added, "You are a parent and must know what a parent feels when a child is about to be launched into the world." [45] Finally, on December 6, Irving dispatched the last bit of his work on Columbus, which he had been holding until he had further word from Murray. The tiny script of this letter and those which follow during the next year might suggest that Irving, gripping his pen firmly, was barely able to control his exasperation with his publisher.

23. *To John Murray II*[46]

Madrid, December 6th 1827.

My dear Sir,

I enclose you the preface to the History of Columbus.[47] As I have never had the pleasure of receiving a line from you since you

[43] PMI referred to it, II, 269; "write . . . to Murray sending corrections of ms." Oct. 15, 1827, Myers, "WI's Madrid Journal 1827–1828," 307.

[44] "Made up parcels of the Illustrations of Columb. to go by Mr. Rich tomorrow." Myers, "WI's Madrid Journal 1827–1828," 308. In the final printed copy of JMII's edition the "illustrations" (explanatory notes) and documents covered almost 400 pages and ranged from a discussion of the "Transportation of the Remains of Columbus from St. Domingo to the Havanna" (pp. 65–73) to a printed description (though no facsimile) of the "Signature of Columbus" (pp. 437–39).

[45] Berg Collection, New York Public Library.

[46] Marked in Foreign Post Office in London, Dec. 20 or 30, 1827.

[47] Thomas Lawrence, writing to David Wilkie, Jan. 10, 1828, said: "I rejoice to see that, with the many acquaintances presenting themselves for your selection, you have the more secure comfort of an old friend in Mr. Washington Irving; whose 'Columbus' we are anxiously expecting. The Quarterly (which inserts his admirable preface) promises it in a few days." Allan Cunningham, *The Life of Sir David Wilkie* (London: JM, 1843), II, 494.

have undertaken the work I am in utter ignorance of your intentions concerning it, as to when it is to appear, and in what form. A paragraph in the Morning Chronicle says it is to be published in four octavo volumes.[48] There does not appear to me to be manuscript enough for so many. If such had been your intentions and you had communicated them to me in time I could have pointed out several interesting documents which could have been inserted, but which I withheld through fear of swelling the bulk of the work. There doubtless must be deficiencies in the work which I could easily have supplied if appraised of them in time. I wish for both our sakes you were a little more punctual in your correspondence with me. I am sure in this instance it would have been for your interests. I have never heard whether the illustrations I sent you by Mr Rich came to hand, but presume they did. By the bye Mr Rich has with him a rich collection of curious works in Spanish and other literature, and if you care to be of any service in drawing it to the attentions of Bibliographers I would be greatly obliged to you if you would do so. He is a most obliging and worthy man.[49]

With kindest regards to Mrs Murray and the family I am my dear Sir

Very truly yours,
Washington Irving.

Murray, in the meantime, was experiencing doubts about the wisdom of his purchase. The most painful intelligence came from John Gibson Lockhart, who told Murray that Leslie, during the stagnant period of negotiations in the late summer, had offered

[48] In "The Mirror of Fashion," "Mr. Murray has, it is said, given Mr. Washington Irving three thousand pounds for his 'Life of Columbus,' which is to be published during the present season, in four octavo volumes." London *Morning Chronicle*, Oct. 22, 1827.

[49] In London, Obadiah Rich opened a bookshop at No. 12 Red Lion Square and became a legend in American bibliography. The British Museum's collection of his sales catalogues indicates the very high quality of his wares. See especially *Catalogue of Books Relating to America* (1832) and *A Catalogue of a Collection of Manuscripts Principally in Spanish, Relating to America . . .* (1848). Rich's library is described in J. Sabin *et al.*, comps., *Bibliotheca Americana: A Dictionary of Books Relating to America . . .* (New York: J. Sabin & Sons, 1868-1936), XVII, 206–10, and Adolph Crowell, *Book-Trade Bibliography in the United States in the Nineteenth Century* (New York: The Dibdin Club, 1898), pp. xlv–xlviii.

the Columbus manuscript to Colburn for fifteen hundred pounds, but that that cagey publisher was unwilling to consider it at any price.[50] In addition to this, at least one of Murray's valued critics contributed to the woeful situation by advising caution—after the "accident" had already happened:

> Will you pardon a well-meant line? Have you finally concluded about the "Columbus"? If not, will you excuse me if, from the extract I see in the Literary Gazette,[51] I am induced to ask, what has it of the superb degree as to make it fully safe for you to give the price you intend for it? I see no novelty of fact, and, though much ability, yet not that overwhelming talent which will give a very great circulation to so trite a subject.[52]

But Irving knew nothing of this.

The new year brought no news of Columbus, but it did bring news of Murray: he declined to publish Alexander Hill Everett's latest book, *America: or A General Survey of the Political Situation of the Several Powers of the Western Continent, with Conjectures on their Future Prospects.* Irving seemed to take the rejection of his friend's work as a personal affront to himself.

24. *To John Murray II*[53]

Madrid, Jany 14th 1828.

My dear Sir,

I understand from Mr Everett that he had offered you his book on America for publication, but that you have declined undertaking it, fearing that it might not prove profitable. Of the state of public demand for works of this kind you of course are the best judge,

---

[50] Smiles, II, 256. No available evidence suggests that there is any truth in this rumor.

[51] On Feb. 2, 1828, *The Literary Gazette*, pp. 65–67, published a review which included large extracts from the *Life.* "This work will appear in the course of the ensuing month," the article, reportedly by Lockhart, began.

[52] Sharon Turner to JMII, Dec. 1827. Smiles, II, 257. The date is apparently in error, for there are no samples of the *Life* in *The Literary Gazette* before Feb. 2, 1828.

[53] Quoted, with the omission of a few insignificant words, in STW, I, 470, n. 32.

but if, as I am inclined to believe, there is a lively interest at present in England as to the situation and prospects of the various American Empires, and their influence on European affairs, I cannot but think the work of Mr Everett would be highly acceptable to the public. His situation in public life for a number of years, and his habits of observance have afforded him opportunities of acquiring extensive and familiar acquaintance with his subject, and have opened to him high sources of information not often accessible to others. His work appears to me to abound with new and extensive views; and ingenious and animated speculations; there are several public characters sketched with great spirit and candour; the political tenants [tenets] are urged with frankness and firmness, but without bigotry, so that one of a different faith may listen to them without hostility. The style is at all times clear, expressive, flowing and harmonious, and often possesses great vigour and eloquence. I cannot help thinking that a work of the kind, on so fresh, important, and interesting a subject, would take with the English public, if introduced to them in a way to attract attention. It is not often that they get information concerning America from so able and authentic a source.

As to Mr Everett himself, he is a person with whom I should think you would be glad to establish a correspondence.[54] He greatly resembles his brother whom I believe you were acquainted with when he was in England.[55] Like him he is an accomplished scholar, and remarkable for the variety, extent and accuracy of his information. They have both distinguished themselves in various departments of elegant literature so as to stand at the head of our national writers; while both having devoted themselves to public life are in a fair way to attain to the highest honours of our nation. Mr Everett has been for several years in diplomatic situations at various courts of Europe and I should not be surprised if before long he should be transferred to the Court of St James. Now that

---

[54] According to Smiles, II, 83, JMII had met Everett several years before and had been responsible for introducing him to Scott.

[55] Edward Everett, Harvard professor and editor of the *North American Review*, had visited England toward the end of the previous decade. He was later (1841–1845) U. S. Minister to the Court of St. James.

Mr Gallatin[56] has withdrawn we have no diplomatic character so deserving of the station.

I have been looking for some time past for a letter from you in reply to repeated enquiries which I have made both by letter and through my friends. I have been desirous of knowing something relative to the publication of my work, but have found every attempt to get information unavailing, until a few days since I accidentally saw it advertised as in the press. I must say to you that I feel excessively hurt, for it seems to me as if this neglect is something more than accidental. I cannot suppose however that any remonstrances on my part would have any effect and therefore shall spare them.

With my kindest remembrances to Mrs Murray and the family I am my dear Sir,

Truly your friend,
Washington Irving.

P.S. I wish a copy of my work to be presented to Col. Aspinwall, and another sent to Henry Van Wart Esq., Birmingham. I shall be excessively anxious to receive a copy of it here; but fear I shall look for it as vainly as I have looked for letters from you.

Irving's letter must have influenced Murray, for he did publish Everett's work.[57]

Murray was working hard, the shadows of 1826 still hanging over 50 Albemarle Street. The death of Archibald Constable, who was trying in 1827 to re-establish himself in the trade, was a personal blow to Murray, whose publishing career had previously paralleled that of the Czar of the North. In 1828 Murray had two major schemes underway: a new life of Byron and an experiment in "cheap" literature. On March 30 he signed an agreement with

56 Albert Gallatin had retired from the diplomatic service in Nov. 1827 after a tour as U. S. Minister to the Court of St. James. See Beckles Willson, *America's Ambassadors to England (1785–1928): A Narrative of Anglo-American Diplomatic Relations* (London: JM, 1928), pp. 165–97.

57 On July 31, 1828, with *America* in the press, WI wrote to Everett: "I observe from your letter that Murray has not written to you on the subject of your work. I do not wonder at it. He is the most negligent man in his correspondence (for a man of business) that I ever had any dealings with. I have felt extremely vexed at times, until I found that he was so with everybody." PMI, II, 335.

Thomas Moore whereby the poet would prepare a monumental life of Byron for Murray's imprint.[58]

By the beginning of the summer months, plans were becoming definite for Murray's Family Library, "a serial publication by means of which good literature and copyright works might be rendered cheaper and more accessible to a wide circle of readers than they had hitherto been." Appearing monthly, Murray's Family Library would cover "a variety of subjects including History, Biography, Voyages and Travels, Natural History, Science, and general literature"—to be written by the leading authors of the day.[59] The first volume was to be an "epitome" of Scott's *Life of Napoleon Bonaparte*, prepared by Lockhart.

A History of the Life and Voyages of Christopher Columbus was published on February 8. On the whole it was received favorably, the bulk of criticisms falling on the physical aspects of the work. Published in four slender octavo volumes, in large print and with vast margins, this first edition was priced at two guineas. Murray's intention clearly had been to produce a quality book which would serve for years as a standard reference source, but unfortunately it was seriously hurt by "the gross typographical errors with which it abounded." As Pierre M. Irving noted, "Mr. Irving had given no direction on the subject [of proofreading]," [60] the type-setters had interpreted his handwriting as best they could, and a reader with no special knowledge of the subject had read the proofs for obvious errors. As the months went by, Murray's regrets about this particular venture increased; the failure hurt more and seemed greater because he had expected it to be one of his monuments. Certainly there had been some grounds for high hopes in the beginning. Rich reported to Irving in a letter dated February 12: "On Friday last Murray had one of his periodical sales and (as I have been confidentially informed) disposed of 4000 copies." [61]

[58] Smiles, II, 312. At the outset Moore was advanced sufficient money to repay his 1824 debt to the Longmans.

[59] Smiles, II, 295–96.

[60] PMI, II, 279. STW, II, 296–308, discussed the critical reception of this work.

[61] MS Division, New York Public Library.

Not until March 7 did Irving actually see a printed copy of the *Life of Columbus*, which was forwarded from Madrid to Seville, where he settled in the early spring to continue work on his story of the conquest of Granada. Peter had left him to return to Paris in February, but Washington was not alone for long. In Seville he met David Wilkie, who sketched the local color and made two drawings of Irving before he reluctantly moved on. After Wilkie's departure, Irving found a home in Mrs. Stalker's boarding house, a remarkedly British establishment in which "God Save the King" was often sung in grand unison. He worked hard making corrections in the text of the biography, using the original material in the Bibloteca Colombia. The Archives of the Indies, he felt, would add to his collection, but his application for admission was not favorably received. On August 5 he dispatched the corrected volumes of Columbus to Murray.[62] From August 11 to August 15 he made a pilgrimage west of Seville in search of traces of the subject of his biography. He found plenty of relics: Don Juan Fernandez de Pinzon, the descendant of Columbus' friend, was his guide to "the convent where the explorer had begged water and bread for his child" and "the church of Santa Clara, where all night Columbus had kept vigil." [63] All the while he feverishly wrote in his notebook. Returning to Seville, he learned that, by special permission of the king, he had been granted access to the Archives of the Indies.

25. To John Murray II[64]

Seville, August 19th 1828.

Dear Sir,

Inclosed you have a bill of lading of a box lately shipped from

[62] *Washington Irving Diary, Spain, 1828–1829*, ed. Clara Louisa Penney (New York: Hispanic Society of America, 1930), p. 48. Hereinafter cited Penney.

WI had received no direct communication from his publisher: "As to Murray, he sends me a verbal message by Mr. Rich, requesting alterations and corrections, instead of writing particularly to me on the subject. I have always foreseen that there would be many corrections required in the second edition, and would have been glad to have had any errors I had committed clearly pointed out that I might amend them." WI to A. H. Everett, April 23, 1828. PMI, II, 313. This "verbal message" was apparently the basis on which he sent the corrected copy.

[63] STW, I, 340–41.

[64] Marked in Foreign Post Office in London, Sept. 8, 1828.

this port, containing a copy of the history of Columbus, with copious corrections. As the volumes have many loose pages in manuscript inter bound in them great care must be taken that they do not get displaced.

Since dispatching the books I have met with documents in the Archives of the Indies which will oblige me to make further corrections in the early part of the first volume. I have not a copy of the work by me at present; and it will be some days before I can arrange the corrections. Should you put the second edition to press before the receipt of these corrections you had better begin with the second volume to give time for the receipt of them.

With kind remembrances to Mrs Murray and the family I am dear Sir

Very truly yours &c.
Washington Irving.

On August 24, having hastily surveyed the Archives of the Indies, Irving left Seville, moving south to Puerto de Santa Maria, where he expected to finish *A Chronicle of the Conquest of Granada*. The first installment he sent to Murray by way of Aspinwall on September 1, "at the same time authorizing him to dispose of copy right at 2,000 guineas or as near thereabout as he could procure." [65] To his agent he also wrote: "I am thoroughly dissatisfied with him on account of the manner in which he has acted while publishing Columbus, never answering my letters nor giving me any information concerning the work, nor in short acting toward me either as a friend or a man of business." [66]

26. To John Murray II[67]

Port St Marys, Septr 6th 1828.

My dear Sir,

I forwarded you not long since a copy of Columbus, with many alterations and corrections. I will thank you to have the foregoing inserted as a note at the end of chap. V, book V in place of the note

[65] Penney, p. 64. This journal entry began: "Sent off parcel to Col. Aspinwall, containing a part of MS. of Conquest of Granada to go by steamboat Duke of York, write to him...."
[66] WI to Aspinwall, Aug. 31, 1828. Alderman Library, University of Virginia.
[67] Marked in Foreign Post Office in London, Sept. 29, 1828.

that appeared there in the first edition.[68] I have one more correction, or rather addition to make, but as it is an illustration, for the fourth volume, and, from filling a few pages, would cost heavy postage, I shall endeavour to find some private mode of forwarding it.[69]

I have lately forwarded part of the MS. of a new work to my friend Col. Aspinwall to dispose of for me, and hope you may find it to your interest to become the publisher.

With my best regards to Mrs Murray & the family

I am very truly yours &c.

Washington Irving.

Involved with a multitude of business problems, Murray had no time to linger over Irving's alterations and corrections. His Family Library had to be seen to; Moore had to be pressed for copy. The scurrilous writing of Molloy Westmacott, he decided, had to be publicly ignored. Of the latter Irving was surely informed by a gossipy letter from Newton or perhaps in some matter-of-fact news from Aspinwall. Beginning on August 31, 1828, and continuing at intervals through August 16, 1829, Westmacott, a Tory journalist of black reputation, wrote for the scandal-minded *Age* a column entitled "Murrayana," a collection of outrageous anecdotes, puns, and near vulgarities involving John Murray II. This was apparently one of Westmacott's early ventures into blackmail—and perhaps his most unsuccessful one.[70] A contemporary described his manner of working: he "writes to you—'Sir, I have received some anecdotes about you, which I

[68] Concerning the Pinzon family and contemporary Palos, the original note (JM ed., I, 415–16) had cited information taken from Juan Bautista Munoz's *Historia del Nuevo Mundo* and "particulars . . . furnished me by a friend, and which he had gathered in a voyage on board of the steam-boat between Seville and Cadis." The substitution was two paragraphs based on his conversations with the Pinzons (in Aug.) and his own observations. See revised Amer. ed., 1831, I, 177.

[69] The "illustration" on Martin Alonzo Pinzon greatly expanded WI's original note (JM ed., IV, 193–96). The new version appeared in revised Amer. ed., 1831, II, 261–63.

[70] The best-known instance of his practicing his black art was in connection with WI's friend Countess Blessington in 1831–1832. See Michael Sadleir, *Bulwer: A Panorama* (London: Constable & Co. Ltd., 1931), pp. 336–46; Michael Sadleir, *Blessington-D'Orsay: A Masquerade* (London: Constable & Co. Ltd., 1933), pp. 138ff., 241–42.

would not publish for the world if you will give me ten pounds for them.' " [71] John Murray did not pay, and "Murrayana" was received by the reading public with relish. It must have been a bitter draught for the subject of the series.

Away from the sophisticated problems of London, Irving took a house in the country, perhaps a mile from the center of *el Puerto*. In this haven Irving worked, making daily excursions to visit new-found friends in the city: Johan Nickoulaus Bohl von Faber, a German scholar pursuing the profession of wine-making, and his daughter Cecilia, later to take her place in literary history as the novelist Fernan Caballero.[72]

Everett forwarded two letters from Murray to Irving's country address. Why this awakening of interest? Stanley T. Williams speculated darkly that the publisher had ulterior designs on Irving's pen, that he was trying to involve the writer in "hack work." [73]

Lacking copies of Murray's letters, we can only guess their seductive contents from Irving's reply and from his outline of their contents in his letters to other correspondents.[74] The first letter indicated that the publisher still planned to issue a corrected unabridged edition of the *Life of Columbus* and, perhaps, a popular one-volume duodecimo abridgment, the latter to be an early feature of the Family Library—to which Irving might wish to contribute further items.[75] In this letter he also asked for graphic

71 Edward Bulwer, *England and the English* (London: Richard Bentley, 1833), II, 235.

72 WI's influence on the later novelist has been the subject of considerable discussion. See STW, I, 490–91.

73 *Ibid.*, 343.

74 PMI, II, 343–45.

JMII had bought from Wilkie a sketch of WI drawn in April 1828, which he intended to use as a frontispiece for the second edition of the unabridged *Life*. The original is still at 50 Albemarle Street.

75 The overture—in every way complimentary to the American—points to the major prerequisite for making a success of an extended series of cheap original editions. Murray explained to Charles Knight that the main problem with "big deals" like the Family Library was the shortage of capable writers to furnish regular copy for the press. *Passages of a Working Life* (London: Bradbury & Evans, 1864), II, 48.

illustrations for the new editions of the Columbus biographies and for a life of Cervantes being prepared by Lockhart.[76]

The second letter contained the "hack work" proposal.

The last letter I have received from Murray [wrote Irving] is the best critique I have ever had as to my general reputation with the public. He is about to set up a monthly magazine, free from any political or party bias, purely literary and scientific.[77] He has offered me a thousand pounds a year to conduct it, besides paying me liberally for any articles I might contribute to it.[78]

If this were not enough, the publisher further offered Irving "one hundred guineas an article for contributions for the Quarterly Review." [79]

27. *To John Murray II*[80]

Port St Mary, Octr 16th 1828.

My dear Sir,

I have recently received two letters from you; the last dated Septr 24, and am happy to find the corrected copy of Columbus has come safe to hand. I notice by one of your letters that you had wished the work to be curtailed, whereas I have, if any thing, rather enlarged it. While writing the work I was aware that by abbreviating it in some places I might make it more entertaining,

---

[76] WI to A. H. Everett, Oct. 21, 1828. "I have had two letters from Murray lately, in which he seems disposed to make up for past neglect. He is about putting a new edition of Columbus to press, and is eager for all kinds of graphical illustration, facsimilies, &c., that can be procured for love or money. Had he written this some time since, I could have procured him something of the kind; now it will be difficult. He wishes also similar illustrations for a Life of Cervantes that Mr. Lockhart is writing, and wishes me to employ any competent person to take fac-similes of letters, unpublished poems, drawings of Cervantes' house, apartment, &c., giving me *carte blanche* as to expence. Do you know if anything of the kind is to be had?" PMI, II, 347.

[77] This was the third (and last) time since JMII had given up his share of *Blackwood's Edinburgh Magazine* that he had seriously considered the possibility of founding his own magazine.

[78] PMI, II, 345.

[79] Penney, p. 73. After telling Aspinwall about Murray's offers, WI concluded: "A publisher's offers are the sure gauges by which an author can ascertain his stand with the public. They are beyond criticism." Letter, Oct. 16, 1828. Berg Collection, New York Public Library.

[80] Marked in Foreign Post Office in London, Nov. 4, 1828.

but upon mature consideration, and upon consulting with others in whose judgement I confided, I determined to be full & minute at the risk of being prolix. The work professed to be a complete & circumstantial account of Columbus & his voyages, and were any thing omitted that was to be found in other works concerning him, it might have been noticed and cancelled it [the professed completeness of the biography]. As the work seems to have interest & entertainment enough to give it currency with the mere readers for amusement, I do not doubt that, in the long run, you will find its fullness to be of an advantage. It satisfies that class who look for exact information; and the suffrages of that class are all important to an historical work. The work would admit to a popular abridgement, but that I have not time to make. If it could be done by any judicious hand, (as a job) retaining all the important and popular points of the work, I should have no objection to look over and touch up the abridgement and sanction it with my name. I regret extremely that I did not receive at an earlier date your request to produce drawings, facsimiles &c. &c. for illustrations. I am now living in the country, out of the way of procuring any thing of the kind. I have seen things from to time that might have been interesting, but, never hearing any thing from you on the subject of the work, I grew discouraged and indifferent about it. I shall probably soon return to Seville, where in the Cathedral library & in the Archives of the Indies I may probably meet with something. Mr Rich I think would be able to furnish you with something of the kind. He is knowing in every thing relative to Columbus, & has curious works in his own possession, some of which contain pictures. If you could procure a sight of the old work of De Bry, with fine old wood cuts. /It must exist in the British Museum & in private collections./ There is a fine old engraving of the scene of Columbus breaking the egg & there must be others that are curious.[81] These however are fanciful sketches & not properly illustrative. The map or globe of Martin Beham's ought to be inserted, as it must be pretty

[81] The British Museum has copies of Theodore de Bry, *Americae Pars Quarta. Sive Insignis & Admiranda Historia de Reperta Primum Occidentali India a Christophore Colombo anno M.CCCXCII* (Frankfort, 1594), in several translations. The print of Columbus making the egg stand on its end (by smacking the end slightly) to show a group of ill-mannered noblemen that they were not as smart as they thought they were is No. VII in this collection. The story of the egg incident is referred to in JM ed., I, 432–33.

much the idea Columbus had of the world before he made his voyage & must resemble the map of Toscanelli by which he sailed. A copy of that map is in a work in Mr Rich's possession called "Investigaciones Historicas par—— Cladera." [82]

It will give me great pleasure if I can be of any service to Mr Lockhart in his life of Cervantes, and when I go to Seville I will make diligent search for any thing that may serve as illustrations. He has a noble subject for his pen, rich in character, incident and various views of life, and I make no doubt he will produce a highly popular work. Cervantes is one of those characters that belong to the world & in whom all civilized nations take an interest.

The periodical work you propose to set on foot appears to me to be judicious in its plan, from the abundant literary aid you have at your command, cannot fail to be carried on with spirit. The terms you offer me are liberal in the extreme, and, were I other than I am, or otherwise situated, would be powerfully tempting. But I have an insurmountable repugnance to binding myself to any periodical task, or in fact to any thing that should control my free agency and mode of living. I cannot, above all, undertake any thing that should oblige me to reside out of my native country; to which, though I so long remain absent from it, I have a constant desire to return. Besides I have literary undertakings in my mind, which, if followed up, will sufficiently occupy all the time and industry I can devote to the pen, and which, if successful, will I trust render sufficient profits for my moderate wants. For [cut out under seal] other reasons which it is superfluous to mention, I must decline

[82] Martin Behem (or Behaim) was a German geographer who in 1492, while Columbus was on his first voyage, constructed a terrestrial globe which is still preserved in Nuremburg. WI's illustration No. XII (JM ed., 1828, IV, 205–12) is devoted to a discussion of Behem.

"The learned Paulo Toscanelli of Florence . . . sent him [Columbus] a map, projecting partly according to Ptolemy, and partly according to the descriptions of Marco Polo, the Venetian. . . . Columbus was greatly animated by the letter and chart of Toscanelli, who was considered one of the ablest cosmographers of the day." JM ed., 1828, I, 66–67. In a footnote WI pointed out that there were no known copies of the Toscanelli map.

Christobal Cladera's *Investigaciones Historicas* (Madrid: Don Antonio Espinosa, 1794) has this large fold-out map fastened into the binding of the back of the book. When O. Rich published his major catalogue, *Bibliotheca Americana Nova* (London: O. Rich, 1835), I, 389–90, he still had a copy of this work.

your very flattering and certainly very liberal offer. Whenever I can find time to write the kind of articles you mention for the Quarterly Review I shall be happy to do so, though, during my sojourn in Spain I fear I shall be too completely occupied with other literary matters to be able to furnish contributions. When you set up your new magazine I shall probably have it in my power to furnish you with frequent articles for it. I could often get up an article from my notes & memorandums, for a work of that kind, when I could not furnish the bulky article required for a review.

By a letter just received from Col. Aspinwall I find he has received and put in your hands the early part of the MS. of The Conquest of Granada.[83] I hope it may meet your approbation & you may feel disposed to undertake it. I have the rest of the MS. waiting for the sailing of a ship, from Cadiz for London. It makes in all upward of 1000 pages of the Sketch Book, and may be published in three volumes if advisable. Should you purchase it let me hear on the subject whether you want graphical illustrations &c.

With kindest remembrances to Mrs Murray & the family I am my dear Sir

Very truly your friend,
Washington Irving.

The thought behind Murray's proposed magazine, "free from any political or party bias," needs to be discussed, for the facts may indicate that too much has been made of Murray as a Tory publisher. Professionally—as befits a professional—he was a publisher for all, issuing in the years of his strongest party associations works by such important Whigs as Lord Holland, George Lamb, and Lord John Russell. As early as 1821 he had protested good-naturedly to Lord Byron against the automatic linking of his name with Toryism.

My connections are, I believe, even more numerous amongst the Whigs than the Tories. Indeed the Whigs have nearly driven away the Tories from my house; and Jeffrey said, "If you wish to meet

[83] "Receive letter from Col. Aspinwall by Duke of York Steam boat, has received MS. of Granada." Penney, p. 73.

the most respectable of the Whigs, you must be introduced to Mr. Murray's room." [84]

In political thought, as in other subjects, he took some pleasure in publishing both sides of a controversy.[85] In 1828, as evidenced by a letter to Henry Hallam, Murray was somewhat disenchanted with his Tory compatriots:

> I feel it is a duty to publish, with equal integrity, for Croker and Leigh Hunt, Scott and Moore, Southey and Butler, Hobhouse and Gifford, Napier and Strangford. I have received many personal civilities, and I own obligations to the Whigs, but the Tories! I paid to the utmost their under-secretaries of state, secretaries of state, bishops, and even two prime ministers, for [*QR*] articles advocating their own cause. They took my money, but never did they confer the slightest favour in return either upon Gifford or myself. So much for my Tory relations.[86]

At the same time, the Reverend Mr. H. H. Milman, valued contributor to the *Quarterly Review*, was agitating with Lockhart and Murray, insisting that that publication should reflect greater independence in the future.[87] Certainly all of this and the continued sniping of Westmacott from within the Tory camp contributed to the publisher's way of thinking as he looked over the contemporary scene and considered the possibilities of new publishing ventures.

Also, he must have sensed the trend toward the popular magazine, which would offer choice bits to the literate classes, prose and occasionally poetry designed to appeal to their fancy and inform without taxing their powers of concentration.[88] Among Murray's acquaintances, only Washington Irving had the poten-

[84] Smiles, I, 424.
[85] See *ibid.*, II, 237.
[86] *Ibid.*, 263.
[87] *Ibid.*, 269.
[88] The trend away from the review and the rise of "popular" magazines such as *Sharpe's London Magazine* (1829), the *Metropolitan* (1831–1857), and *Fraser's Magazine* (1830–1882)—to mention only a few—is discussed in Walter Graham, *English Literary Periodicals* (London: Thomas Nelson & Sons, 1930), pp. 271–310.

tial to fit perfectly into the editorship of such a magazine. Free of British party alignments, Irving had a ready reading public and a wide circle of writing friends, all of whom could be expected to support his editorship. Further, his offer could be interpreted as yet another effort by Murray to draw the American once again into light literature, back to the familiar essay of *The Sketch Book*, above which he had never risen in experimentation in other genres. That Murray abandoned the idea of the magazine after Irving declined to accept the editor's chair indicates how closely he associated the American with the project.

In the wind at this time was another project that Murray soon found advisable to give up. In November 1828 he was a member of the Society for the Diffusion of Useful Knowledge, agreeing to act as the publisher for its Library of Entertaining Knowledge, an experiment not unlike his Family Library. Perhaps it was for this reason—or to avoid the risk of sinking himself too far into speculation on "cheap literature" for the public—that he withdrew amiably as the society's publisher.[89]

From Cadiz, Irving mailed his letter of October 16 and the remainder of *A Chronicle of the Conquest of Granada* "by the brig Placida" on October 18. [90] That job finished, he returned to Seville early in November.

Irving's offer to allow Murray to have an abridgment of Columbus made had hardly reached London when the biographer received news that someone in the United States had already announced the intention of publishing such a work there. To offset this, Irving began at once to make his own version for the American press; the same copy would serve for Murray's purposes.[91]

About this time Irving received from Murray a packet of the publisher's latest imprints, including W. F. P. Napier's *History of the War on the Peninsula and in the South of France, from* . . .

[89] Knight, II, 116–17.
[90] Penney, p. 74. The *Placida*, mastered by a Mr. Cole, docked in London Nov. 21, 1828. Records of Lloyd's, London.
WI's manuscript of this work has been bound into three volumes and is preserved in the Murray Archives.
[91] See PMI, II, 352–53.

1807 to ... 1814, and James J. Morier's *The Adventures of Hajji Baba, of Ispahan, in England.* To tell Murray about the forthcoming abridgment of Columbus, to thank him for the consignment of books, and—most importantly—to remind him of the business transaction hanging fire, Irving wrote his publisher.

28. *To John Murray II*[92]

Seville, Novr 23rd 1828.

My dear Sir,

I wrote to you some time since from Port St Mary in which I suggested that you might get the history of Columbus abridged by some job writer and that I would afterwards revise & retouch it. A few days since, however, I was induced to take it in hand, and have already proceeded some distance in an abridgement. I will reduce it to one good sized volume, which will contain all the pith and marrow of the larger work, and will I think be very satisfactory to the general reader. In omitting many particulars & amplifications which in the larger work I was obliged to give for the sake of those who want the whole of the matter, I think the work acquires additional force and spirit, while whatever merit it may possess in style is preserved. As soon as I complete the abridgement I will send it to you; which I trust will be before long.

By letters which I have received from Col. Aspinwall I trust you will make an arrangement with him to take the new work I lately forwarded for publication. I desire no terms but such as shall be satisfactory to you as well as to myself. I want to make no hard bargains, and if ever you will shew me that any purchase of my writings has been disadvantageous to you, I shall feel myself bound in honour as well as impelled by inclination to make it up to you. I have felt hurt and offended at times by your neglect of writing to me, which, in my distant and isolated situation, leaves me completely ignorant and at a loss as to my literary concerns; but you ultimately write in a manner to shew that whatever disadvantages & discouraging constructions I may have put upon your silence have been incorrect and you have a gentlemanlike manner of conducting your business that is peculiarly to my taste.

[92] Marked in Foreign Post Office in London, Dec. 10 or 19, 1828. Watermarked "Vanden Ley."

Present my kind remembrances to your family and believe me my dear Sir

Very truly and faithfully,
Your friend,
Washington Irving.

P.S. I had nearly forgotten to thank you for the books you sent me. I have read the volume of Col Napier with great interest and satisfaction. It is extremely well written and bears the stamp of verity that carries conviction with it. I have lent it to General Giron, the Marquis of Las Amarillas, who is nephew of General Castanos[93] and was present at the battle of Baylia. I am anxious to hear his remarks, as the work rather takes down the old General and I believe correctly. Haggi Baba[94] I could read forever, if it ran to a thousand and one volumes, there is so much easy and pleasant humour in it, and such an amusing delineation of Persian character. I have not yet got Salmonia[95] or those from the [illegible][96] for in this country books are such objects of suspicion that they have to be smuggled in peace meal [piecemeal].[97]

Now Irving's daily task was to work on the abridgment of Columbus and to worry about the future of his manuscript on Granada. Not until December 27 did he hear from Murray, who finally accepted *A Chronicle of the Conquest of Granada*, agreeing to pay two thousand guineas for it. A tempest developed on

[93] Francisco Javier de Castanos (1758–1852) commanded the Spanish Army under Wellington at Vitoria (1813).

[94] Hajji Baba had first appeared in *The Adventures of Hajji Baba, of Ispanhan,* which JM published in 1824. WI, of course, knew the Morier brothers and cared enough for this book to keep it for his library at Sunnyside, where this copy can be seen today.

[95] *Salmonia: or, Days of Fly Fishing: in a Series of Conversations: with some account of the Habits of Fishes belonging to the Genus Salmo.* By an Angler [Sir Humphry Davy] (JM, 1828).

[96] One wonders if "those from the [illegible]" might be what WI referred to in a letter to Aspinwall, Feb. 28, 1829: "Your letter dated Nov. 11th and the accompanying books (Don Roderick & Gomez Arias) forwarded by the ship Ann Parry did not reach me until the 14th January." Huntington.

[97] WI was probably remembering an experience that O. Rich had had in the fall of 1826. When Rich was returning from London with official diplomatic dispatches and a collection of books, his books were confiscated at the Spanish border. They were later returned, but only after Everett had protested to the Spanish government. The episode is discussed in Bowers, pp. 7–9.

December 20 when anxious letters from Colonel Aspinwall brought the news that two chapters of the *Chronicle* manuscript had been lost. Irving immediately prepared to go to England to sort things out but abandoned the idea of the long winter trip when he located his draft copy. By December 24 the missing portions had been rewritten and were ready for dispatch to London. Three days later a letter from Murray arrived, accepting *A Chronicle of the Conquest of Granada*—presumably without his having seen the missing chapters—and agreeing to pay two thousand guineas for it. The price is overwhelming, especially when one considers the apt criticism that Lockhart had given Murray concerning it.

> I have read this MS. with my best attention, and would fain read the sequel ere I gave a decided opinion. My impression is that, with much elegance, there is mixed a good deal of affectation—I must add, of feebleness. He is not the man to paint tumultuous wars, in the lifetime of Scott, when Byron is fresh. Southey's "Cid" is worth ten of this in every way. How did that succeed? Surely the Laureate's name is at least equal to Irving's, and what name equal to the "Cid's" can be found in the "Wars of Granada?" This, however, will be the only complete intelligible history of the downfall of the last Moorish power in Europe; and therefore a valuable, and, I doubt not, a standard work. I don't as yet see that, for all this it can be worth 2,000 guineas.[98]

Even printer Davison, after seeing the manuscript, took Thomas Moore aside to suggest that Murray was bereft of his senses for paying this fee for such a weak work.[99]

Lockhart might privately describe his work as feeble, but this Irving did not know; in fact, his election to the Academia de la Historia, where he was championed by Navarrete, gave his work an international boost, suggesting to most people that any publisher might well value his name on a list of authors.

[98] Smiles, II, 258–59.
[99] Moore, *Memoirs*, VI, 64.

29. To John Murray II[100]

Seville, Feby 14th 1829.

My dear Sir,

The above is a receipt of the Captain of the Mary Ellen,[101] for the manuscript of the abridgement of Columbus; which I hope will arrive safe to your hands, and give you satisfaction.

I have been unable to meet with any thing here, to serve as illustrations for Columbus or Cervantes. I wrote some time since to Prince Dolgorouki, Secretary of the Russian Legation at Madrid to endeavour to procure me some facsimiles &c. He is getting a copy made of an Italian engraving of ancient date, said to be after an authentic original of Columbus. It is considered by Mr Navarrete, the Duke de Veraguas & others, as the most *probable* portrait extant; but after all I have my doubts of it; as the text which accompanys [accompanies] the engraving in the Italian work, represents the hair as being black, whereas it is notorious that Columbus had grey hair at thirty years of age.[102] Mr Rich knows the engraving in question as he first shewed it to me in an Italian work in his possession. The Prince will procure for me a facsimile of a letter of Columbus &c. He writes that there is nothing to be found, unpublished, of Cervantes & that all the documents concerning him have been collected & published by Mr. Navarrete. He adds: "De toutes les maisons qu'a habite Cervantes a Madrid il n'y a pas une seule et pas celle même on il est mort, qui ait conserve la meindre trace de son état originaire. De maniere qu'il vaudrait tout autant impro-

100 "Receipt" torn off top of first page of manuscript. Marked in Foreign Post Office in London, March 3, 1829.

101 The captain of the *Mary Ellen* was a Mr. Crutchfield. 1829 edition, *Lloyd's Register of Shipping*. The ship arrived in Seville Jan. 23 and reported into London on its return voyage Feb. 24, 1829. Records of Lloyd's, London.

102 Used as the frontispiece for *Life of Columbus* abridged for JM's Family Library (1830), the portrait was further identified by WI: "The portrait of Columbus is from an Italian work published in Rome in 1596, entitled 'Ritratti de cento capitani illustri, intagliati da Aliprando Capriole.' It is considered by the Duke of Veraguas, the lineal descendant of Columbus, and by other capable judges, to be the most probable portrait extant of the discoverer" (p. vii). The problem of a true portrait of Columbus troubled WI for the remainder of his life. See STW, II, 297.

viser une nouvelle habitation de Cervantes que de donner au public le desin de celle qu'il a effectivement occupeè." [103]

The facsimile of the hand writing of Cervantes in the work of Mr Navarrete is taken from the only morsel that remains of his hand writing.

I have had a long conversation with General Giron (Marquis of Amarillas) to whom I lent the copy you sent me of the first volume of Col Napier's history. He does full justice to the talent with which that masterly work is written, but he complains that Col Napier has written with a prejudiced feeling against the Spanish, and without Spanish documents to aid him. The consequence is many errors in point of fact, and a general colouring of nature disadvantageous to Spain. He has been diligently collating the work with letters, military returns and other documents in his possession and finds a great many statements, founded on French accounts, or on estimates made by reconnoitering parties, totally at variance with facts as existing in official papers. He complains too that Col Napier (P. 140) has mentioned as a circumstance illustrative of corruption and bad faith on the part of the Juntas, that at the end of the war there was not an English musket on the shoulder of a single Spanish soldier. Whereas he affirms that there was scarcely a Spanish soldier whose arms and clothing were not English. A fact, by the bye, which was supported by the testimony of an English gentleman of my acquaintance who was here throughout the struggle and took an active part in it. I mention these things as they may be of service to Col Napier in the progress of his work. The Marquis of Amarillas is a gentleman of high honour and great delicacy of deportment. An admirer of the English nature and a friend of Lord Wellington's. He has spoken on the subject "more in sorrow than in anger," and

[103] In 1822 Lockhart had edited, "with copious notes; and an essay on the life and writings of Cervantes," *The History of the Ingenious Gentleman. Don Quixote of la Mancha* (Edinburgh: A. Constable & Co.). The British Museum catalogue and published Lockhart material offer no additional work relating to Cervantes—though after his death numerous publishers made use of his notes and name to enhance new editions of *Don Quixote*.
WI to Dolgorouki, Seville, Feb. 4, 1829: "As to Cervantes, I had feared the search after any new documents would be fruitless, as I knew Mr. Navarrete had made diligent research, and where he searches, there is likely to be little left to discover by those who come after him. The work of Mr. Navarrete, and its accompanying documents will form I presume the grand foundation and substance of Mr. Lockhart's work." Quoted in STW, I, 493.

as I said before he has acknowledged the great merit of the work of Col Napier.[104]

——In publishing the illustration &c for the 2d edition of Columbus, I wish attention to be paid to the maps, and that they should be corrected by some competent person. The maps containing the routes of Columbus are copies from Mr Navarrete's. Whereas I differ from him in some slight particulars on the second and (I think) fourth voyages, in respect to the Island he made in the Carribbean group, the coasting of Cuba &c. as any person acquainted with maps would perceive in reading my work and regarding the map of Mr Navarrete.[105]

With kindest remembrances to Mrs Murray and the family I am my dear Sir,

Very faithfully,
Your friend,
Washington Irving.

P.S. Tell Mr Lockhart that Mr Clemencin, Secretary of the Royal Academy of History of Madrid & author of an Eulogium on Queen Isabella has for some time been occupied in writing commentaries on Don Quixote.[106] A Mr Felieu also of this place, a politician & statesman of some consequence in time of the Constitution, is making a Dictionary of Don Quixote—explaining all the words of peculiar significance.[107]

I presume the 2d edition of Columbus is printed. If by any chance

---

[104] Smiles, II, 281–87, had much to say about Napier's *History*. The British Museum catalogue lists two columns of blasts and counterblasts concerning it. JMII lost heavily on the first volume and published the remainder of the study (the sixth volume appearing in 1840) for Napier "on his account." Smiles, II, 285.

[105] JMII's abridged ed., 1830, p. 354, contained a map of Columbus' routes "reduced from one made by Don Martin Fernandez de Navarrete." Prepared for JMII, Feb. 1830, it takes into account some exceedingly minor discrepancies in the original Feb. 1828 edition of the same map.

[106] Diego Clemencin in 1820 had written *Elogio de la Reina Catholica Isabel* and was working on *Comentario al Quijote*, eventually (1833–1839) to run into six volumes.

[107] On Nov. 12, 1828, WI had visited Ramon Felieu, whom he described as "a small, dirty, ugly man, abominable mouth, hanging lip, but pleasant eyes—great talent—engaged in a Dictionary of Don Quixote. Lived in palace of the Duke of Medina Sidonia as his stewart." Penney, p. 80. There is no evidence that his work on Quixote was ever published.

it is not I should like to know it, as I would make two or three alterations in the first volume.[108]

Irving continued to work on his historical projects, completing in its first form on March 3 the manuscript of the *Voyages and Discoveries of the Companions of Columbus*. His financial situation was not good in spite of his recent successful arrangements, for the Bolivar mine stock, purchased at Peter's insistence in 1825, regularly made new demands on his purse. Completely exasperated, he finally forfeited the shares altogether; the venture by that time had already cost him "more than the entire profits of the English edition of the Life and Voyages of Columbus." [109]

Murray, for his part, must have occasionally thought of Irving in monetary terms. The £400 notes covering the protracted payment of the *Life of Columbus* arrived on schedule, and there were four more notes yet to be paid. But the diminishing sales had prompted Murray to abandon any idea of publishing a second edition of the full *Life*, and he must now live with the likelihood that Irving's next work, for which he had pledged a goodly fee, might prove even less rewarding.

When the erratic mail service from England brought no communications from either Murray or Aspinwall, at the end of February Irving sent an unnecessarily carping letter castigating Aspinwall for letting five weeks elapse without writing "though you have one of the most important subjects to write about, viz the publication of my work." [110] He was still boiling the next month, but he did manage to simmer down long enough to address a very civil letter to his publisher:

---

[108] There were four issues of the 1828 JMII ed. in four volumes printed (the first by T. Davison; the remainder by William Clowes), but JMII did not bring out a revised edition of the unabridged *Life of Columbus*. STW and Mary Allen Edge, *A Bibliography of the Writings of Washington Irving: A Check List* (New York: Oxford University Press, 1936), p. 69.

[109] PMI, II, 368.

[110] WI to Aspinwall, Seville, Feb. 28, 1829. Huntington.

30. *To John Murray II*[111]

Seville, March 21st 1829.

My dear Sir,

I sent to you not long since, by a vessel bound to London, the MS. of an abridgement of Columbus. I do not know what stage of publication the second edition of that work is; whether actually printed or about to go to press. If the latter, I wish both it & the abridgement could be kept back for a little [ink blot] time. The third volume of Sen Navarrete's collection of voyages is about coming out. In this I find there will be facts and documents concerning Columbus which it will be very important to notice in a new edition. I have tried, but in vain, to get a copy of the work from Mr Navarrete (which is kept back until a preface can be written). His reply is that the work is printed at the order & expense of the King & that it would be a breach of loyalty to furnish any one else with a copy before it had been presented to his majesty. As soon as this important duty is complied with I am to have a copy.

I have received an admirable copy of an old engraved likeness of Columbus; which is agreed on all hands to be the most probable representation of him extant.[112] I am to receive a facsimile of a letter of his & of the signatures of Ferdinand and Isabella next week and will forward them all to you by the first opportunity.

With kindest remembrances to Mrs. Murray and the family, I am my dear Sir

Very truly your friend,
Washington Irving.

P.S. Will you have the kindness to forward a copy of the Chronicles of Granada to Prince Dolgorouki, Secretary of the Russian Embassy, Madrid? If sent to the Russian Embassy in London the parcel will no doubt be regularly forwarded.

The next letter from the Colonel showed that Murray was not greatly impressed by Irving's displeasure with him. To the author, Aspinwall quoted parts of a personal letter the publisher had writ-

[111] Marked in Foreign Post Office in London, April 7, 1829.
[112] See above, n. 102.

ten to him, words which expressed serious doubts about the value in terms of sales of *A Chronicle of the Conquest of Granada*. Irving was undismayed and set upon his agent again. The "croaking paragraph from Murray's note," he wrote,

> knocked my pen out of my hands for a day, but I resumed it and pursued my plans. It is better, however, not to communicate to me any mere surmises . . . which may have a pernicious effect upon any literary undertaking in hand. Literary excitement is excessively precarious, and there is nothing an author is made more readily distrustful of than the picturings of his fancy. We are mere camelions, fed with air, and changing colour with everything with which we come in contact. We are to be stirred up to almost any thing by encouragement and cheering, but the least whisper of doubt casts a chill upon the feelings and the execution. The Chronicle, I am aware, is something of an experiment, and all experiments in literature or in any thing also are doubtful. It is not however, like the Cid of Mr Southey, a mere translation of an old Spanish chronicle, and of course addressed merely to the taste of those who are curious in literature of the kind (of which I count myself one). But I have made a work out of the old chronicles, embellished, as well as I am able, by the imagination, and adapted to the romantic taste of the day. Something that was to be between a history and a romance. Regarding Mr Murray's suggestion that I ought to write him light work in my old vein. I have some things sketched in a rough state in that vein, but thought it best to hold them back until I had written a work or two of more weight. . . .[113] [Then, remembering Murray's original reaction to his "light work," Irving displayed for the first time, the old wound from 1819, from which he would try to squeeze blood and exhibit as a battle trophy at appropriate times for the remainder of his life.] When I presented the American numbers of the Sketch book, which formed the first volume, Murray, after keeping them nearly a fortnight and consulting his "elbow critics," returned them to me as not possessing sufficient success to induce him to be the publisher, and I actually published them on

[113] "Rough state" should be interpreted as meaning that WI thought he could think up something "in that vein" if he wanted to do so. He had his notebooks, of course, but in these pre-Alhambra days there is no evidence of any light sketches or tales in other than notebook snatches.

shares with Miller. It was not until Murray found the work was making its own way with the public that he became the purchaser of it.[114]

If Murray's man in Seville had nothing good to say about the publisher, even such an adversary as *The Age* (incidentally co-edited by Westmacott and William Maginn, Lockhart's close friend and Murray's former employee) was offering compliments (though backhanded) to the gentleman. On April 19, 1829, giving "Murrayana" a rest, this notice appeared:

In matter of business, he [John Murray II] is, as JOHNSON said of GOLDSMITH, "an inspired idiot." He caught GIFFORD first, then BYRON, and now LOCKHART. The first put him at the head of all periodicals (the Quarterly is worth to Old Muzzy at least £4,000 a-year) the second made him the fashionable and the successful publisher—and now the Scott has started for him the FAMILY LIBRARY, which, if all tales are true, will be as great a hit as either of the others. There were six THOUSAND subscribed the first day; and, beyond doubt, the Life of BUONAPARTE deserved it. If the thing goes on with the same spirit, it must knock BROUGHAM, and the Useful Knowledge scamps, and all such small deer, out of the market as clean as a whistle. MUZZY is doing the genteel thing on the occasion—forking out £500 a volume to the scribes, and employing FINDEN and CRUIKSHANK and other prime fellows as his artists. That after all is the way to do the thing as it ought to be.

Even Irving was pacified temporarily when, six days after his outburst to Aspinwall, he received a pre-publication copy of *A Chronicle of the Conquest of Granada* and a letter from the publisher. Murray told him that he intended to hold back "publication of it in England until the Catholic question is settled, as the public can read, talk, and think of nothing else." With this Irving could not quarrel, for he was aware of the strong feelings behind all sides on the Catholic Emancipation Bill. Murray further reported that the first volume of Moore's *Life of Byron* was in the

114 WI to Aspinwall, Seville, April 4, 1829. Huntington.

hands of the printer, adding that in this job Moore "had executed his task in the most masterly manner, and it will be, I feel confident, one of the most interesting pieces of biography that ever was written." [115]

Murray's edition of the *Chronicle*, as Washington reported it to Peter, was done "in a beautiful style." But he added indignantly:

> I observe he has altered the title page. I had put "A Chronicle of the Conquest of Granada by Fray Antonio Agapida." He has inserted my name; I presume to make the work saleable, but it is an unwarrantable liberty, and makes me gravely, in my own name, tell many round untruths. I here openly make myself responsible as an author for the existence of the manuscript of Agapida, &c. &c. Literary mystifications are excusable when given anonymously or under feigned names, but are impudent deceptions when sanctioned by an author's real name.[116]

On May 1 Irving, in company with Prince Dolgorouki who had come from Madrid, left Seville for a spring ramble. Their destination: Granada. This was to be an important period of the American's life, for after Dolgorouki and the other traveling companions had left him, he settled into the Alhambra to live, dream, and write among the Spanish ruins and people. Here he wrote the early versions of the material later to be incorporated into *The Alhambra*. Here, too, after Murray's "unwarrantable liberty" had preyed on his mind for several weeks, he wrote the publisher a strong letter, one which Murray must have brooded over, for—two years later—he would throw some of Irving's own words from this letter back at him.

31. *To John Murray II*[117]

Granada, May 9th 1829.

My dear Sir,

I forwarded to you about three weeks since by Mr Clements of

---

[115] PMI, II, 375.
[116] *Ibid.*, 376.
[117] Portion beginning "I have been annoyed . . . ." printed in Smiles, II, 259–60. Marked in Foreign Post Office in London, May 29, 1828.

the 43rd regt[118] a pacquet containing a copy of an engraved likeness of Columbus, published originally in an old Italian work, the
title page of which accompanied the copy. The likeness is at present
considered the *most probable* by Mr Navarrete, the Duke of Veraguas and other competent judges.[119] In the same pacquet was a
facsimile of a letter of Columbus, a printed copy of which you will
find in the first volume of Mr Navarrete's collection. This facsimile
is curious in itself as a work of art, for not merely the hand writing,
but the very colour of the paper, the folds, accidental stains &c. are
copied with such exactness that it is difficult to distinguish the
counterfeit from the original even when they are together. The
fidelity of the copy is testified by Mr Navarrete, and the Duke requested him to write his testification on the copy itself, lest hereafter it should be passed off for the original. The difficulty and
slowness of getting anything executed in Spain has prevented my
procuring other illustrations; besides I do not know whether they
would be in time for the second edition, since, notwithstanding my
repeated enquiries, you give me no information whether it has actually gone to press or when it is about to be published. The same
doubt & darkness in which I have been left prevents me from attending to several important corrections which I ought to make in
consequence of having received the third volume of Mr Navarrete's collection of documents, in which are several articles relative to Columbus.

I have received a copy of the Conquest of Granada and am much
pleased with the style in which it is got up; but I must protest
against the alteration you have made in the title page. I do not con-
ceive that the purchase of the work gave you any right to make
such alteration. I put in the title page the name of Fray Antonio
Agapida as author of the chronicle. You must have perceived that
this was a nom de guerre to enable me to assume greater freedom &
latitude in the execution of the work, and to mingle a tinge of romance and satire with the grave historical details. By inserting my
name in the title page as the avowed author, you make me personally responsible for the verity of the facts and the soundness of the

---

118 William Syd. Clements, Lieutenant in 43d (or the Monmouthshire)
Regiment of Foot. *A List of the Officers of the Army and Royal Marines,
on Full, Retired, and Half-pay* (London: H. M. Stationery Office, 1830), p. 208.
119 See above, n. 102.

opinions of what was intended to be given as a romantic chronicle. I presume you have done this to avail yourself of whatever attraction my name might have in drawing immediate attention to the work; but this might have been effected in some other way, without meddling with the work itself, which ought never to be touched without the knowledge and consent of the author. I am sorry to make these complaints, but these matters displease and annoy me. I have been annoyed too by your forebodings of ill success to this work. When you have the spirit to give a large price for a work, why have you not the spirit to go manfully through with it, until the public will determine its fate. These croakings get to my ears, and dishearten and interrupt me for a time with other things which I may have in hand. Remember, you doubted the success and declined the publication of the Sketch Book, when I offered you the materials for the first volume which had been already published in America, and it was only after it had been published in London by another bookseller & had been well received that you ventured to take it in hand; remember too [under seal] you lost heart about the success of Columbus, and dropt a tho [under seal] copies of the first edition after you had printed the first volume, and yet you see it continues to do well. I trust that you will be equally disappointed in your prognostications about the success of the Conquest of Granada, and that it will not eventually prove disadvantageous either to your purse or my reputation. At any rate, I should like hereafter to make our arrangements in such manner that you may be relieved from these apprehensions of loss and from the necessity of recurring to any management of the press to aid the publication of a work of mine.

I shall probably pass three or four weeks in Granada, but wish all letters to me still to be addressed as before to the care of Don Miguel Walsh &c. &c., Seville.[120]

With kindest remembrances to Mrs Murray & family I am my dear Sir,

> Very faithfully your friend,
> Washington Irving.

News from Aspinwall that the *Chronicle* would not be pub-

[120] British Consul in Seville. See PMI, II, 314.

lished until the last of June brought from Irving another diatribe against Murray:

> He has been playing fast and loose in such a manner with this work, now advertising it for publication and now holding it back, that we are likely to get at cross purposes in the matter. I find that the booksellers to whom I gave permission to publish it in America, when they should receive certain intelligence of its having been published in London, have issued it about the 20th of April, no doubt having been misled by Murray's advertisements.[121]

On July 4 Irving wrote again to Aspinwall, bitterly denouncing the publisher's "deep and parliamentary calculations" behind the delayed publication of the book.[122] Irving's squeaking quill jabs at Murray might pierce the walls of the Alhambra, but the publisher rested securely in London. On March 5 he had deposited eleven copies of *A Chronicle of the Conquest of Granada* with the Registrar of Stationers' Hall and on that date, at least, publication was official.[123] This copyright was as safe as any other Murray purchased from Irving, but he apparently never bothered to enlighten the author.[124]

In July, Irving's storybook existence ended. The offer of the secretaryship of the United States Legation in London drew him away from his reverie. On July 28, he left for Paris, where Peter was waiting. Irving enjoyed the comradeship of his brother for a fortnight before proceeding to his new post in the services of the new Minister to the Court of St. James, Louis McLane.

The requirements of setting up the Legation put the new Secretary to work immediately. His first address was 3 Chandos Street, Cavendish Square, opposite the Legation. There, after an absence from London of over five years, he received Moore, Mills, Leslie, all the chums, who publicly declared that time had not touched him and turned aside to sigh privately that it had handled

---

121 WI to Aspinwall, June 23, 1829. Huntington.
122 Huntington. STW, II, 308–14, discussed the reception of *A Chronicle of the Conquest of Granada.*
123 See Appendix V.
124 See Letter 64.

them all without favor. Clothes-conscious Irving needed a new wardrobe suitable to London. To Nugee, the illustrious tailor of St. James's Street, he turned, but he may have left with less enthusiasm than he had entered the shop. Perhaps the tailor showed him that the measurements of Washington Irving of 1820, carefully kept on file through the years, bore no relation to the Washington Irving of the autumn months of 1829. Everywhere he turned, on the faces of his friends and in the news from America, were the signs of the passage of time. He might have denied the validity of his mirror, but Nugee's measuring tape told a story he could not deny.

John Murray II was away on an extended tour of Wales and the west of England. After his return, Irving called and managed to have a few words of business before the interview turned into a planning session for a welcome-back dinner for the author. Before Irving could get launched into his carefully worked-out protest against Murray's inclusion of his name as author on the title page of the *Chronicle,* the publisher, in his disarming way, agreed that some readers no doubt did misunderstand the philosophy of composition because of his intrusion in this matter; to rectify matters would Irving consider preparing, for the sum of fifty guineas, an article to appear anonymously in the *Quarterly Review* explaining the ideas behind the *Chronicle?* Irving would. The remainder of the discussion must have been strangely anticlimactic to Irving, who had anticipated a showdown with Murray for weeks. The proposed study of the voyages of Columbus' companions and the life of Mahomet the publisher viewed favorably as possible volumes for his Family Library, but what really appealed to him was the suggestion that the traveler had in the offing a group of tales or essays, not unlike *The Sketch Book* pieces, dealing with Spanish subjects. The visit ended with the publisher and the author agreeing on October 5 as the best date for their celebration.

CHAPTER FIVE

BACK AFTER A FIVE-YEAR ABSENCE

Monday, October 5, 1829

Leslie, Newton, Moore, Rogers, Lockhart, James Smith, a young American—a clergyman named Edmund Griffin—, and a few of Murray's own special friends made up the guest list. From the beginning, at the dinner table, Moore took the floor, but his supremacy as a talker was ably challenged by James Smith's quick mind and tongue. Amid the roast fowl and fresh fruits they scattered their anecdotes to the delight of the entire party.

Moore began: a lady chattering to Charles Lamb at a dinner party attempted to chastise him for not attending to her words. "You don't seem," said the lady, "to be at all the better for what I have been saying to you!" "No, Ma'am," he answered, "but this gentleman on the other side of me must, for it all came in at one ear and went out at the other."

"Good creature! Good creature!" applauded one of the publisher's friends, as the party roared its approval of Moore and Lamb.

Smith retorted: John Bannister's melancholy increased with each passing year. When he was sixty-five, exactly the number of the address of his house, he was often seen shaking his fist at the plate on the door: "Aye"—Smith assumed, to the delight of all, the familiar stance and unmistakable intonations of the late comedian —"you needn't tell me, I know it; you told me the same thing yesterday." The diners momentarily ceased eating, their laughter indicating the general appreciation of Smith's mimicry.

Seated as he was, exactly opposite, John Murray could easily study the features of the portly American across the table. Washington Irving was no longer young. The flesh on his face hung heavily from his cheek bones and his skin appeared gray in the artificial light; his hair was brushed differently (to conceal the thinness on top), and his smart new frock coat for comfort's sake made ample concession to his expansive figure. Even his countenance, mild as always and occasionally detached, had changed; he responded appropriately to all remarks, but, at times, especially after the cloth had been removed and the decanters set out, he seemed to be sliding hopelessly into sleep. Murray chuckled, no doubt remembering what Disraeli had written in Vivian Grey *about Irving's falling asleep at a party.*

After dinner, the group having adjourned to the drawing room, tiny Moore played on the pianoforte, accompanying James Smith, whose lively songs contributed to the speed of the movement of the still-circulating decanters. Smith composed his song on the spot, humming the tune first in an overtone so that Moore's acute musical ears could catch and transfer it to his dexterous fingers. Smith called the ditty "Contradiction."

> *Mr. Metcalf ran off upon meeting a cow,*
> *With pale Mr. Turnbull behind him.*

So went the first verse; the last one left the listeners stamping their feet with laughter:

> *Over poor Mr. Lightfoot, confined by the gout,*
> *Mr. Heaviside danced a bolero!*

The tone of the gathering changed from frivolity to sentimentality. Moore sang one of his own Irish melodies, his head cast backwards, his eyes upward, his whole body in the very stance of an ancient Irish bard.

> *'Tis the last rose of summer*
> *Left blooming alone;*
> *All her lovely companions*
> *Are faded and gone....*

Not a sound from the transported audience.

> *. . . Oh! who would inhabit*
> *This bleak world alone!*

This broke even the steely composure of Lockhart. There was not a dry eye in the room, and Irving's quiet dignity seemed likely to develop into sobbing hysteria when the poet suddenly burst into a jig and began cavorting about the room, lustily singing:

> *Wreath the bowl*
> *With flowers of soul,*
> *The brightest wit can find us;*
> *We'll take a flight*
> *Towards heaven to-night*
> *And leave dull earth behind us!*

Still singing, he seized a decanter from a table and danced around Irving's chair.

> *Should Love amid*
> *The wreaths be hid*
> *That Joy, the enchanger, brings us,*
> *No danger fear*
> *While wine is near,*

He waved the decanter, and Irving, understanding his meaning, held out his empty glass.

> *We'll drown him if he stings us.*

In the brief pause of pouring, the American interjected his only comment of the evening intended for the ears of the entire group. "Yes, I'll have a little more."

"A little Moore!" shrieked Newton, and a pandemonium of laughter shook the crystal chandelier as Moore, himself shaking with mirth over Irving's magnificently executed pun, went back into his jig and the chorus of his song.

Young Griffin viewed with interest, if not admiration, the activities of the evening. He had left the United States and come to England in search of culture and refinement; this party at 50 Albemarle Street must have been a revelation. Perhaps it was the complete absence of profound thought or lengthy discussion on any important issues which produced the disappointed look on his long face. As Moore began "Come O'er the Sea . . . ," Griffin moved across the room with a purposeful not-to-completely-waste-the-evening stride to where John Murray was sitting beneath the precise stare of Lockhart's portrait; the publisher's smile froze on his face as Griffin introduced the possibility of his issuing an English edition of the travel journals which he planned to keep throughout his European tour.

Sources for Vignette

This was probably the most fully described function that WI attended at 50 Albemarle Street. The Rev. Edmund D. Griffin died shortly after he returned to the United States. His journal, carefully describing this party with occasional sour notes, was included in *Remains of the Rev. Edmund D. Griffin*, comp. Francis Griffin (New York: G. & C. & H. Carvell, 1831), II, 260–63. (Smiles, II, 234–35, erroneously dated Griffin's visit in 1827–1828.) Moore, *Memoirs*, VI, 85, told of the event from his viewpoint, and Leslie left two descriptions, one in a contemporary letter to his sister (II, 200); the other in his autobiography, written several years later (I, 226). For Nugee, see PMI, IV, 177, and Peter Irving to Thomas Aspinwall, Jan. 23, 1829 (New York Public Library). Moore's "Irish Melodies" are included in *The Poetical Works of Thomas Moore* [Albion Edition] (London: Frederick Warne and Co., n.d.), respectively, pp. 224, 238, and 229.

*I*f we are to believe Charles MacFarlane, the period between 1829 and 1833 was the most satisfying at 50 Albemarle Street.[1] The flamboyant Byron was gone, and Scott, like all the regulars, had aged, but more than ever John Murray II was the "Emperor of the West [End]," on whose head the crown rested

[1] *Reminiscences of a Literary Life* (London: JM, 1917), p. 20.

more easily than in days of earlier struggles. As a mentor of the trade, Murray was a leader of the London Booksellers' Committee, which on December 9, 1829, agreed to force controls on retail prices of books.[2] But the economic scene, though black at times, never darkened completely the life at Murray's establishment, as had happened in 1826, and the publisher seemed to find in the companionship of his old friends the only true relief in his fight against a variety of physical pains.

The tone of his social gatherings had changed. The afternoon drawing-room groups were less spectacular and the dinner parties were more select and included mainly old friends. One senses, in reading accounts of Murray's dinners from this period, a serenity never present in the *arrivism* of the first years of Murray's residence in Mayfair. The new spirit was as much the product of the regular guests as of the host, for they had proved their worth and now rested in the familiarity of long acquaintances. This does not mean that the principals had settled into staid middle-age. Indeed, referring to this general period, George Paston gave John Murray II yet another nickname: "The Playbody of the Publishing World." [3]

"High jinks" was the term MacFarlane used to describe the parties, remembering a typical one in this way:

> The bard of "Hohenlinden" [Thomas Campbell] for many years wore a wig. . . . It was a wig not at all suited to his age and complexion; it was a fine black wig with Hyperion curls, and generally well oiled and perfumed. One night, after a very jovial dinner at old John Murray's, and while the claret-jugs were still in rapid circulation, Theodore Hook was called upon to sing one of his improvised songs. He was in "keff" and in vein; he sang three songs in succession, and really excelled himself. Campbell, considerably more than three-parts "fou," went off into an ecstasy, and taking his wig off his head, he threw it across the table at Theodore, shouting, "There, you dog! Take my laurels! They are yours!"

2 James J. Barnes, *Free Trade in Books: A Study of the London Book Trade since 1800* (Oxford: The Clarendon Press, 1964), pp. 1–18.
3 Paston, *At John Murray's*, p. 6.

The laughter was uproarious, and it did not cease until long after the elder bard had recovered his wig, and had covered his bald, shining pate. Washington Irving laughed until his sides ached, and then with a sly, demure face told Campbell that he had never before fancied that those poetical looks were not of his own growth.[4]

At Albemarle Street a new personality had come onto the business scene. Having just gained his majority in 1829 and completed his formal education, John Murray III became officially a part of the organization. Earlier in this year he had gone abroad, returning with voluminous notebooks which would eventually bring additional fame and fortune to the House of Murray. The younger Murray began the first series of *Guides* or *Handbooks* for travelers, methodically covering most of the civilized world during the remainder of his active life. In his sojourns, his much-traveled friends provided him with valuable information and letters of introduction, Washington Irving always lending a willing hand.[5]

Away from 50 Albemarle Street, Geoffrey Crayon had been a literary lion in 1820, but "Mr. Irving of the American Legation" was an even greater personage in London in 1829. His later works, though less financially successful than his publisher might have hoped for, had solidified his reputation; many of his English and diplomatic friends of earlier days had themselves matured and settled into high places from which they now reached out to him; and finally his official position in the diplomatic corps gave him a wider range of acceptability than mere authorship had ever afforded him. His days were filled with work—for though his heart was not always in it, the daily drudgery and occasional crisis of the Legation had to be tended to—and his nights were devoted to society. Louis McLane and his family took their countryman into their midst with a familiarity that later gave rise to the rumor

4 MacFarlane, pp. 19–20.
5 See "The Origin and History of Murray's *Handbooks for Travellers*" in JMIV, *John Murray III, 1808–1892: A Brief Memoir* (New York: Alfred A. Knopf, 1920), pp. 39–49. See JMIII's letter, July 17, 1830, concerning a contact in Bordeaux made through WI's efforts. *Ibid.*, pp. 50–51.

of a romance between him and one of the McLane daughters.[6] What part Irving played in McLane's diplomatic bargaining which opened the West Indies to American shipping is open to conjecture, but certainly the author's prestige did no harm to his superior's maneuvering among the British ministers.[7]

Irving's trunks still held bundles of unfinished business: the copy of *Voyages of Companions of Columbus;* sheaves of notes for a biography of Mahomet; the collection he had worked on at the Alhambra; and other odds and ends so varied that they mystified even his imagination.[8] The demands of job and friends, however, left him little time to think of his literary career—though his two-thousand dollar annual salary hardly met the financial demands of his taste in living. He worked when he could on his own projects, but now, as always, he spared no efforts to aid his fellow authors.[9]

Through Ebenezer in New York, Washington was able to secure an American publisher for Moore's *Life of Byron,* and in so doing he posted himself as the agent responsible for securing copy for the transatlantic edition. This would be, for several months, a thorny problem for Irving and a tight situation for Moore, who was depending on his payment from the American

[6] STW, II, 46.

[7] The long official correspondence between McLane and Lord Aberdeen, British Foreign Secretary, began on Dec. 12, 1829. See *America: Domestic* (F. O. 5/256, 263) in Public Record Office. Much of the correspondence is in WI's handwriting. Of special interest is McLane to Aberdeen, March 10, 1830 (F. O. 5/263, pp. 39–75), in which the arguments for opening trade are put forth in a style smooth enough to suggest that WI may have contributed to the composition as he penned the sentences. For a review of McLane and Irving's "mission," see Willson, *America's Ambassadors to England,* pp. 185–94.

[8] On Nov. 6, 1829, WI wrote (for McLane to sign) to Lord Aberdeen requesting the usual diplomatic courtesy that "three trunks containing books and papers belonging to Washington Irving Esquire, Secretary of the Legation" be released without any duties from the custom house in London (F. O. 5/256, p. 130). PMI, II, 373–74, gave a full catalogue of the material "in a crude state" in his trunk.

[9] See my "Irving's Literary Midwifery: Five Unpublished Letters from British Repositories" in *Philological Quarterly.* The five letters, covering the period 1829 to 1846, show WI's efforts to help William Godwin, Thomas Moore, Fitz-Greene Halleck, Francis L. Hawks, and two of his British nieces in their literary endeavors.

edition to repay a loan Murray had made to finance repairs on Moore's Sloperton cottage.

32. *To John Murray II*[10]

Chandos St.
Tuesday, Decr 15th [1829].[11]

My dear Sir,

The sheets came a couple of hours too late for the dispatches, but will be forwarded by the next packet, next week. I observe that Pages 557, 558 & 560 are wanting. Will you have the goodness to supply them in time, that the work may be completed.

Very faithfully yours &c,
Washington Irving.

33. *To John Murray II*[12]

Thursday, Feb 5 [1830].[13]

My dear Sir,

I send you the MSS. of the American tales &c. Mr Jones,[14] the

---

[10] Used by permission of The Clifton Waller Barrett Library of the University of Virginia Library. The MS bears the inscription "Presented to us by J. Murray Jun. Esq."

[11] According to *Atherton's Calendar Chart, 1800–2000* (London: Herbert Atherton, n.d.), Tuesday, Dec. 15, was in 1829.

[12] Used by permission of the Harvard College Library.

[13] Docketed "1830" at 50 Albemarle Street.

[14] James Athearn Jones (1791–1854) in 1826 had published in Philadelphia *A Letter to an English Gentleman, on the Libels and Calumnies on America by British Writers and Reviews. Tales of an Indian Camp* had been published anonymously in London by Colburn in 1829, but neither the British Museum nor the Library of Congress has copies; the Library of Congress, however, does have a copy of a translation (*Sagen der Nordamerikanischen Indianer. . .* [Altenburg: J. Helbig, 1837]) and the later British edition which Sabin *et al.*, comp., *Bibliotheca Americana . . .* (New York: J. Sabin & Sons, 1868–1936), IX, 322, list as *Traditions of the North American Indians: Being a Second and Revised Edition of "Tales of an Indian Camp"* (London: Henry Colburn and Richard Bentley, 1830), describing it as "a curious and rather apocryphal performance." In 1831 his *Haverhill: or, Memoirs of an Officer in the Army of Wolfe* was published in London by T. & W. Boone (Sabin, IX, 322). This hardly fits the description of the MS which WI sent JMII; one imagines, therefore, that his collection of "American tales" was never published.

On July 6, 1830, following a discussion on the merits of American literature, WI sent Samuel Rogers a copy of *Tales of an Indian Camp* as proof of the worth of his native culture. Clayden, *Rogers and His Contemporaries*, II, 44. On July 15, 1835, WI wrote to Aspinwall in London asking for a copy of this work

person of whom I was speaking to you, does not claim to the merit of being more than the Selector. It is his intention to review them carefully in the course of publication, and to weed out any words, or paragraphs that may be offensive to English taste.

I have read half of the first volume of the Tales of an Indian Camp published by Colburn for the same author. The perusal of them convinces me that he is a person well worth your securing.

Very faithfully yours,
Washington Irving.

The society world was not the only one that honored the American. In April 1830 he was awarded the Gold Medal of the Royal Society of Literature, a distinction which Sir Walter Scott had attained only three years earlier.

In stolen moments he closeted himself to work on unfinished manuscripts at 8 Argyll Street, where he had moved earlier in the year to get away from his business address. His new residence placed him almost exactly halfway between the United States Legation and John Murray's. On Argyll Street, Irving polished the last paragraphs of *Voyages of the Companions of Columbus*, which he understood Murray intended to use as a volume in his Family Library. He wrote and rewrote the article discussing *A Chronicle of the Conquest of Granada* for the *Quarterly Review;* it was intended to appear anonymously and to rectify the damage he felt the publisher had done by putting the author's true name on the title page.[15]

34. *To John Murray II*[16]

Argyll St
July 6, 1830.

My dear Sir:
I have been rather interrupted for some days past by the busi-

---

—"subsequently the title page was altered to Traditions of the North American Indians—(or some such title). It was published by Colburn & Bentley about the year 1830." Barrett Collection, Alderman Library, University of Virginia.

Vols. II and III (London, 1829) are among the books from WI's private library still preserved at Sunnyside.

[15] XLIII (May 1830), 55–80.

[16] Written on mourning paper used for official embassy correspondence during July and Aug. after the death of King George IV. Sealed with black wax.

ness of the office or should have had the volume of voyages ready for the press. In fact I could furnish copy to the printers immediately, but every day that I withhold it makes the work better. You spoke sometime since of writing me a "Business Letter." I wish you would do so at once, and let me know what you can offer for this work. It will form one volume, and may be printed uniform with the octavo edition of Columbus, and also in a smaller form as one of the Family Library. I cannot but think it will be found interesting & readable. The singular narratives of these voyages, have to me, even in the crude state in which I found them entangled in the old Spanish writers, all the charm of wild tales of romance; and I have endeavoured to set them off in the clearest and most striking manner.

I am my dear Sir

Yours faithfully,

Washington Irving.

P.S. As we are sending off dispatches this day I will thank you for any additional letter press of Moore's work that may be printed.

One would suppose from Irving's definite tone that the manuscript of the *Voyages* was safely in hand. Such was not the case. In fact, it would be almost two months before he could get it into good enough shape to put it into the care of a printer, and even then the introduction was not complete. In the meantime, however, he played a hard author-publisher game with Murray, whose disposition was growing daily more sour, inspired by his poor health, a multitude of business problems,[17] and the current financial depression.

The newspapers and the gossip of the diplomatic corps were suddenly focusing their attention on France, where King Charles X was struggling to hold his power against the pressure of demands for greater public freedom. Irving's attention was focused there also because he wished to visit Peter and his old haunts. The

[17] See, for example, *Report of the Trial of Mr. John Murray, in the Court of King's Bench, at Westminster-Hall, the 19th December 1829, on an Indictment of Libel on Messrs. Lecesne and Escoffery, of Jamaica* (London: Bagster and Thomas, 1830), concerning George Wilson Bridges' *The Annals of Jamaica*, which JM had published. JMII was fined one shilling and commended for his action by the court.

eruption of the political ferment into a brief shooting war only increased Irving's desire to go to Paris. On the eve of his departure, he attempted to come to terms with Murray concerning the *Voyages*.

35. *To John Murray II*[18]

> F. L.[19]
> Argyll St
> Tuesday, Aug. 3d.

My dear Sir,

I am extremely sorry to say that the terms you mention as having given to others are much below what I had expected. I speak not from any reference to the value of my work, but to the offers made me by others, who may be supposed to have a knowledge of the literary market. When Dr Lardner[20] applied to me to write for his series he offered me five hundred guineas per volume. On my declining, it was intimated that I might have 700. I know that the latter sum per volume is given by him to some of his authors, and that Moore is to receive 1000 guineas for his Hist of Ireland in one volume.

Should you be disposed to give me five hundred guineas for my volume of voyages we may settle the matter at once, and a note sent to my lodgings any time before 5 o'clock PM. will find me. I leave town in the Southampton coach at 6.

> I am my dear Sir
> Ever most faithfully yours,
> Washington Irving.

The messenger arrived from Albemarle Street. John Murray agreed to Irving's terms. Irving would have his fee—when the publisher had the copy for the *Voyages*. Mr. and Mrs. Murray

---

[18] On mourning paper.

[19] First Letter. Filing comment written at Murray's.

[20] Dionysius Lardner (1793–1859), Professor of Natural Philosophy and Astronomy at the newly founded University of London, in 1829 began his *Cabinet Cyclopaedia*, published by Longmans. He secured the best writers of the day (Scott on Scotland, Moore on Ireland [*The History of Ireland. From the Earliest Kings of that Realm, Down to its Last Chief*, 4 vols., 1835–1846]). H. F. Fergus prepared a two-volume *History of the United States* (1830), this being the subject Lardner had asked WI to treat.

were on the point of departing for an extended tour of Scotland, during which they expected to visit the Lockharts and the Scotts. Notes of £175 each, payable at six, nine, and twelve months, would be drawn and left with young John, with whom Irving should deal in the absence of the older Murray.

36. *To John Murray II*[21]

Argyll St
Aug. 3d 1830.

My dear Sir,

I am happy to receive your letter agreeing to my proposal. The notes can be drawn and left with your son as you suggest. I take the earlier part of the MS. with me to Paris, to make some trivial corrections & will send it on to him through the ambassador's bag, as I get it ready.

I have recd also the letter of Mr Lockhart which you forwarded me, which incloses your check for 50 gs for the article in the Review.[22] As I am in a great hurry & on the point of setting off I have not time to write to Mr Lockhart to acknowledge the receipt of it, but will do so when I have more leisure. I beg you to give him my kind regards. He is a man whom I shall ever be proud to call my friend.[23] With kindest remembrances to Sir Walter Scott & family when you see him,

I am my dear Sir
Every very truly
Your obliged & faithful friend,
Washington Irving.

In Paris, at the Chamber of Deputies, Irving witnessed the new king, Louis Philippe, taking his oath and sampled briefly the delights of the city which had only days before been in the process of overthrowing the national government. By August 28 he was back in London, grappling with reality in the form of his manu-

[21] Watermarked "J Whatman 1830"

[22] Irving's piece on *A Chronicle of the Conquest of Granada*.

[23] Writing to JMII, July 9, 1830, JGL had asked: "What is W—Irving, good fellow true, about." Murray Archives.

script commitment to Murray. Through September, October, November, and into December, Irving continued, as he described it to Peter, "jogging on with the printing of the voyages." [24]

Meanwhile, the Murrays were enjoying their extended tour of Scotland, traveling in "a handsome barouche drawn by four spirited horses." [25] In Edinburgh the publisher gave a dinner for the book trade at the Royal Hotel. The bill was £108, seemingly a fabulous expense, but, according to one report, he received orders for twenty thousand pounds worth of Byron's works alone. [26]

37. To John Murray III

> Argyll St
> Aug. 28th 1830.

My dear Sir,

I send you the MS. of the Voyages for the printer[27] to make his estimate. Should I not furnish sufficient letter press I can readily furnish more in the appendix, from curious documents illustrative of the voyages. I have retained in my hands for correction the introduction & some of the early part, making together about 110 pages similar to those sent. I shall be able to furnish the early part for the press on Monday morng & then to continue the supply as wanted.

> Very truly yours,
> Washington Irving.

38. To John Murray III

> Monday morning
> [Sept. 6, 1830].[28]

My dear Sir,

I want a duplicate of the proof, to send off with this day's dispatches to America. The lad who brings this note will go to the

24 PMI, II, 442.
25 Grant, II, 15.
26 *Ibid.*, 14–15.
27 C. Roworth, Bell Yard, Temple Bar.
28 Dated at Murray's.

printers for the proof, if you will give him the requisite order & directions.[29]

Very truly yours,
W Irving.

Though his writing moved slowly, because of his numerous responsibilities, Irving's spirits were good. Murray returned in late October from his visit to Edinburgh and professed great plea-sure over the progress that had been made in the preparation of the *Voyages*. Too, Irving heard the rumor that the abridgment of his *Columbus* (for which he had charged Murray only the cost of copying) had sold out the entire first edition of ten thou-sand copies.[30] His position with his publisher was surely secure. The long doubtful years that followed the appearance of *Tales of a Traveller* now seemed very far away.

Getting Moore's *Life of Byron* through the presses of the brothers Harper in New York was becoming more and more of a problem. The American publisher had signed an agreement to pay Moore three hundred pounds for his work, if they were not superseded by a pirate publisher in the United States.[31]

39. *To John Murray II*

Argyll St
Thursday, Oct.[32] 4 [1830].

My dear Sir,

The following is an extract from a letter written by my agent in N York dated Oct. 7.

"I fear that another blunder has been made in forwarding sheets of the 2d vol. of Moore's Life of Byron. I lately received pages 737 to 768. The previous part of the vol. as far as page 560 had duly

[29] Carey and Lea of Philadelphia were probably using the C. Rosworth proofs as the copy for the American first edition.
[30] PMI, II, 442.
[31] Eugene Exman, *The Brothers Harper* (New York: Harper & Row, 1965), p. 23. By this time a few enterprising American publishers with piratical tenden-cies had hit upon the idea of employing printers to set books in type aboard ships during the western voyage. Ladas, I. 26.
[32] An obvious error by WI. The month was Nov. 1830.

come to hand, but from 561 to 736 inclusive has not made its appearance.

"I was in hopes that the missing sheets of the first vol. would have been sent to me to tender to the publishers, to obviate any possible attempt on their part to contest the payment of the money, as you will recollect by the words of the contract the money is only due on my furnishing them with the first complete copy of the work here."

The sheets missing of the first vol. were twenty eight, being from Page 408 to 521. If the printer can furnish them by Saturday, the 6th I will forward them with the dispatches which we make on that day to the U States.

Very truly yours,
Washington Irving.

40. *To John Murray II*[33]

Argyll St
Sunday [Nov. 7?][34] [1830].

My dear Sir,

The deficiences of the 1 vol of Moore's Byron are *twenty eight sheets* or from *Page 408 to 521*. I will thank you to let me have them, together with the remaining sheets of vol 2d early in the course of tomorrow.[35]

Yours truly,
W Irving.

[33] Used by permission of the Berg Collection, The New York Public Library, Astor, Lenox and Tilden Foundations.

[34] Most probable reading.

[35] PMI (II, 420–21), STW (II, 17–18, 332), and a recent scholar (Thomas A. Kirby, "Irving and Moore: A Note on Anglo-American Literary Relations," *Modern Language Notes*, LXII [April 1947], 251–55) rhapsodize over all the money WI put into Moore's purse by this venture. Yet Moore clearly stated in his *Memoirs*, June 1831: "From the delay of the work, the money, of course, did not come" (VI, 194). In his study of Harpers, Exman implied that the £300 was paid to Moore, though he never actually stated this as a fact: "The real pirating began before the Harper two-volume edition was fairly marketed, the work being reproduced in several forms in 1830 by several American publishers, including Munroe & Francis of Boston. This unhappy experience, early in their publishing career, taught them a lesson about English reprints that they never forgot" (p. 23). I have discussed this transaction in "Irving's Literary Midwifery," *Philological Quarterly*. Since all of Harpers' old records were de-

Amidst his numerous projects and jobs Irving took on, of his own free will, another task: he secured (as he reported it)[36] Murray as the English publisher for Alexander Slidell's *A Year in Spain*, revised the American edition for the British public, and corrected the proofs as the volumes went through the press. In addition to this, he agreed to write a lengthy review of the work for the *Quarterly Review*.[37]

41. *To John Murray III*[38]

> Argyll Street
> Saturday morng
> [Dec. 18, 1830].[39]

My dear John,

I send you a number of pages of the work, which I corrected last night in bed. They will do to begin with, and I shall send more, as fast as I correct it. I am quite delighted with the book, it is so lively, so minute and so accurate. I had only seen portions of it before, in reviews. I wish the copy to be returned to me that I may transmit it to the author, that he may see the liberties I have taken with him, with which I trust he will not be displeased.[40] I wish also to have proofs as fast as they can be furnished, that I may go on with a review of it, which I shall immediately commence.

> Very truly yours,
> W Irving.

Tell your father I received the notes of hand, for which he has my acknowledgements.[41]

---

stroyed in a fire in 1853, it is likely that further information will never come to light on this matter.

[36] PMI, II, 450.

[37] See below, n. 50.

[38] "Lt. Slidell's Spain" written in pencil at top of page in another hand. Watermarked "R Tassell 1830"

[39] Dated at Murray's.

[40] See my "WI's Edition of Slidell's *A Year in Spain*," *Bulletin of the New York Public Library*, LXXIII (June 1969), 367–73.

[41] Notes completing the business transaction of Aug. 3. See Appendix IV, item 9.

Voyages of the Companions of Columbus was published on Dec. 30, 1830, as No. 18 of Murray's Family Library. Its reception followed the pattern of acceptance set by WI's previous work: laudatory recognition without excite-

42. *To John Murray III*

Thursday morng
[Dec. 23, 1830].[42]

My dear John,

I send you a part of the 2d vol. in case your father should think proper to print both at once. There are about 60 pages remaining of the 1st vol. which you shall have in time.

I have thrown over board much of the heavy gazetteer matter. Chap. 14, as it is at present lightened, will I think be interesting. It contains a very good sketch of the character & reign of Abderahman, which is not hackneyed, or from gazetteers & is really one of the most interesting reigns during the Moorish domination.[43]

I think it likely that the work, after being trimmed out & lightened, will furnish matter for two volumes.

Very truly yours,
W. I.

Even spending a Yuletide holiday in the country home of the Mansfields, Diggswell House,[44] in Hertfordshire, he took time to continue his work on behalf of Slidell's reputation.

43. *To John Murray II*[45]

Diggeswell, Dec. 26th 1830.

My dear Sir,

I send you a part of the review, as far as I have been able to write it from the materials in hand.[46] You will perceive there is danger of its over running, from the richness of the materials for extract-

---

ment or high praise. Typical of the British reviews was the three-installment article in *The Literary Gazette*, Jan. 1, p. 8; Jan. 8, pp. 22–23; Jan. 22, 1831, pp. 55–56.

[42] Dated at Murray's.

[43] In JM ed., chap. XIV is in II, 105–26.

[44] John Mansfield's beautiful wife was the daughter of Gen. Samuel Smith of Baltimore. Diggswell House, four miles north of Hatfield, is now the headquarters for the Diggswell Arts Trust.

[45] Watermarked "R Tassell 1830."

[46] The entire review was written on folded gilt-edge sheets, watermarked "R TASSELL 1830." Judging from the ink and WI's own pagination [1–12], the portion included with this letter ended with "by a master hand" in *QR*, p. 329.

ing: as there are many long passages in the residue of the work, extremely interesting, entertaining & characteristic. It had better be set up in slips, where it can be pruned and altered as may be deemed expedient. I shall return to town on Tuesday so there is no need of sending me any thing here.

Very faithfully yours,
Washington Irving.

Back from Hertfordshire and a subsequent visit to Birmingham, Irving settled into a routine of business and pleasure, working whenever possible on his life of Mahomet and the Alhambra tales. The publication problems of others continued to take his time, a fact made clear by his letters to Murray.

44. *To John Murray II*[47]

Argyll Street
Jan. 13th 1831.

My dear Sir,

When I was at your house this morning I forgot half of my errand, which was about a poem which I left at your house a day or two since. It appears to me to be a singular production with a great deal of wild power and exuberant splendour. As the authoress has been most particularly recommended to me I feel committed to make some exertion to serve her.[48] I have given her brother a note to you which he will present in person.

---

[47] Postmarked at 8 A.M. in London, Jan. 15, 1831. Watermarked "R Tassell 1830."

[48] The authoress in question was Maria Gowen Brooks, described by Rufus Wilmot Griswold in 1842 as "the foremost American poetess." For details concerning Mrs. Brooks and her relations with WI and Southey, see *DAB*, II, 81–82; Ruth Shepard Grannis, *An American Friend of Southey* (New York: The De Vinne Press, 1913), pp. 19–22; and PMI, II, 453–54. Dedicated to Southey, the manuscript finally got into print as *Zophiel: or The Bride of Seven*, by Maria del Occidente (London: R. J. Kennett, 1833).

On March 3, 1831, WI wrote to Brevoort, then on an extended visit to Paris: "I received your letter by Mr. Gowen, the gentleman who brought the poem some time since. There was a long letter, too, from the authoress, which it was quite out of my power to answer. I left the poem with Murray, on my going out of town, saying everything I could in its praise. He wrote me word that he had declined publishing it, as he did not think it calculated to advance either the author's interests or reputation. I am continually applied to by writers to help

I beg you *as a personal favour to me*, to see him, and give him an answer as early as possible. The poem I have had barely time to glance at. It may prove good on being pruned—or perhaps the authoress may produce something else, that would be attractive.

I am my dear Sir

In great haste
Yours faithfully,
Washington Irving.

45. *To John Murray II*[49]

Argyll Street
Jany 13th 1831.

My dear Sir,

This will be handed you by Mr Gowan, brother of the authoress of the Poem I left at your house a day or two since.

As I feel particular interest in this matter I beg you will give Mr Gowan as early an answer as possible on the subject of the poem, and that you will do all in your power to promote the success of the work.

Ever my dear Sir
Yours faithfully,
Washington Irving.

46. *To John Murray II*

Birmingham, Jany 18 [1831].

My dear Sir,

I send you the residue of Vol. 2d of the "Year in Spain." I have recd no proofsheets since my arrival here, & hope there has been no mistake in the direction as there was while I was at Diggeswell. Any letter or parcel should be addressed to me care of Henry Van Wart Esqr, Birmingham.

---

their works into the press. Now there is no person less able to do so than I. My only acquaintance among the publishers is Murray, who is the most difficult being on earth to please." PMI, II, 453–54.

[49] Watermarked "R Tassell 1830." Inscribed on the back of the letter at John Murray's: "Mr. Gowan's address—Care of Messrs. Brown Danson Willis & Co., Bishopsgate Church Yard—London." This was a company of general merchants, with whom Mr. Gowan probably did business. *Robson's London Directory . . . for 1832*, Pt. V, 227.

The critique will be ready for you whenever you wish it.[50]
I am my dear Sir

Very truly yours,
Washington Irving.

47. *To John Murray III*[51]

Argyll Street
Friday morng
[Feb. 18, 1831] [52]

My dear John,

What I spoke to your father about, yesterday, was a copy of the "Companions of Columbus" neatly bound, to send to the Royal Academy of History at Madrid.[53]

If you can furnish me with a copy of the large edition of Columbus, that may be cut up, if necessary, to enlarge the new abridgement,[54] I will thank you.

Yours very truly,
Washington Irving.

P.S. I understand Moore's sudden visit to Dublin is on account of the illness of his mother, who is said to be on her death bed.[55]

---

[50] *QR*, XLIV (Feb. 1831), 319–42. The MS of this review is still in the Murray Archives. A collation of WI's MS and the *QR* text shows that there were several revisions made in print, probably the work of Lockhart, who was perhaps no less a polisher than Gifford had been. To begin with, most of WI's opening sentence was omitted: "This is, altogether, one of the most amusing book of travels that we have read for a long time; and what is more, it relates to a country which though by no means distant, is comparatively but little known—a country, in fact, where the 'far wandering' foot of the all pervading Englishman but seldom rambles."

[51] Watermarked "R Tassell 1830." In the second paragraph "the large edition" is underlined and in the same ink someone at JM's wrote "gone" in the margin.

[52] Dated at Murray's.

[53] The Librarian of the Academia de la Historia, Madrid, informs me that a copy of WI's *Voyages and Discoveries of the Companions of Columbus* with JM's imprint is in his collection. Letter of Nov. 5, 1965.

[54] If WI's reference was to the new edition which JM was bringing out, there is no evidence to suggest that he actually made any changes. The first edition had been printed by Davison; the second by W. Clowes, Stamford Street. The only obvious difference in the two editions is minor textual shifting done by Clowes. There seem to be no authorial changes. In the United States, however, in 1831, G. & C. & H. Carvill brought out "A New Edition, with additions and improvements by the Author."

[55] Moore left Sloperton Cottage on Feb. 11, having heard from his sister "an alarming account of my dear mother's state of health." His mother revived and by Feb. 22 Moore was in London calling on JMII. *Memoirs*, VI, 167–77.

48. *To John Murray II*

Argyll Street
March 15th 1831.

My dear Sir,

I inclose a bill exchange drawn on me for £ 10.11.8., which I paid a few days since, being for the expenses of the painter & the sketches which he made at Palos, for the illustrations of "The Companions of Columbus." [56] If you can pay the amount to the bearer of this note you will oblige.

Yours very truly,
Washington Irving

P.S. I also send you some manuscript tales sent to me by the author to dispose of. Will you let me know, as soon as convenient, whether they will tempt you to become the purchaser? It is probable that a very brief glance at them will enable you to determine.[57]

49. *To John Murray III*[58]

Tuesday morng [1831].

My dear John,

We are sending off dispatches to America today. If you can let me have a copy of the Year in Spain to send out to the author's family I should be glad to have it in the course of the morning. Perhaps you can send it to me by the bearer.

Yours truly,
W Irving.

[56] The sketches included the frontispiece "Convent of La Rabida at Palos, where Columbus asked bread and water for his child" and "Town of Palos, with the Church of St. George," opposite p. 309, both sketched by Ignacio Wagner and later engraved for the book by E. Finden.

[57] Lacking further clues, we can only speculate as to the nature of these tales. The most likely explanation is that they were from the pen of John Fanning Watson, whose *Historic Tales of Olden Times* was published in New York in 1832. On March 30, 1831, WI wrote Watson thanking him for a book (whether printed or in manuscript is not clear) and encouraging him to continue his writing (MS in The Historical Society of Pennsylvania, Philadelphia). A copy of Watson's *Annals of Philadelphia* (Philadelphia, 1830) is in WI's private library as preserved at Sunnyside. JM did not publish Watson's book or any other title which could have been the MS WI sent him at this time.

[58] Used by permission of The Clifton Waller Barrett Library of the University of Virginia Library.

50. *To John Murray III*

Argyll Street
April 6, 1831.

My dear John,

As I am sending off dispatches &c. to the United States today, I should be glad to have the reviews of the "Year in Spain" about which you spoke.[59]

Though communicating mere empty praises to an author is something like "filling a man's belly with the East Wind," yet it may do for the present, until your father shall make up his mind as to the "handsome thing" to be done in the matter, according to your intimation to me prior to my preparing the work for the press.

Yours very truly,
Washington Irving.

51. *To John Murray II*[60]

Argyll Street
Monday Morng
Apr. 1831.

My dear Sir,

I am extremely sorry that a previous engagement prevents my having the pleasure of dining with you tomorrow.

Very truly yours,
Washington Irving.

---

[59] Among the reviews that JMIII would have wanted Slidell to see were the serial in *The Athenaeum*, Feb. 25, March 5, 1831, pp. 135–36, 146–47, and the article in *The Literary Gazette*, Feb. 26, 1831, pp. 132–33. The latter began: "We have been somewhat anticipated by an anticipatory and well-written review in the Quarterly, in which the personal adventures of the gallant lieutenant are brought forward in a style worthy of his countryman, Washington Irving."

[60] Used by permission of the MS Collection, Russell Sage College, Troy, N. Y. This letter was a part of the Margaret Venables Autograph Collection which dated back to the 1820's, when William Venables was Lord Mayor of London. Also in the group were letters to JMII from Croker (Nov. 1, 1830), Moore (Nov. 17, 1830), and Henry Hallam (May 19, 1831). Apparently, all had been contributed by one of the Murrays as autograph specimens.

The collection was broken up and sold as individual pieces in June 1966 by Michael Lewis, 45 Roath Court Road, Cardiff, Wales. See his Catalogue No. 23, items 1 through 102. WI to JMII, number 42, erroneously dated Sept. 1831; it sold for £5 5s. 0d.

McLane's recall to become Secretary of the Treasury in June 1831 left Irving as chargé d'affaires at the Legation, a job which quickly ate up the few minutes he had previously been able to steal for composition. But even with official engagements at the Palace and conferences at Whitehall, he gave his friends literary assistance.

52. *To John Murray II*

Argyll Street, July 5th 1831.

My dear Sir,

My friend Professor Renwick of New York is engaged on a work which he wishes me to offer to you for publication. I give his own account of it. "I am engaged in writing a 'Treatise on Theoretic and Practical Mechanics,' which I consider will be as[61] well suited to the English public, as I hope to make it for the American. It will be ready to go to press about 1st October next.

"My object in writing this work is to condense into a form suited for public instruction or private study the researches & investigations of the best writers of the continent of Europe, uniting the three subjects which they keep distinct, namely *Mecanique, Physique* & *Machines*. I shall avoid as much as possible the direct use of English authorities, and hope to place it on a level with the present state of Science, which the only English work of analogous character (Gregory's Mechanics)[62] is not. The work will consist of 500 pages of the form of the American Quarterly Review, with 6 or 8 plates and *2* or *300* woodcuts. It will make two very sizeable volumes, 800 if printed as such works are in England.

"Should you open a negotiation with Mr Murray I presume I am not wholly unknown to him, having contributed several articles to the Quarterly Journal of Science.[63] This work will combine the results of ten years laborious studies."

61 In copying WI inserted the *as* after *well*.
62 Olinthus Gilbert Gregory, *A Treatise on Mechanics, Theoretical, Practical, and Descriptive* (London: George Kearsley, 1806).
63 Before the financial crisis of 1826 JMII had been the publisher of the *Quarterly Journal of Literature, Science and the Arts*. Henry Colburn took it over in 1827, reversing *Literature* and *Science* in the title. James Renwick contributed at least two articles to the publication: "Report on the Subject of Weights and Measurements made to the Commissioners for Revising the Laws

Mr Renwick is also well known as a man of Science to John Frederick Daniell Esqr F.R.S., to Captain Chapman of the Royal Artillery—who is on the publishing committee of the Royal Institute[64]—and reference may be had to them for his qualifications for the task he has under taken. My own opinion of him is very high, from long & intimate friendship with him; and he has a very high character throughout the United States.

I should like to have an answer from you as early as possible, whether you are inclined to treat for the English copy right of this work, as I wish to write to Professor Renwick by the Packet Ship of the 16th inst, & must send my letter from London by the 14th. If you are disposed to undertake the work I wish likewise to know whether it will be requisite for him to send a manuscript, or whether the printed proof sheets of the American edition will be sufficient.[65] The latter would be preferable, as the first correction of the proofs of the mathematical part can hardly be done with exactness by any one but the author.

> I am my dear Sir
> Very truly yours,
> Washington Irving.

Still trying to help Moore, Irving schemed to secure "a little bag of money" for the sale of his *Life of Lord Edward Fitzgerald* in America.[66] At the same time he was working in behalf of his friend, United States diplomat Henry Wheaton. Earlier in the year Irving's hand had been involved in securing Murray as the publisher for the British edition of Wheaton's *A History of the Northmen*. Although Irving appears to have done no editing on the work, wily Murray may have included in the bargain a review

---

of the State of New York," N.S. I (Jan. 1827), 101–16; "An Account of Some of the Steam-Boats Navigating the Hudson River in the State of New York," N.S. II (July 1828), 1–9.

[64] John Frederic Daniell, physicist, appointed Professor of Chemistry at Kings College, London, in 1831. *DNB*, V, 483. John James Chapman attained rank of captain April 21, 1820, and went on half pay from Royal Artillery, June 2, 1829. *A List of Officers of the Army, 1830*, p. 331.

[65] See below, Letter 57.

[66] WI to TM, July 9, 1831. Quoted in *Catalogue of the Loan Collection of Relics of Thomas Moore* [Moore Centenary Celebration in Dublin, 28th May 1870] (Dublin: Joseph Dollard, 1879), p. 10.

When Irving chose, his writing could
look like an example from a calligrapher's handbook.
Usually, however, his letters to John Murray II—like this
one, which is transcribed on the following page—show
haste and the assurance that penmanship alone did
not impress his publisher. *Courtesy of the
University of Virginia Library.*

from Crayon's pen for the *Quarterly Review,* as he did in the case of Slidell's *A Year in Spain.*

53. *To John Murray II*[67]

Argyll Street
July 27th 1831.

My dear Sir,
    I send you part of the article on Mr Wheaton's work. I will send you the residue in the course of a day or two. There will be about fifteen or twenty of my pages more.[68]

Very truly yours,
Washington Irving.

The new Minister, Martin Van Buren, arrived on September 13 and moved into quarters Irving had reserved for him at Thomas' Hotel on Berkeley Square. The chargé d'affaires did not see him that first evening because he was dining at the Palace and charming King William IV. When they did meet the next day, each was agreeably surprised. Van Buren regretted strongly that Irving insisted on retiring immediately from the Legation. Irving, however, was determined. *Mahomet* was in sorry form, with much work to be done on it before publication (he saw it as a likely choice for a volume in Murray's Family Library); the Alhambra tales were in an even worse shape. Irving could get away from

---

[67] Used by permission of The Clifton Waller Barrett Library of the University of Virginia Library. According to a catalogue in WI Miscellany, MS Division, New York Public Library, this letter was advertised for sale by James F. Drake, Inc., 24 West 40th Street, New York, in 1934 (Catalogue 237, p. 30).

[68] On Sept. 1, WI forwarded the entire review to Lockhart. "My object," he said, "has been to be entertaining rather than erudite. I beg you not to lop down this article in your cursed bid of Precaution as you did its predecessors. I have not exceeded the bounds Murray allowed me, and within them you must let me have fair play. The touch of republicanism in the prelude is more for my own sake than for the sake of the author. I am vehemently suspected from the company I keep, and the Tory review in which I occasionally write." He continued good-naturedly, "I wish to god I could be more political in my walks and associates, and could keep from contracting so much personal regard for individuals in this Tory society in which I am so often thrown." Cover letter among the Lockhart Papers, National Library of Scotland. Included in my "WI's Amiable Scotch Friends: Three Unpublished Letters to the John Gibson Lockharts," *Studies in Scottish Literature,* IV (Oct. 1966), 103.

the work of the Legation by resigning, but he could escape the sweet demands of London society only by leaving town. On September 28 he had dinner with the Lockharts, seeing for the last time Sir Walter Scott, and, as preparation for his extended sojourn away from London, took himself to 50 Albemarle Street the next afternoon to talk business with the "Emperor of the West."

Completely absorbed in his own plans, Irving did not understand that Murray's pleasant social front had been a veneer for several months as he watched the trade dwindle in the face of the political unrest with its accompanying economic hazards. His health and disposition had remained stable, though delicately balanced on the edge of a precipice. Lockhart had grumbled to Milman that he no longer had influence with the publisher, rather ungenerously attributing the situation to Murray's physical disability, which the editor diagnosed as gout, the result of his high living.[69] On September 16, aware of the decline in the sales of the *Quarterly Review*, Lockhart suggested that Murray "may find it necessary to lower the scale of remuneration to editor as well as author, and I am quite willing to abide by your decision in the matter."[70] The publisher, rather characteristically, refused to consider the idea.

If he would not cut down the expenses of the *Review*, Murray must make adjustments in other areas of his business. The list of book titles scheduled to appear under his imprint was reduced to three major undertakings: the beginning of a proposed fourteen-volume edition of Byron's complete writings, a six-volume collection of Gifford's essays, and a continuation of the Family Library.[71] For a time he toyed with the idea of publishing a manuscript entitled *Sartor Resartus*, the work of one Thomas Carlyle, presented with high recommendations by Francis Jeffrey. In a letter of September 19, Carlyle plied Murray with compliments:

I had heard you described as a man of honour, frankness, and even

[69] Letter dated 1830 in Murray Archives.
[70] Smiles, II, 377.
[71] *The Athenaeum*, Nov. 5, 1831, p. 723.

generosity, and knew you to have the best and widest connections; on which grounds, I might well say, and can still well say, that a transaction with you would please me better than a similar one with any other member of the Trade.[72]

But the negotiations collapsed with some bitterness on the parts of both men, Carlyle taking his manuscript and returning to Craigenputtock to write the editor of the *Edinburgh Review* that "the Charon of Albemarle Street durst not risk it." [73]

So, though things were tight, visitors at 50 Albemarle Street sensed neither panic nor despondency in the faces of the professionals there. Thomas Frognall Dibdin could report after personally surveying the scene that, by virtue of Murray's careful planning, "the great *Family* [Library] man in Europe" was resting safely "surrounded by an extensive circle of little ones." [74] Irving, with two contributions already a part of Murray's Family Library, seemed to be in a safe position in Murray's "extensive circle."

[72] Smiles, II, 353.
[73] *Ibid.*, 355.
[74] *Bibliophobia* (London: H. Bohn, 1832), p. 31.

CHAPTER SIX

ESTRANGEMENT AND RECONCILIATION

Wednesday, September 28, 1831

John Murray II was in another part of the building. Irving, self-consciously resting his folded hands on the brass head of his new cane, exchanged civil remarks with Dundas, the clerk who was working over a pile of Murray's correspondence at a table set up by the fireplace. When the publisher did appear, it was evident that he was experiencing more pain than usual in walking. After he stiffly lowered himself into a chair, he asked about Sir Walter Scott, indicating that a note from Lockhart had told him of the supper party the previous night. When Irving reported on Scott's sad mental and physical deterioration, Murray shook his head, a pained expression on his face, as he adjusted his feet on a low stool.

To other matters Irving abruptly changed the conversation. Having resigned from his responsibilities at the Legation, he planned to devote full time to polishing the two manuscripts about which he had talked with Murray on several occasions. The first, a biography of Mahomet, he described as in such an advanced state of preparation as to be ready for the printer in a few days' time. This excellent title for the Family Library, Irving would let Murray have for 500 guineas. Aside from a slight tightening of the mouth, the publisher showed no reaction to the offer but continued to listen to the author.

The second work, a sort of "Spanish sketch book" (Irving accentuated the last two words and was rewarded by the flicker of a smile from Murray) would require considerable effort, but it would be ready for publication before the end of the year. For this—Irving hesitated—probably because of the scope and nature of the work, he would have to have 1,000 guineas. The only sound came from the amanuensis who, overhearing Irving's figure, broke his quill.

Murray gazed hard at the American. He opened his mouth as though to speak, but instead turned his head to watch the copyist busily sharpening the quill.

When Murray did speak, he was the charming publisher of old —in conference with an author aspiring to publication. He hoped, he said, to continue as Irving's British publisher. Both works interested him greatly. Another Sketch Book *would be most welcome on his list—a dose of medicine for the sluggish book trade. He said, "Let me see the manuscripts. . . ."*

Irving broke in, explaining his traveling intentions and the necessity for definite publication arrangements at this time.

Murray hesitated, a deep frown on his face. The American repeated his promise to get the manuscript of Mahomet, *at least, to Albemarle Street within a matter of days. The publisher grimaced, removed his feet from the stool. "Very well, very well," Murray's voice rose as he lifted himself lamely to a standing position.*

Irving's face showed relief: it was clear that he considered his business satisfactorily concluded, but he found it necessary to repeat his plea for immediate publication plans. Murray's every move, however, indicated that he wished, for whatever reason, the interview to end without further discussion. Clutching his unaccustomed cane, Irving made ready for his departure. "I'll be anxious to get this matter settled," he admonished the shaky man, "for I am firm in my resolve to return to the United States as quickly as I can get these books through the press."

"Yes, I'll write you!" Murray replied, as Dundas accompanied Irving to the front door.

Sources for Vignette

MacFarlane, p. 100; PMI, II, *passim;* STW, II, *passim;* Smiles, II, *passim.*

Back at 8 Argyll Street, Irving wrote to Colonel Aspinwall, apprising him of the situation: "I have made a bargain with the Murray for a brace of volumes I am preparing for the press, but will get you to call on him and arrange the terms of payment &c. &c. and the legal writings &c. when I have my batch of MS. ready for delivery."[1] On October 4, from the Van Warts' in Birmingham, Irving dispatched twenty-one chapters of *Mahomet* to Aspinwall for delivery to the publisher.[2] At the same time, he addressed a letter to Murray.

54. To John Murray II [3]

Birmingham, Oct. 4th 1831.

My dear Sir,

In the hurry of leaving town I had not time to make a written agreement for the works about which we bargained. I have therefore requested my friend & agent Col. Aspinwall to call upon you and arrange in my name the terms of payment, and reduce the whole to writing. In our conversation you will recollect it was agreed that I should receive 500 gs for the Legendary Life of Mahomet, and 1000 gs for the miscellaneous volume. Each work to be a volume containing about as much as a volume of the Conquest of Granada. Col. Aspinwall will hand you the first 21 chapters of Mahomet. There will be about 70 chapters in all and the rest will be forwarded as fast as you can need them. I will thank you to have the work put to press as soon as possible and furnish proof in slips, as I may wish

[1] Sept. 29, 1831. Princeton University Library.
[2] Huntington.
[3] Postmarked in Birmingham, Oct. 5, and again in London, Oct. 6, 1831. At Murray's someone wrote, using red ink, "Mahomet" on the back of the sheet. Watermarked "Gater 1828."

to make occasional alteration & additions. I will commence sending MS. of the miscellaneous volume shortly, so that both works may be out before Christmas.

My address is to the care of Henry Van Wart Esqr, Birmingham.

I am my dear Sir
Yours very truly,
Washington Irving.

On October 22, in Sheffield visiting his nephew Irving Van Wart,[4] Irving wrote to Aspinwall, enclosing a letter for Murray. He said to Aspinwall:

I enclose a letter for him [Murray], which I think will rouse him, if he is desirous of having the works. . . . The Mahomet is entirely ready, and the other I can furnish as fast as it could be wanted. . . . If Murray bargains for the Mahomet he must pay the whole by the end of the coming year. The fact is Mr Murray's irregular mode of conducting business has always been an annoyance to me, and of late he has been wanting in consideration and punctuality in money matters. He never paid me a farthing (for the author) for the year in Spain, nor for my trouble in correcting it for publication & while going through the press—nor the review I wrote for it, nor for a review I subsequently wrote on Mr Wheaton's work. —and I know that he is behindhand with other persons. I am not in a very favorable mood therefore to put up with any more of his delays and negligencies, and would be quite willing to deal with some other bookseller who is a mere man of business. [He added as a postscript:] Seal the letter to Murray & put it in the twopenny post.[5]

The Colonel apparently delivered the letter personally to 50 Albemarle Street hoping to use it as a means of getting to see Murray. At any rate, Irving's ultimatum to the publisher bears

---

[4] WI's twenty-four-year-old nephew was a merchant in partnership with a man named Naylor. *History and General Directory of the Borough of Sheffield*, comp. William White (Sheffield: Robert Leader, 1833), pp. 276, 335.

[5] Used by permission of The Clifton Waller Barrett Library of the University of Virginia Library. Postmarked in Sheffield on Oct. 22, in London on Oct. 24. Col. Aspinwall made a neat copy of WI's letter to JMII on the inside folds of the second (cover) sheet.

no postal markings, and Aspinwall and the publisher apparently never discussed this matter.

55. To John Murray II

Sheffield, Oct. 22d 1831.

Dear Sir,

I wrote to you between two and three weeks since wishing the arrangement to be closed with my agent Col. Aspinwall about the publication of the two works which I have ready for the press and which for various urgent reasons I wish to have published immediately. I have since authorized Col. Aspinwall to make further propositions to you concerning one of these works. I find however by a letter from him dated the 21st that he has not been able to see you on the business. As this delay is excessively annoying to me and impedes all my plans and movements, and as it is very probable that you may not be desirous of publishing at this moment, I am perfectly willing that what has passed between us on the subject should be considered as null and void, and in such case will thank you to return to Col. Aspinwall the MS. already left with you. Should you still be disposed however to publish that work (Mahomet) and to put it to press forthwith it is at your service at the price agreed upon (though it rather exceeds the quantity of MS. I mentioned). As to the other work, I do not think there is any likelihood of your being able to get it out as early as I wish. I trust, therefore, you will not take it amiss if I seek some other person or mode to publish it. Nothing but the peculiar circumstances which hurry me at this time would make me quit my usual channel; but time is every thing with me just now.

I am my dear Sir
Very truly yours,
Washington Irving.

Never had Irving so miscalculated. John Murray was having too many other problems to mince words or worry about the feelings of the fretting American in the English Midlands. His reply deserves to be quoted fully.[6]

6 From the file copy in Murray Archives.

Albemarle Street
Oct. 25. 1831.

My dear Sir,

My reply was "Yes, I'll write to you," and the cause of my not having done so earlier, is one for which I am sure you will make allowances. You told me upon our former negociations, and you repeated it recently, that you would not suffer me to be a loser by any of your Works; and the state of matters in this respect, I am exceedingly unwilling because it is contrary to my nature to submit to you, and in doing so at length, you will I am sure do me the justice to believe that I have no other expectations than those which are founded upon your own good feelings. The publication of Columbus cost me. Paper—Print—Advertising—Author £5,700 and it has produced but £4,700—Grenada cost £3,073 and its sale has produced but £1,830, making my gross loss of £2,250.—I have thought it better to communicate with yourself direct, than through the medium of Mr. Aspinwall.—

Let me have time to read the two new MSS—and then we shall not differ I think about terms.

With sincere regard,
I remain,
My Dear Sir
faithfully yours,
(signed) John Murray

Washington Irving Esqr
Henry Van Ward [Wart] Esqr
Birmingham

(Copy Extract)[7]

"Granada &c.
"May 9. 1829

"At any rate, I should like hereafter to make our arrangements in such manner that you may be relieved from these apprehensions of loss, and from the necessity of recurring to any management of the press to aid the publication of a work of mine."—
To John Murray Esqr.

The portly American was certainly stunned but in no way

---

[7] See above, Letter 31.

cowed by Murray's letter, which he received at Barlborough Hall, the Derbyshire home of the Rev. Mr. Reaston Rodes.[8] The usually amiable and mild-mannered guest must have been livid. In such a mood no doubt he unburdened his mind to his sympathetic host, beginning with the *Sketch Book* experience of 1819–1820. It is easy to see Irving as he brooded overnight, tossing sleeplessly in his great bed. In the morning, perhaps before the principals of the household were astir, Irving had settled in the easy light of the window to write a letter.

56. To John Murray II

Barlborough Hall, Chesterfield
Oct. 29th 1831.

My dear Sir,

Your letter of the 25th did not reach me until last evening. When I left town I supposed the terms for my two new works agreed upon. I had accepted your offer of 500 guineas for "Mahomet" & you had assented to my demand for 1000 guineas for the miscellaneous volume of Spanish Tales and Sketches. The works were to be printed as fast as I should furnish the MS. and proof on slips to be sent to me for correction. All dispatch was to be used, as I intimated that time was precious with me. Nothing apparently remained to be settled but the dates of payment, and as you did not appear prepared on that point on my leaving town I left it to be adjusted by my friend & general agent Col. Aspinwall.

I accordingly sent you a portion of the MS. of Mahomet, anticipating a prompt return of proof sheets. By your letter of the 25th however I find you do not consider any arrangement existing between us. You now say "let me have time to read the new MSS. & then we shall not differ I think about the terms." No stipulation of the kind was ever hinted at when we made our bargain; and depending on the indulgence to be given me of having my works printed on slips, I left my manuscripts in the rough intend-

---

[8] Cornelius Heathcote Reaston (1792–1844) inherited the Barlborough Hall estate from his uncle in 1825, taking at that time the name of his uncle, Rodes. Barlborough Hall is minutely described in *The History and Gazetteer of the County of Derby* . . ., ed. Thomas Noble (Derby: Henry Mozley & Sons, 1833), Pt. I, Vol. II, 89–90. In a letter to one of his sisters, WI declared that Barlborough "might have stood for a model" of Bracebridge Hall. PMI, II, 460–61.

ing to make final corrections in the proof sheets. I could not prepare them for critical examination without a loss of time that
would alter all my plans. As it is the delay that has already occurred will oblige me to change my scheme of publication.

I do not know whether you intend the statement you give of
loss on two of my works as your reason for departing from the
present arrangement, but on that point I will observe that Columbus and the Conquest of Granada are copy right works, the sales
of which cannot be considered as at an end; especially as they are
on historical subjects, which, though they may not have the immediate sale of works of fiction, are more permanent in their circulation. Neither do you take into your estimate the abridgement
of Columbus, for which I charged you nothing, which has already
gone to two editions and must remain, from the nature of the subject & the size of the volume, a saleable book. Neither do you recollect that I have just put into your hands the "Year in Spain"
which I corrected and improved with great care & trouble and
conducted it through the press, so as to ensure it a very successful
run & yourself very handsome returns. Nor have you recollected
that I have furnished you with two copious articles for your review; for all which productions and labours I have received nothing.[9] All these and other items I might mention tell something
against the estimate you make of loss upon two works that are
yet but young in existence. The miscellaneous work I am now preparing will probably awaken new interest respecting the Conquest
of Granada, as will other writings that I have in preparation. If
you would give me & my works a fair chance, I have no doubt you
would find both of us to work well in the long run, but you must
not always expect to clear the price of a farm by the first year's
crop.

As I observed before, the delay in the publication of these works
obliges me to alter my plans respecting them. I wished to hurry

[9] WI had been paid for the review of the *Chronicle* (see letter 35 and WI to
Aspinwall, Aug. 3, 1830. MS Division, New York Public Library). He was not
paid, however, for the review of Slidell's book or for the piece on Henry
Wheaton's *A History of the Northman*, which was never used by Murray.
"This last article, though written for the *Quarterly Review*," WI explained to
PMI years later, "did not appear in that publication, but was published in the
North American Review." PMI, III, 267. Perhaps this letter caused JMII to direct
Lockhart to return the MS to WI.

them at once into print, that I might leave England. I now post-
pone for a time the publication of Mahomet, and shall confine myself for the present to getting the miscellaneous work ready for
the press, so as to be out by Christmas. It will either be in one
volume, the size of those of the Conquest of Granada or I may
extend it to two light volumes of about 320 pages each, the pages
the size of those of the Sketch Book. My price will be 1000 guineas
if in one volume and 1600 guineas if in two. The payment to be
made in bills each for a quarter of the amount at six, nine, twelve
& fifteen months dating from the first of January next. If on these
terms you are disposed to purchase the work I shall be happy to
hear from you. Our mutual friend Mr Lockhart may arrange for
matter between us, as I have the utmost confidence in his judgement and his good taste. In the mean time I will thank you to seal
up the MS. of Mahomet and send it, addressed to me, to the
Legation of the U.S., Stratford Place, where any letters addressed
to me will be promptly forwarded.[10]

> I am my dear Sir,
> Very truly yours,
> Washington Irving.

This exchange of letters, the climax to their uneasy business
relationship, characterizes these two men. That Murray, in his
developing pique, chose to accuse Irving of being a financial drag
is unfortunate because the American could easily enough have
annihilated this suggestion—though the idea would be perpetuated
by virtually every Murray biographer in later years.[11] Murray's
real objection could have been that in those hard times in the book
trade Irving seemed unrealistic in his demands as the quality
of his work waned from title to title. The fragmentary parcel
he called *Mahomet* was an insult to Murray. Perhaps Murray
had not even looked at it; this could account for the amazing

---

10 Van Buren had leased this luxurious building at the cost of $2,500. Denis
Tilden Lynch, *An Epoch and a Man: Martin Van Buren and His Times* (New
York: Horace Liveright, 1929), p. 347.

11 James Grant characteristically argued in 1841 that WI's *Columbus* was one
of JMII's three great failures, the other two being *The Representative* and
Napier's *History of the Peninsular War*. He also erroneously said that JMII paid
£4,000 for *Columbus* (II, 19, 22–23).

restraint of the publisher's letter, for after all temper was one of Murray's personal trademarks. The second paragraph of Murray's letter (which Irving in his fit of temper probably didn't bother to try to understand) clearly left the door open, and, remembering Murray's recent experiences in which Irving sold manuscripts still in his head, the reader cannot avoid sympathizing with the publisher. A decade earlier Murray had offered to take original manuscripts from the American sight unseen, but the 1830's was a different era. Not even Geoffrey Crayon need think that twenty-one hastily scribbled chapters (of a proposed seventy) and the promise of a collection of Spanish tales were sufficient evidence to cause the "Emperor of the West" to scramble for his check book. Instead, he asked of Irving the impossible. He wanted to see what he was buying, but Irving couldn't show it to him: it wasn't written yet.

By November 1 Irving was back in London, working fitfully on the Spanish miscellany (*Mahomet* had gone back into storage in his much-traveled trunks) and conferring busily with his friends about the injustices of 50 Albemarle Street. Murray, for his part, made no secret of the way he felt about Irving. Moore agreed with everything Irving could say against Murray,[12] adding illustrative stories from his own experience, but Benjamin Disraeli would make sport of the author and approve of the publisher.[13] Samuel Rogers would nod in agreement with the American's bitter words at his breakfast table,[14] but in the Albemarle

[12] This division, like the others in London society, tended to follow generally political party lines. Whig Moore's ambivalent relationship with JMII had left him with personal grudges that he never failed to exhibit at any opportunity in his journals and—we can suppose—in private conversation. See Moore's *Memoirs*, VI, 236 *et passim*.

[13] "Washington Irving's works have been read of late only by the author, who is daily more enamoured of these heavy tomes. He demanded for the new one a large price. Murray murmured. Irving talked of posterity and the badness of public taste, and Murray said that the authors who wrote for posterity must publish on their own account." *Lord Beaconsfield's Correspondence with His Sister, 1832–1852* (London: JM, 1886), p. 6.

[14] Samuel Rogers, the scion of Holland House's Whig circle, had on more than one occasion inveighed against JMII's treatment of his authors. See the bitterly anti-Murray account of Rogers' activities on behalf of Luttrell's *Crockford House* in *The Age*, March 25, 1827. Rogers also clashed with JMII over

Street drawing room John Wilson Croker could dismiss with a sneer (not worth the effort he had expended on Keats) the "soap and water bubble" writer.[15]

To the frayed fabric of London society, worn threadbare by the political strains of the Reform Bill and the pressure of fear occasioned by the cholera epidemic creeping from the North, the Irving-Murray split was simply another rent in the design, which at this very moment had been drastically torn by the scandal of Lady Blessington's step-daughter, who abandoned her husband, the exotic Count D'Orsay, to the comfort of her ladyship's care.[16] One searches in vain for a season in London (short of civil war) when society presented such a condition of unrest. *The Athenaeum* heard with its keen ears of Irving's plans and protests and declared in its "Weekly Gossip" that it did not wonder that he

> is said to be on the point of sailing to America, and we think he is right: extinction of literature, and depression of art, riots and bloodshed, and finally the Cholera in Sunderland, shut up from escape by sea, with full liberty to march whither it pleases by land, are, on the whole, no cheering prospects.[17]

The Christmas of 1831 Irving spent at Barlborough Hall, where he introduced Van Buren to an old-fashioned English Yuletide. Early in 1832 he moved on to Newstead Abbey, Byron's ancestral home.[18] There he visited for several days as the guest of the new owner, continuing to rail against Murray. To Leslie he wrote:

> I am determined to have nothing more to do with him [Murray].

---

playwright C. R. Maturin and William Wordsworth (Roberts, *Samuel Rogers and His Circle*, pp. 148, 168).

15 Of all the frequenters of JMII's drawing room, Croker was the only one who seems never to have entertained a pleasant thought concerning WI. See Myron F. Brightfield, *John Wilson Croker* (Berkeley: University of California Press, 1940), p. 352. In the Murray Archives, a letter from Croker to JMII, Jan. 18, (or June) 1825, is decidedly unappreciative of WI and his writings.

16 See Chap. VII, "The Autumn of 1831" in Sadleir, *Blessington-D'Orsay: A Masquerade*, pp. 157–91.

17 Nov. 12, 1831, pp. 740–41.

18 WI told of this visit to *Abbotsford, and Newstead Abbey*, published in 1835.

He is either inexcusably remiss or very deficient in good faith in business—and either is enough to unfit him for a publisher.[19]

Then from the poet's historic home, he made a point of dispatching a letter to the address of the poet's official publisher.

57. To John Murray III

Newstead Abbey, Jany 21st 1832.

My dear John,

Before leaving town about six weeks since I sent to your father a portion of the proof sheets of a work on Mechanicks, by Professor Renwick of N. York, which your father agreed early last summer, to republish.[20] Not having heard from him since on the subject I presume he does not intend to republish it. May I request that favor[21] of you, therefore, to deliver the proofsheets to the bearer, that I may, if possible, prevent the interest of Professor Renwick from being sacrificed by this delay.

I will thank you at the same time to give the bearer the sketch in Indian ink of one of the walls of the Alhambra, which I left with your father last autumn.

Very truly yours,
Washington Irving.

Within a week Irving was back in London, where he found himself in a rather embarrassing situation. Among the American literati the image of Irving as a friend and cohort of Murray's was widespread. This was an idea that Irving had been building and fostering for most of the past fifteen years. Irving naturally (as these letters have shown) had been called upon by American authors to intercede on their behalf with Murray. Unaware of any discord between the publisher and the author, America's leading poet, William Cullen Bryant, sent a copy of the American edition of his collected poems to John Murray, hoping that he would contract with Irving to bring out an English edition. On December 29, 1831, the poet wrote to Irving:

[19] Jan. [1832], in WI Miscellany, MS Division, New York Public Library.
[20] *The Elements of Mechanics* was published in Philadelphia by Carey & Lea in 1832. Apparently there was no British edition.
[21] It is amusing to notice that WI had now assumed the American spelling.

I have taken the liberty, which I hope you will pardon a countryman of yours, who relies on the known kindness of your disposition to plead his excuse, of referring him [Murray] to you. . . .
May I ask of you the favor to write to Mr. Murray on the subject
as soon as you receive this? . . . I should be glad to receive something for the work, but if he does not think it worth his while to
give anything, I had rather that he should take it for nothing, than
that it should not be published by a respectable bookseller.[22]

Irving had just given up the Murray imprint; now Bryant reminded him of something which previously had been a motivat-
ing factor in his dealings with the publisher: Murray's imprint
could be of more value than money.

In a letter, not preserved in the Murray Archives, Irving ad-
vocated Bryant's cause to John Murray II. His reply from John
Murray III left little hope for such a venture.[23] Finally, by agreeing "to edit them, and write a dedication" for the poems, Irving
was able to secure a publisher, John Andrews, described by
Pierre M. Irving as "a fashionable bookseller." [24]

As the southward-moving cholera epidemic reached London,
Irving finished *The Alhambra* which, by March 23, Colonel
Aspinwall had sold to the newly formed firm of Colburn and
Bentley for one thousand guineas. Ignoring the "infectious diar-
rhea" all around him, Irving abandoned himself to enjoying Lon-
don—get-togethers with the "Lads," breakfasts with Samuel
Rogers, an excursion with Moore, the theater with Frank Mills.
But he did not include John Murray II of 50 Albemarle Street.

On April 2, Irving left London by coach for Southampton.
From there he crossed the channel to visit Peter in Havre, finally
leaving France aboard the packet *Havre* on April 12.[25] The west-

22 PMI, II, 472.
23 Jan. 30, 1832. Yale University Library.
24 PMI, II, 474. The volume was dedicated to Samuel Rogers.
25 WI in mid-Atlantic, *The Age* (quoting *The Globe*), on April 22, p. 130,
offered him a compliment, perhaps intending at the same time to twist Murray's
nose. It suggested that WI's *Sketch Book* had "equalled, if not surpassed" the
sales of Scott and Byron, and that "from the new 'Sketch Book' which is forthcoming from the same author, the publishers calculate, allowing for the altered
state of the times, a sale of not less than 20,000."

ward journey was noteworthy for at least one reason. He met two adventurers who were soon figuring in his literary endeavors: English traveler Joseph Latrobe and a young Swiss entrusted to his care, Count de Pourtales. The two young men were planning to make a tour of the North American West.

Washington Irving touched American soil after an absence of seventeen years. There was a difference now. The young man of 1815, uncelebrated except in his immediate locality, had sailed from the same port; he returned just less than an international hero. There were friendly parties, printed welcomes, and, on May 30, a public dinner (at which Newton, in the United States to take a wife, sat reassuringly close by him).

Trips to Washington, Boston, and upper New York State filled Irving's summer; his mind was filled with a desire to satisfy the demands of his American public, which wanted a book from him on native material. On September 2, 1832, he set out from Cincinnati, Ohio, in the company of Latrobe, Pourtales, and a government commissioner, Henry Leavitt Ellsworth. Their destination was Arkansas, where Ellsworth was supposed to attend a meeting of various Indian tribes.

It was a new experience for Irving. The rigors of the trip were demanding and the author did not have the stamina of a young man. Adding to his problems was the fact that his traveling companions turned out to be something less than kindred spirits. Twenty-one-year-old Pourtales, sent to America to sow his wild oats, set about seducing every Indian maiden who crossed his pathway. Soon, to the author's mortification, the immoral reputation of "the Irving party"—for such the group had been dubbed by the journalists—spread into even the remote prairie settlements. Once, Irving ordered the Swiss to leave the camp. He went, followed by Latrobe, but both men soon returned and were accepted back into the party. By the middle of November, Irving had had his fill of frontier life.

By way of Louisiana, Georgia, Virginia, and the District of Columbia, Irving returned to New York, his notebooks primed for action. Working on his new project, he was often distracted by connections from his British years. In 1833 he saw lovely Fanny Kemble, the actress daughter of Charles, who declared the sight of him was like seeing "a bit of home, England." [26] Following in Irving's transatlantic wake, Leslie settled his family at West Point, where he took the Professorship of Design, but they remained there only a few months, forsaking the culturally barren Military Academy to return to the society of London and the British Academy.[27] Disquieting stories came from England concerning Newton, who had returned with his American wife to London and suffered a mental breakdown which resulted in his confinement in a mental institution near Regent's Park and, within months, his death.[28]

Rumors persisted that Murray was having financial troubles, the main evidence being that he had sold the entire stock of his Family Library, amounting to some 100,000 volumes, to Tegg, the remainders man, for one shilling each.[29] But Irving worked on, trying to produce a book that would satisfy his American public. The result was by November 1834 *A Tour on the Prairies*. To this he added—in an attempt to strengthen by variety —two volumes, presenting the whole as *The Crayon Miscellany*. The second was *Abbotsford, and Newstead Abbey*, based on his notebooks of 1817 and 1831–1832; the third was *Legends of the Conquest of Spain*, pulled in bits and pieces from his trunks.

Would these volumes have an English publisher? Aspinwall might approach John Murray, Irving suggested. He wanted five

[26] Frances Ann Kemble, *Record of a Girlhood* (London: Richard Bentley & Son, 1878), III, 279.

[27] Leslie, I, 125.

[28] *Ibid.*, 137–39.

[29] Scott Bennett, "The Family Library, 1825–1835: The Uses of Literacy in a Revolutionary Age" (unpublished Ph.D. thesis, Indiana University, 1967), provides a concise history of the Family Library. It failed, he said, sometime in the late summer or early fall of 1832, though several numbers were issued after that time. A reprint of WI's *SB* appeared as Vols. XXXIX and XL in Jan. 1834. (Records of A. & R. Spottiswoode [B. Mus. MSS. 48819, ff. 101, 102–103, 106] indicate that JMII had 5,500 copies in two printings, Dec. 1833.) On Dec. 4, 1834, JMII wrote to Lockhart indicating that he was completing his business with Tegg. The financial aspects of the transactions remain cloudy. Bennett concluded, "the Library was sold with minimal loss or marginal profit, and by the new year Murray and Lockhart were free of it" (p. 222).

hundred guineas, "but," he added, "make such bargain as you can." [30]

Though Irving did not know it, this was an auspicious time for a reconciliation. Improved in both health and finances, Murray was mending his personal and business tears of recent years. In a letter to author H. H. Milman, who had formerly been out of Murray's good graces, Lockhart commented on the publisher.

> I am rejoiced that Emperor John & you are at one again. Nobody means better than he habitually does but he is liable to strange starts & flows of something that I won't call meanness. Rogers has a Yankee name for it *squigglishness*. . . . I see he [Murray] is launching . . . grand schemes. [31]

John Murray II was receptive to Irving's advances, perhaps dreaming of involving the old Geoffrey Crayon in one of the elusive "grand schemes" to which Lockhart referred.

When the American Consul replied in the affirmative, Irving was clearly pleased and a bit surprised. "You may tell him [Murray] for me," he wrote Aspinwall, "that I am really delighted to renew my old connections with him, and that it will give me the sincerest pleasure to promote his interests in any way in my power." Then, echoing the words which he had bantered about on the night of his first visit to 50 Albemarle Street: "In fact, from the rapidly growing and improving literature of this country I think I shall be able occasionally to put some good things in his way." [32]

The split was healed. The particulars of the Murray-Aspinwall bargaining can be pieced together from some scattered fragments which have survived. On February 5 Murray agreed to publish *Tour on the Prairies,* paying to Irving two-thirds of the net profit on the work. Aspinwall demurred and finally on March 2 the publisher bought outright the copyright for £400. [33] It was pub-

---

[30] WI to Aspinwall, Feb. 2, 1835. Sunnyside.

[31] Nov. 29, 1834. Murray Archives. This is in a packet of Lockhart-Milman correspondence purchased by Sir John Murray some time ago.

[32] WI to Aspinwall, April 8, 1835. Ella Strong Denison Library, Scripps College, Claremont, Cal.

[33] See Appendix III, items 10 and 11.

lished in London almost a month earlier than in the United States. On April 11, 1835, Washington wrote to Peter:

> I am glad to be once more in dealings with Murray, and am well satisfied with the terms of sale. . . . The price is not so high as I used to get, but there has been a great change in the bookselling trade of late years. The inundation of cheap publication, penny magazines, &c., has brought down the market.[34]

Encouraged by Murray's acceptance of the first volume, Irving instructed Aspinwall to try to get five hundred guineas for *Abbotsford, and Newstead Abbey*. Although this was a much thinner volume than the previous one, it dealt in a personal way with subjects close to 50 Albemarle Street. Lockhart read the manuscript and insisted that Murray must publish it,[35] but the publisher balked at the price. Aspinwall described the final bargain to Irving in this way: "I have agreed with him for £600, payable in the following manner, viz.: £400 at six and nine months after the day of publication, and £200 at six and nine months after the day of publication of a second edition—the first edition to consist of three thousand copies."[36] Irving was well pleased with the agreement, though it appears that he never realized more from it than the payment of £400 for the first edition.[37]

For the hodgepodge *Legends of the Conquest of Spain* Murray held out against Irving's price—five hundred guineas. This was the figure the author quoted to Aspinwall in July 1835, but he had gone on to say that everything should "be done to Mr Murray's satisfaction." Then he added, "It really gives me a great pleasure to be again in business relations with him."[38]

Of the actual bargaining for this work there is little information. Worth noting, however, is Lockhart's evaluation of the author and text, written on August 25.

34 PMI, III, 66.
35 Smiles, II, 261.
36 PMI, III, 70–71.
37 See Appendix III, item 12, and PMI, IV, 410.
38 WI to Aspinwall, July 15, 1835. Barrett Collection, Alderman Library, University of Virginia.

171

I have looked over Irving's *very rough* proofs & am sorry to say I think the whole affair feeble & vapid. Neither learned enough to be the historian, nor imaginative enough to be the poet of the Roderick & Julians he gives matters to us sufficiently familiar in a middle style which seems to me, as in the case of the Conquest of Granada, devoid of any one characteristic worthy of his reputation. Seriously, his mind and taste seem to be weakening in America. Even he can't help writing down I suppose to a scale of intelligence miserably below that of the poor old world.[39]

Again Murray disregarded his advisors concerning Irving's writings. On December 15, 1835, he registered the title under his imprint in the official book at Stationers' Hall.[40] From the British publisher Irving realized £100 on this, the weakest of the three volumes of the *Miscellanies*.[41]

So John Murray was once again the publisher of Geoffrey Crayon. The American writer considered the revived association both profitable and desirable. What of the British publisher? Obviously, Irving's friends in London congratulated Murray on the wisdom of his purchases.[42] Scott's family and friends were brought to tears by the memories excited by the second volume,[43] and the British reviewers, if they could not always loudly applaud the individual volumes, could find no reason to condemn them.[44] These titles "by the AUTHOR of the 'SKETCH BOOK'" (that was still a magic phrase) John Murray advertised prominently on a full-page advertisement of suggestions of "Literary Presents" in the Christmas issue of *The Athenaeum*, December 19, 1835.[45]

[39] JGL to JMII. Murray Archives.
[40] PMI, III, 76, indicated that "in consequence of an unlucky hiatus in forwarding the proof sheets to London" the volume lost its copyright value for a British publisher. See Appendix V.
[41] PMI, IV, 410.
[42] Cf. Leslie, II, 227–28.
[43] PMI, III, 72.
[44] STW, II, 319–23, considered the reception of these volumes. Concerning the *Legends of the Conquest of Spain*, *The Athenaeum* slyly observed: "we wish the author would do as much for America as he is doing for Spain." Dec. 12, 1835, p. 922.
[45] Also on the list was John T. Irving's *Indian Sketches*, which JM had pub-

In the meantime, Irving continued his customary socializing, but financial thinkers replaced his literary and artistic friends, the supreme example being John Jacob Astor, into whose home Irving had settled in August 1835 to prepare the first biographical study of the tycoon. Astor's library was almost as rich in its holdings of pertinent source material as Rich's Madrid collection had been for Irving's purposes in 1826. On February 14, 1836, he finished *Astoria*.

58. *To John Murray III*[46]

New York, Feb. 24th 1836.

My dear Sir,

I have read your letter of Decr 20 and am glad to find that the booksellers orders for the Legends of Spain have encouraged you to publish a larger number than had been at first intended. I shall send you before long a work in two volumes (moderate octavo) which I trust will prove interesting. It relates to this country and contains much picturing of life in the wilderness, in portraying which I have had access to journals as well as have been benefited by oral accounts of our hardy traders beyond the Rocky Mountains.[47]

I find you did not undertake Slidell's American in England, and in fact I hardly supposed you would so do from the tenor of some part of his work.[48] He has recently put to press another work, however, of which you ought to be the publisher. It is called "Spain Revisited" and contains an account of his journey to Madrid and back again when he went from England. I have just read it in proof sheets. It is capital. As minute and graphic and faithful as his Year in Spain, and, in my mind, superior in some respects. He crosses the Pyrenees and makes his way by hook and by crook, through the belligerent provinces during a time of civil war. It is just the work to be beside the Year in Spain and to complete the picturing

---

lished with WI's encouragement. The fact that the author was "a nephew of Washington Irving" seems to have added some market value to the work. See *The Athenaeum*, Aug. 1, 1835, p. 588.

46 Marked in London, March 17, 1826.

47 *Astoria, or Anecdotes of an Enterprise beyond the Rocky Mountains.*

48 Slidell's *The American in England* (New York: Harper & Brothers, 1835) did not present a very sympathetic picture of England or English life.

of the Country.[49] I find he has sent the work to a Mr George Wildes, 12 Chester Terrace, Regent's Park,[50] with instructions to dispose of it for him and has pointed out Bentley as one who might undertake it. I talked with Slidell yesterday on the subject and he now wishes you to take it in hand should you feel inclined.

I would advise you to do so by all means. You can send to Mr Wildes, who may not have made arrangements with Bentley, as the latter is rather a baffling personage.[51] The work cannot but make a hit.

With kindest remembrances to your father and family I am my dear Sir

Yours very faithfully
Washington Irving.

Murray did not buy *Astoria*. He wisely speculated that Irving's American subject would be of even less interest to the British public than his recent Spanish tales had been. The work went to the adventurous Bentley, who paid £500 for the copyright.[52]

Next, Irving turned to a job which was an outgrowth of the previous work: *The Adventures of Captain Bonneville, U.S.A.*, based on the actual journey of the captain whom he had met in Astor's library. Irving described it to Aspinwall:

It relates to the Rocky Mountains and shows up scenes of wild life among trappers, trader[s] and Indian banditti, of which the world

[49] The Harpers published the two-volume *Spain Revisited* and Slidell's own revision of *A Year in Spain* in 1836.

[50] Probably this was the home address of the merchant head of George Wildes & Co., 19 Coleman Street. *Pigot & Co.'s London . . . Commercial Directory for 1836*, p. 184.

[51] Richard Bentley had freed himself from the uncomfortable yoke of his partnership with Colburn in Sept. 1832. Of the two men, Bentley would seem to have been the more business-like and in no way "baffling" (see Gettmann, pp. 15–27). WI may have had upsetting experiences with the firm in connection with the publication of *The Alhambra*, or perhaps this was a gesture from WI, intending to imply Bentley's inferiority to Murray.

Spain Revisited was published by Bentley on March 12, 1836, which, the reader will note, was five days prior to the arrival of this letter in London. Letter from Professor Royal Gettmann, Feb. 16, 1966.

[52] PMI, IV, 410. Gettmann, p. 190, suggests that this book made "an unexpected profit" because the title was changed to one "which if it did not actually invite the public to think it was a romance, certainly did not inform them that it was a dull book of travels."

174

has little idea. . . . It is full of adventure, description, and stirring incident; with occasional passages of humour.[53]

Again—for the same reason—Murray declined Aspinwall's offer, and Bentley accepted the challenge, paying £900.[54]

This was Irving's first book written at Sunnyside, the house he had bought in 1835 and had been remodeling to be a home for himself, for Peter, whose health had finally enabled him to make the long sea voyage back home, and for other members of the family who needed a haven. Here he received personal friends and literary pilgrims for the remainder of his life. In literary history, as surely as 50 Albemarle Street means John Murray II, Sunnyside means Washington Irving.[55]

Irving visited New York City frequently, but he hurried back to Sunnyside to Peter and to his nieces, who were becoming for him a close family such as he had not previously known. Offered the position of Secretary of the Navy in the Cabinet of President Van Buren, Irving declined on April 23, 1838, in the face of persuasive arguments from political friends. He chose the security of his family and Sunnyside, though the tight circle was soon to be broken by Peter's death on June 27, 1838.

The expenses of Sunnyside were not small. It was a generous household and the several nieces (at times as many as six) were largely dependent on his pocketbook. The depression of 1837 did not spare Irving, and his letters until 1842 rarely failed to mention financial difficulties. A typical lamentation read: "I have to find the ways and means to make both ends meet, and hard it is in these precarious times and with my precarious resources."[56]

---

53 Feb. 9, 1837. New York Historical Society.

54 Bentley lost £400 on this deal. His reader had warned him that he should not pay more than £500 for the "rummagings of his [WI's] portfolio." Gettmann, p. 190.

55 Through the generosity of the late John D. Rockefeller, Jr., Sunnyside was purchased in 1945 from collateral descendants of WI and opened as a historical home of public interest. The Curator, Mr. Joseph T. Butler, has prepared an illustrated booklet, *Sunnyside: Washington Irving's Home* (Tarrytown, N.Y.: Sleepy Hollow Restorations, Inc., 1962), which provides a thorough description to the house.

56 Quoted in STW, II, 95.

In desperation he began to search through his faithful trunks. There was enough material there to give him courage to agree to contribute in 1839 regularly to the *Knickerbocker Magazine*, breaking his earlier resolution to avoid such periodical entanglements.[57]

Irving had no more dealings with 50 Albemarle Street, but on occasions, when an especially close friend announced his intention to visit London, Irving bestirred himself to offer a letter that would introduce the American into the wonders of the Murray drawing room.

59. *To John Murray II*

New York, Oct. 1, 1840.

My dear Sir,

Permit me to present to you my young friend and countryman Mr Charles Bristed,[58] a young gentleman of fortune; grandson of the celebrated Mr John Jacob Astor, founder of Astoria. Mr Bristed visits Europe for the purpose of instruction and the gratification of a liberal curiosity. He has already given evidence of literary talent for which we indulge strong hopes. Any attention you may find it convenient to bestow on him will add to the many obligations of

Yours ever very faithfully,
Washington Irving.

60. *To John Murray II* [59]

New York, April 4th 1842.

My dear Sir,

Permit me to introduce to your acquaintance and recommend to your civilities Mr Henry R. Schoolcraft;[60] a gentleman of celebrity

[57] WI later used most of the *Knickerbocker* essays in *Wolfert's Roost and Other Papers*.

[58] Charles Astor Bristed (1820–1874) was preparing to matriculate at Trinity College, Cambridge, when WI gave him this letter of introduction. This period of his life he described in *Five Years in an English University* (New York: G. P. Putnam, 1852). See also, *DAB*, II, 53–54.

[59] Mailed to 50 Albemarle Street, using a one-penny Victoria stamp.

[60] Henry Rowe Schoolcraft (1793–1864) spent much of his mature life as an explorer and ethnologist among the American Indians. As early as 1821 he had published material relating to these interests. *DAB*, XVI, 457.

in this country, and who, during his residence of many years as Indian agent, among our aboriginal tribes, has made great researches into their manners, customs, traditions, oral tales &c. &c. These he intends to throw into a collective form and publish under the title of *Cyclopedia Indianaeasis*.[61] Any good offices you may find it convenient to render him in the prosecution of his plan and any personal attention, which from his private worth and general intelligence he well merits, will be considered favours done to myself.

Ever my dear Sir with great regard
Yours faithfully,
Washington Irving.

In 1842 Irving was experiencing one of his periodic mental depressions. His favorite niece Sarah Paris had left Sunnyside to marry young Thomas Wentworth Storrow, the little boy the author had known in Paris in the 1820's. The couple established their home in the French capital, and to Mrs. Storrow in Paris Irving often directed his thoughts. Without Sarah's personal encouragement, his financial obligations seemed greater than ever. His literary troves, the trunks, provided no easy solution to his problems, but an unexpected champion did. Through the efforts of Secretary of State Daniel Webster, Washington Irving was appointed Envoy Extraordinary and Minister Plenipotentiary from the United States to the Court of Spain. The position offered financial security for himself and his Sunnyside brood, and it bolstered his international reputation as nothing else could have done. English and Spanish friends were exuberant; even Benjamin Disraeli, now a rising politician, found the appointment one that did honor to all parties concerned.[62]

His staff of three young men—including the son of Henry Brevoort—selected, his official papers in order, his trunks con-

---

[61] Schoolcraft abandoned this pretentious title, but the work was published in six parts (Philadelphia: Lippincott, Grambo & Co., 1851–1857) as *Historical and Statistical Information Respecting the History, Condition, and Prospects of the Indian Tribes of the United States.*

[62] *Harper's Weekly* [Supplement], May 27, 1871, p. 494.

taining unexploited tidbits shipped to Cadiz,[63] Irving sailed for his diplomatic post. His journey was by way of England and France. "It is not too much," Stanley T. Williams wrote, "to say that his sailing on April 10th was [for the United States, at least] the event of the month." [64]

Irving's party landed at Bristol and on May Day entrained for London, where four hours later they prepared to take rooms at Thomas' Hotel, Berkeley Square. On May 3, having paid his respects to Edward Everett, United States Minister to the Court of St. James, and Lord Aberdeen, Victoria's Foreign Minister, Irving called at 50 Albemarle Street.

63 PMI, III, 224.
64 STW, II, 118.

CHAPTER SEVEN

THE LAST YEARS

Tuesday, May 3, 1842

The doorway, at least, was unchanged, Irving could see. The familiar portal must have been a friendly sight in this great city which had undergone so many changes during the ten years since his departure. There was an unseasonable chill in the air which, no doubt, was responsible for the occasional shudder that had shaken his ample frame on his thoughtful walk from Berkeley Square. Aside from Lord Aberdeen he had as yet seen no one who harked back to those Heliconian days of ten to twenty years earlier. For a man of Irving's sensibilities, even a doorway might be charged with emotional impact under such circumstances.

The door opened. The entrance hall, the stairway, finally the drawing room: the world he had stepped from on September 18, 1831, was as he had left it. At a glance he surveyed the room: Byron's portrait was in its accustomed spot over the fireplace; the others, including his own 1820 likeness by Newton, held their usual places on the walls.

The announcement of his arrival brought young John to the drawing room first. The thirty-four-year-old man greeted him cordially, but before they could exchange adequate opening remarks, old John appeared, helped by the faithful butler who had become his constant aid as rheumatism crippled him more and more. His eyes sparkling, John Murray II took Irving's hand and held it firmly, his pleasure at seeing the American obvious. Thus they stood for a moment, the author unable to find words.

179

Mrs. Murray's entrance and her gracious welcome to one of her all-time favorite guests forced the stout American to control his emotions and enter into a conversation.

Old John held the floor with news of the old frequenters of the drawing room: Hallam, Lockhart, Moore, and others. They must, of course, have a reunion. There was a considerable amount of activity to report in the publishing world: the unfortunate prudish vogue had played havoc with the Byron editions, but there were good things to report. Did Irving know that Allan Cunningham was writing a biography of David Wilkie (who had died the previous year), which Murray's planned to publish? Had Irving heard of Murray's new discovery, George Borrow, whose Spanish interests were gaining much attention for him? Listening to the publisher's voice, Irving might have allowed himself to forget that since his last visit he had passed from the ranks of the middle-aged into the role of an exalted senior citizen. Here, it would have been easy for him to brush aside the years because he found the Murrays almost as unchanged as their residence.

Old John was less mobile, but otherwise he seemed to be as loquacious as ever. Young John had developed from a serious young man into a mature figure whose every motion suggested steadfastness and capability, the solid doggedness in his character contrasting with his father's colorful nature. Mrs. Murray was as charming a listener as she had been in 1817.

Finally, Irving had to leave his friends to keep an appointment with Everett, but the Murrays would not let him pass out of the drawing room until they had made definite plans to host a party for him.

Irving stepped briskly into Albemarle Street and strolled toward Piccadilly. The chill of the day probably seemed less severe; indeed, he may have been quite unaware of any sensations of cold. On the corner he passed a "bobby" who gave him a smart salute—if not in recognition, because such a stately figure progressing with such a purposeful gait had to be a personage of some importance.

Sources for Vignette

This scene is based on Trent and Hellman, II, 197, 200; Paston, *At John Murray's, passim;* Marion Lochhead, *Elizabeth Rigby, Lady Eastlake* (London: JM, 1961), *passim;* STW, II, *passim;* A. Edwin, Weather Diary for 1842.

Irving's old London began to open up for him after his visit to 50 Albemarle Street. Wiry Samuel Rogers could not resist embracing his portly figure. Lady Holland was only slightly less excited at seeing him again. Leslie, Lord John Russell, Lockhart, Hallam, Frank Mills, Aspinwall: one by one they managed to see him, bringing along other notables, such as Wordsworth. Twice he was presented to Queen Victoria.[1]

The Murrays' dinner on May 10 brought him face to face with Moore again. "The man of all others I wanted to shake hands with once more,"[2] exclaimed Moore. Lockhart and Leslie sat beside him while Moore exercised his musical magic as of old, bringing the entire assemblage to tears with his sentimental ballads. Over claret Irving was convinced by his friends that he should attend the banquet of the Literary Fund Society the following night.[3] This event proved to be a high point in Irving's professional career. With Prince Albert looking on, the author-ambassador accepted a toast from Sir R. H. Inglis on behalf of American literature.[4] After a journey to see the Van Warts in Birmingham and a short visit to Sulgrave Hall, the English home of George Washington's ancestors, the new United States Minister to Spain took up his course again.

On May 26, Irving reached Paris. His purpose was a reunion

[1] See Trent and Hellman, III, 196–202; PMI, III, 193–203.
[2] Moore, *Memoirs*, VII, 319.
[3] PMI, III, 199–201.
[4] All of the major London papers carried an account of the banquet. A typical description appeared in the *Morning Chronicle*, May 12, 1842, p. 6.

with his niece Sarah, but the diplomatic world had greater plans for him. The United States Minister to France, General Lewis Cass, whirled him through a round of introductions including a pleasant informal audience with the King, whom he had seen crowned in 1830, and other members of the royal family. Here, too, he became acquainted with W. H. L. E. Bulwer, who would appear in 1843 as Victoria's representative to the Court of Isabella II. It was not until July 25 that the new Minister could write to his family and friends that he had arrived at his Spanish destination.

Even if Irving had come to Spain on a private visit, he could have expected a full social schedule, for enough of the Madrid of the 1820's remained to assure him of a familiar welcome and, further, those prominent people who had not known him personally during his earlier visits now knew him as a celebrity and a Hispanophile. Days and nights were busier than he had expected them to be, as the social courtesies of old and new friends competed with the necessary demands of his official life.

He had hoped to work on a biography of George Washington (his trunks contained notes on American research as well as the remains of the historical and literary diggings of almost two decades), but the author's pen was virtually stilled as he slipped without resistance under the romantic spell of political intrigue. The struggle between Maria Christina, the Queen Mother, and General Baldomero Espartero, regent for the child Queen, became a part of his daily life.

On June 27, 1843, Irving wrote to Sarah in Paris: "We are in the midst of plots, conspiracies, and insurrections, and know not what a day may bring forth." [5] As he wrote of his exciting experiences in Spain, the life of John Murray II was coming to an end at 50 Albemarle Street. Murray's death, *The Athenaeum* reported, "was occasioned by general debility and exhaustion, but he had rallied so often that no fears were entertained by his family or his physicians until Monday morning, when all hope

[5] PMI, III, 281.

was at an end." [6] When news of the drawn curtains at the Murray establishment reached Madrid, the American was engulfed in the Spanish civil war with hardly enough time to linger over the obituary notices in the publications arriving at the British Legation or to reminiscence with Bulwer over his memories of Murray. The account in *The Athenaeum*, reprinted in numerous other publications, must have come to his attention, giving the United States Minister, even in his present situation, a great deal of pleasure by the personal associations he drew from it:

> Five hundred anecdotes of the great spirits of his time died with Mr. Murray—enough to make a second Spence, or another Boswell. ... His little back parlour, in Albemarle Street, was a sort of Will's, or Burton's: his "Four-o'clock visitors" embracing the men of wit and repute in London. Few men distinguished in literature, in art, or in science, but have partaken of the hospitalities of Mr. Murray's table. If Tonson had a gallery of portraits,
> With here a Garth and there an Addison,
> so did Mr. Murray; but Tonson's Kit-Kat Club pictures were all *presents*—Mr. Murray's kit-kats were all commissions; commissions to men like Lawrence, Phillips, Hoppner, Newton, Pickersgill, and Wilkie; and portraits, too, of Byron and Scott, Moore and Campbell, Southey and Gifford, Hallam and Lockhart, Washington Irving and Mrs. Somerville—a little gallery in itself of British genius. . . .[7]

In early July, fearing for the safety of the thirteen-year-old Queen Isabella in the besieged city of Madrid, Irving joined forces with the British Minister to attempt to guarantee her safety. She did, in fact, come through the struggle unharmed; Espartero was defeated; and the Cortes declared Isabella of age, thus dispensing with a regent. A sort of stability was thereby achieved and shakily maintained throughout the remainder of Irving's mission. With the young Queen he was a favorite—as he was with much of

---

[6] July 1, 1843, pp. 610–11.
[7] The full notice was included in *Gentleman's Magazine*, N.S. XX (Aug. 1843), 210–12. One notes with interest the inclusion of WI among "British genius."

Madrid society. At times his health was a problem, but any hostess was willing to provide a couch for him to recline upon amid the sparkling gaiety.

He made several private visits to Paris to see Sarah. On the first, in August 1843, his carriage narrowly missed running down an elderly pedestrian, who turned out to be eighty-year-old Samuel Rogers. From then until late November when Irving returned to Madrid, they were together frequently, full of talk about the present and the past—about Moore, about Mills, about Leslie, and about old John Murray, whom they had last seen in a seemingly fit condition, and young John Murray, who was so different from his flamboyant father.

Perhaps Irving's greatest diplomatic service during the years of his mission to Spain was rendered in England rather than on the Iberian Peninsula. Summoned hastily to London late in 1845 by McLane, once again Minister to the Court of St. James, Irving took part in the negotiations of the touchy Oregon boundary dispute over which Great Britain was ready to go to war. It was a hurried trip with little time for personal activities, but Irving took time to call at 50 Albemarle Street—it was his last visit. In the drawing room the portraits were in their usual places; a fire glowed in the grate; widow Murray, herself within the shadow of death, sat on the couch and graciously acknowledged his well-chosen words. With John Murray III he talked about Spain, about Murray's new Home and Colonial Library (inexpensive issues similar to the Family Library) to which *Bracebridge Hall* had recently been added as Volume XI, about his projected life of Washington, and about a prospective title for Murray's list—a book his nieces in the Midlands were working on.[8] The big door with its brass name plate "Mr. Murray" closed behind him. It is not unreasonable to imagine that Irving, with his overdeveloped sense of nostalgia, left 50 Albemarle Street for the last time with a full heart. In 1842 his heart had leaped to find it all unchanged;

8 WI to Rosa Van Wart, Feb. 12, 1846. The John Rylands Library, Manchester, England. The letter is included in my "WI's Literary Midwifery," *Philological Quarterly.*

now it was a different place without the personality of the "Emperor of the West."

Irving left London that day, returning to Madrid only to get the affairs there in order, for his resignation was already on the way to Washington. In the late summer of 1846 he passed swiftly through London, weary and anxious to see his beloved nieces and Sunnyside again. He did not take time to see Leslie and the other "Lads," who had long anticipated a last reunion.

Back at Sunnyside, Irving found life to be as good as he had hoped it would be. He resumed his patriarchal position in American letters. On Irving Societies which sprang up he benevolently bestowed his blessings from afar, but he remained aloof from the demands of public involvement, even declining the presidency of the American Shakespeare Society.[9] The task of every well-traveled gentleman—that of writing letters of introduction to foreign acquaintances for their friends going abroad—frequently claimed a few minutes of his time. It is likely that he penned several such communications to 50 Albemarle Street during this period, though the following note is the only example which has been preserved.

61. To John Murray III

Sunnyside, May 8, 1847.

My dear Sir,

Permit me to recommend to your kind civilities Mr St George T. Campbell,[10] who visits Europe on a tour of health. He is a gentleman of intelligence and worth and nephew to Mr Dallas, the Vice President of the United States. Any attentions you may find it convenience to bestow upon him will be considered as personal favors rendered to myself.

With kind remembrances to your family

Yours ever very faithfully,
Washington Irving.

---

[9] See STW, II, 389, for the unusual honors which came to WI at this phase of his career.

[10] Campbell's obituary notice in the Philadelphia *Evening Bulletin*, March 21, 1874, neatly summed up his life.

Irving was figuratively at the head of his native literature, but he was not without his detractors. Since the British success of *The Sketch Book* and its sequel, with their fond references to England, Irving was never—even in the case of such an American product as *Tour on the Prairies*—free from suspicion of being an Anglophile. After the publication of *Tour on the Prairies* he had been attacked because he used different prefaces for the English and American editions: "One preface for my countrymen, full of *amor patriae* and professions of home feelings, and another for the London market, in which such professions are studiously omitted." [11] Of all the charges directed against him this was one of the most inept. His American preface (dropped after the first edition because it was no longer timely) was intended to serve as a friendly note to his fond American readers who had been demanding an American book from him. The English preface did no more than fulfil the conventional requirement of a preface at the beginning of the volume.

Later, in 1842, after Irving's departure for Spain, the long-brewing chauvinistic animosity had boiled over. The firebrand who provided the necessary heat was the Reverend Mr. Rufus W. Griswold, later to gain infamy as the falsifying biographer of Poe. In a review for *Graham's Lady's and Gentleman's Magazine* of some of Walter Scott's writings, Griswold took the opportunity to cast a shaft at Irving who, he said, had been guilty of "writing laudatory notices of his own works for the reviews" and thus receiving "pay for whitewashing himself." He added, "We do not imagine that . . . there was any great injustice in the self-praise, but certainly Mr. Murray should not have been solicited to pay the 'guinea a page.' " [12]

In the absence of the accused party, Pierre wrote immediately

[11] WI's summation of the accusation, quoted in PMI, III, 106. The preface of the JM ed. alluded to the two Miscellanies to follow and extended the portfolio imagery, in which the British critics took special delight: "It is the intention of the author to give the accumulated contents of his portfolio, as well as the casual lucubrations of his brain, in occasional numbers, published as circumstances may permit" (p. v).

[12] XVI (Oct. 1842), 219.

to Griswold demanding to know his authority. The editor replied that his information was from "A Mr. E——,[13] an English gentleman, with whom his acquaintance was limited to a single interview." [14] The informer had told Griswold that Irving had written reviews of the *Life of Columbus* and *A Chronicle of The Conquest of Granada* for Murray's periodical.

Little effort was required to prove to Griswold that the *Quarterly Review* contained no article on the *Life of Columbus* and that the piece on the latter book was explanatory rather than critical. Griswold "rather ungraciously" retracted his statement, but he remained unimpressed, privately communicating his feelings "that he had strong ground for supposing Mr. Irving to have been a *frequent* contributor to the London Quarterly." [15] Indeed, in view of Irving's highly advertised association with the publisher, Griswold's supposition would seem to be a safe one to individuals not initiated in the more involved aspects of the Irving-Murray relationship.[16]

In 1848 American publisher G. P. Putnam and Irving felt that the time was ripe for a standard edition of his writings. Putnam discussed the venture with John Murray III (the two men had

---

13 With access to all of Griswold's literary remains, his biographer, Joy Bayless (*Rufus Wilmot Griswold* [Nashville: Vanderbilt University Press, 1943], pp. 62–63) was unable to identify "Mr. E."

14 PMI, II, 265.

15 PMI, III, 266. Griswold's retraction consisted of the following comments: "We learn with pleasure, from one who speaks on the subject by authority, that Mr. Irving is guiltless of the imputed self laudation. He did indeed write the article in the London Quarterly on his 'Chronicles of Grenada,' and received for it the sum we mentioned; but, like so many of the modern 'reviews,' it had but very little relation to the work which gave it a title, or to its author." *Graham's Lady's and Gentleman's Magazine*, XVI (Dec. 1842), 344.

16 Griswold further reminded Pierre that the *QR*, "more than any other [periodical] in Europe, was distinguished for its unprincipled hostility to the United States" (III, 266). Writing the biography of his uncle approximately twenty years later, in the second volume Pierre anticipated Griswold's statement to appear in the third volume: He justified WI's contributions of 1830–1831 to the *QR* on the grounds that Gifford had been responsible for the early hostility of the *QR* to the U.S. and he was "now dead" (II, 450). Pierre was, no doubt, echoing the words he had heard from the late WI—a sad turn when one realizes that the last words Gifford wrote for the *QR* may have been his farewell salute to WI, March 1825, p. 487.

been friends since the late thirties, when Putnam was in London where his publishing house had a branch office until 1847 [17]), but even if the Englishman had wished to associate himself with the full venture, the fact that Bentley held some of the Irving copyrights for British publication would have excluded him. On July 26, 1848, Irving signed a contract with Putnam, agreeing to supervise a collected revised edition of his work, to which would be added several new titles. By the end of the summer of 1850 all of Irving's old works (excepting the *Oldstyle Letters* and *Salmagundi*) had been reissued to an American public which had been reawakened by the accompanying publicity to the worth of the author.

That John Murray II was never far from the author's thoughts is evidenced by the preface of new edition of *The Sketch Book*. From his trunks Irving salvaged the first letter Murray had written him, that communication of October 27, 1819, in which he had declined to publish what would be Irving's major British success. With almost jocular peevishness Irving inserted the letter in its entirety in the preface of the edition which posterity would know as the standard text.[18] It served no purpose there except to give Irving a subtle revenge on the publisher, against whom he had harbored some flickering resentment all those years. This exhibition of sly public malice—so unlike the amiable Irving who in 1826 had twice warned Payne against "petulant prefaces" [19]— must have had a complete cathartic effect on the writer, for he concluded the preface with a tribute to John Murray II, "The Prince of Booksellers." [20] One searches in vain among Irving's letters and papers after 1848 for a reference to John Murray II which was not one of nostalgic friendliness. The memories of Murray and his drawing-room circle grew dearer to the aging author with each passing year.

Other volumes of the new edition were related in a variety of

[17] George Haven Putnam, *Memories of a Publisher, 1865–1915* (London: G. P. Putnam's Sons, 1915), pp. 53–54.
[18] AREd., II, viii.
[19] *Scribner's Magazine*, XLVIII, 609, 614.
[20] AREd., II, xii.

ways to John Murray. *Bracebridge Hall* was almost a verbatim text of the Murray edition, which the author had seen through the press in 1822. The greeting to the readers was the same, including the statement, not in the earlier American editions, that "England is as classic ground to an American as Italy is to an Englishman; and old London teems with as much historical association as mighty Rome." [21] *Tales of a Traveller*, retouched under pressure from the publisher in 1824, became in the Author's Revised Edition a copy of the original British version, complete with Buckthorne's too-good-to-be-true parson and the cathedral cities.[22] Finally, from among the previously published works, *A Chronicle of the Conquest of Granada* sported a lengthy note which began: "Many of the observations in this note have already appeared in an explanatory article which, at Mr. Murray's request, the author furnished to the London Quarterly Review." [23] In prefaces and notes and on the pages of the texts the traces of John Murray II lingered.

In the titles that appeared for the first time in this edition, the House of Murray also figured. "During a visit to London in 1851," George P. Putnam wrote, "I arranged with Mr. Murray, on the author's behalf, for an English edition of the new works, 'Mahomet' and 'Goldsmith,' to be issued from the American stereotypes." [24] In his preface Irving made it clear that *Mahomet and his Successors* (2 vols., 1849–1850) had its origin in material intended for a volume of Murray's Family Library.[25] Indeed, he missed no opportunity to explain that the work had been "composed some years since for popular circulation and originally intended for Mr. Murray's family library; circumstances prevented

---

21 *Ibid.*, III, 10.
22 See *ibid.*, VII, 198–202, 215.
23 *Ibid.*, XIV, xv-xix.
24 "Memories of Distinguished Author: WI," *Harper's Weekly* [Supplement], May 27, 1871, p. 495. The court records of JMIII's action against Henry Bohn in 1850 stated: JMIII "is now by purchase from the said Washington Irving the proprietor of certain works entitled as follows 'Lives of Mahomet and his Successors[']—in two volumes and—['] Oliver Goldsmith[']" C14/1162/105 in Public Record Office.
25 AREd., XII, ix-x.

its publication at the time; it has been revised and almost rewritten in consequence of after views taken of the subject." [26]

Oliver Goldsmith: A Biography (appearing as both a hardback issue and a title in Murray's Home and Colonial Library) had had its unexciting beginning in the Galignani volume of 1825. It grew in 1837 when Irving prepared a two-volume edition of Goldsmith's work for Harper's Family Library, adding a lengthy sketch incorporating material from the biography by Sir James Prior. The American's final version (1849) gained impetus, at least, from Forster's *Life and Adventures of Oliver Goldsmith*. Although Irving made no secret of his debt to his British sources, there was much grim mumbling—especially in England—about his "piracy." [27]

Murray might be unable to participate fully in the Author's Revised Edition because of the British copyrights held by Bentley, but he was legally qualified to issue any of the other titles. This he did, probably with the co-operation of Irving. Stereoplates of *Knickerbocker's History of New York* were paid for by Murray in March 1849,[28] but for some unknown reason this edition was never printed. More decisive action was taken regarding *The Sketch Book* (AREd., II) and the three-volume *Life and Voyages of Christopher Columbus, Together with the Voyages of His Companions* (AREd., III-V), both of which appeared at 50 Albemarle Street in 1849; *Bracebridge Hall* (AREd., VI) and *A Chronicle of the Conquest of Granada* (AREd., XIV) followed in 1850.

The revival of interest in Washington Irving was one of the

---

[26] A. L. S., dated April 12, 1847, and printed in *Carroll A. Wilson: Thirteen Author Collection of the Nineteenth Century and Five Centuries of Familiar Quotations*, ed. Jean C. S. Wilson and David A. Randall (New York: Charles Scribner's Sons, 1950), p. 169.

[27] One of the interesting items to come out of these plagiarism charges was an avidly anti-Irving and anti-American letter (British Museum, 1414, i. 1. [8]). Published without a signature, it was, according to the introductory note, the work of "a gentleman of high character in the literary world." The letter accuses WI of merely rewriting Sir James Prior's *The Life of Oliver Goldsmith, M.B., from a Variety of Original Sources*, published by John Murray in 1837.

[28] The cost of the plates was £67 8s. 6d. The plates were finally melted in 1910, having never been used. Murray Archives.

major features of the book trade in both America and Britain at the beginning of the second half of the nineteenth century. A new generation was being introduced to the satire of Diedrich Knickerbocker, the charm of Geoffrey Crayon, and the romanticized history of Fray Antonio Agapida. In America, Putnam watched the sales of the volumes of the Author's Revised Edition increase and realized that his association with Irving was one of the most lucrative of his career. But in London, where the demand for Irving's writings was almost as great as in the United States, John Murray III found himself in a position which was in complete contrast to Putnam's.

Irving's success had alerted other British publishers to the financial value of his works on their lists.[29] Murray (and Bentley) claimed ownership of the British copyrights to most of the titles, but the whole question of international copyright was vaguely understood. Maintaining that Irving was a citizen of a foreign nation and consequently not entitled to the protection of British copyright laws, publisher H. G. Bohn took the field in 1850, issuing an unauthorized collected edition based on Putnam's text.

Henry George Bohn had achieved his first success in the remainders trade, buying up not only surplus stock but also copyrights to the material. In this way he amassed a wealth of selections from which to choose when he began to publish his cheap reprints in related groupings called "Libraries." [30] His inexpensive ten-volume *Complete Works* of Irving (each volume sold separately in Bohn's *Cheap Series* for one shilling; double volumes were an additional six pence) flooded the British market, undercutting the quality editions the House of Murray was sponsoring.[31] Young Murray did not take Bohn's infringements lightly.

29 For an indication of the number of publishers reprinting WI's writings and the range in prices, see Anon., *The London Catalogue of Books, 1816–1851* (London: Thomas Hodgson, 1851), pp. 289–90.

30 F. G. M. Cordasco, *The Bohn Libraries* (New York: Burt Franklin, 1951), provides a good look at the scope of Bohn's reprints. For Bohn's WI volumes, see pp. 48, 49.

31 See advertisement dated Feb. 21, 1850, inserted by Bohn in *Life of Mahomet* (B. Mus. 12296–d. 16).

That he meant to gain the issue was indicated by his excellent choice of counsel, Sir Fitzroy Kelly, whose "practice at the bar," the *Dictionary of National Biography* modestly declared, "was very large and lucrative, especially in the House of Lords and before the privy council, in both of which it was greater than that of any his contemporaries." [32] The struggle to assert Murray's rights to the titles purchased by his firm from Irving can be traced to its conclusion in the following letters.

The news of the copyright war in London may have first reached Irving's attention by way of a letter dated July 26, 1850, from an unknown correspondent, informing him that John Murray III would attempt to justify his copyrights by proving that Irving was a British author because of his British-born parents and his long residency in England.[33] The American, assuming a firm patriotic stance, was repelled by the thought. Moreover, in the far-fetched event that he were proved to be a British citizen, he would lose his American copyrights, which were his source of livelihood. The handsome payments he had received from the British editions had been welcomed, certainly, but that was past business. Nothing could be allowed to interfere with his present lucrative American dealings.

Now came, however, a letter directly from 50 Albemarle Street.[34] John Murray III wrote of the cheap editions of Irving's works which were over-running the British book market, the worst offender being publisher Bohn, against whom Murray was beginning a lawsuit.[35] To help his counsel organize the case, Murray asked for information on the locality of the composition of the pertinent titles and natal data on Irving's parents.

[32] X, 1236.

[33] STW, II, 394.

[34] On May 14, 1850, JMIII had written to Putnam, who assured him that WI would be willing to help JMIII protect his "interests which have been so unscrupulously invaded." G. P. Putnam to JMIII, New York, June 5, 1850. Murray Archives.

[35] The first legal action was on Aug. 7 or 8 before Vice-Chancellor Knight Bruce, who dismissed the case with the understanding that Murray could push his claim in common law. The record is on file as C14/1162/105 in the Public Record Office.

62. *To John Murray III*

Sunnyside, Aug. 8th 1850.

My dear Sir,

I am grieved to find you so much cut up in the publication of my works by the cheap editions with which the market appears to be glutted. Any aid I can give in remedying the evil you may thoroughly command.

In reply to your enquiry about which of my works were written in England—The Sketch Book was written in England—Bracebridge Hall partly in France partly in England. Tales of a Traveller—partly in France partly in England. Companions of Columbus, partly in Spain partly in England. Alhambra, the same. Mahomet partly in England partly in the United States. Successors of Mahomet—the same. Abbotsford and Newstead Abbey—the same.

For the register of the births of my parents you will have to search the opposite ends of the earth. My father William Irving, son of Magnus Irving and Catherine Williamson was born in Shapinsha in the Orkneys August 31st 1731 (Old Style). My mother Sarah Sanders daughter of John Sanders and Anna Kent was born in Falmouth April 14th 1738 (Old Style). My parents were married in Falmouth May 18th 1761 and left England for the United States May 21st 1763.

I shall be ready to sign the deed of assignment of which you make mention, as soon as it arrives.

With kindest remembrances to your family

I remain my dear Sir,
Yours with great regard,
Washington Irving.

Sunnyside, Aug. 8th 1850.[36]

The work entitled the Companions of Columbus was purchased of me by the late Mr. John Murray of Albemarle Street London, and I am ready when called on to make a formal assignment of the same to his heirs.

Washington Irving.

---

[36] This note is written on a separate sheet of paper, inserted in the fold of the main letter, indicating that JMIII probably specifically questioned WI about this title. Perhaps item 9, Appendix III had been temporarily lost.

Before this could reach London, a second letter arrived at Sunnyside from Murray. At counsel's suggestion he requested Irving's power of attorney in case it might prove useful in presenting the lawsuit as publisher (copyright-holder) and author against an illegal publisher. A statement prepared by H. G. Bohn in defense of his case was also included.[37]

63. *To John Murray III*

Sunnyside, Aug. 19th 1850.

My dear Sir,

By the ship which takes this letter you will receive the assignment of copy rights duly executed.[38] The power of attorney which you suggest shall be sent by another opportunity.[39] In a former letter I gave you the information you request concerning the birth places &c. of my parents. I now, however, repeat the same.

My father, William Irving son of Magnus Irving and his wife Catharine[40] Williamson was born in Shapinsha in the Orkneys August 31st 1731, Old Style, married in Falmouth to Sarah Sanders May 18th 1861 [1761].

Sarah Sanders daughter of John Sanders and his wife Anna Kent born in Falmouth April 14th 1738 (Old Style).

My parents left England for America May 21st 1763. I was born in the city of New York 3d of April 1783.

I presume it will be necessary to search for the register of my father's birth at Kirkwall (in the Island of Pomona) which is the county town.

With kindest regards to your family, I remain

My dear Sir, Yours ever very truly,
Washington Irving.

P.S.   The witnesses to the assignment are nephews of mine; both are well known. Pierre M. Irving is United States Pension Agent,

---

[37] No copy of Bohn's statement can be located, but from WI's comments and a later publication of the publisher (*The Question of Unreciprocated Foreign Copyright in Great Britain: A Report on the Speeches and Proceedings at a Public Meeting . . . July 1st, 1851*, with notes by H. G. Bohn, 1851) we can surmise that Bohn thoroughly reviewed WI's alien status, including references to his service in the New York militia as rebellion against the king.

[38] See Appendix III, item 13.

[39] See Appendix III, item 14.

[40] Previously spelled *Catherine*.

and notary of the N York Bank of Commerce. Sanders Irving is Secretary of the Hudson River Rail Road Company.[41]

A third letter had been dispatched from Albemarle Street even before Irving's letter of August 19 was written. This communication included a list of twelve questions concerning each of the copyrights which Irving had sold to John Murray II.[42] In addition to requesting this information, John Murray III asked if the American would come to England to testify on behalf of Murray's claims to Irving's writing. Almost certainly the question carried an offer of financial reimbursement for the traveler.

The sixty-seven-year-old master of Sunnyside did not hesitate a moment. On leaving England in 1846 he had planned that he would return to visit his family and friends there, but his whole mental outlook had changed. Mrs. Van Wart had died in Birmingham in 1849, and virtually every issue of the *Gentleman's Magazine* which came to Sunnyside carried notices of the passing of British friends and acquaintances. He thought of the withered frames and graying heads of his remaining friends in London, of the English nieces and nephews, now approaching dismal middle-age, of the grim fog and the frantic bustle of the populace in wintry London: he would stay at home. He did, however, endeavor to provide Murray with the information he needed.

64. *To John Murray III*[43]

Sunnyside Sept. 22d 1850.

My dear Sir,

The following memoranda partly in reply to enquiries contained in a letter from your house dated the 9th August last—and are

[41] Sanders was the fifth son of Ebenezer.

[42] See Appendix IV. This letter, actually from Robert Cooke of the Murray firm, was directed to WI by way of Putnam. Cooke's cover letter to Putnam is printed in George Haven Putnam, *George Palmer Putnam: A Memoir* (New York: G. P. Putnam's Sons, 1912), pp. 198–99.

[43] George P. Putnam published the portion beginning "It will not be in my power . . ." and ending " . . . publish the work [SB] collectively in London." *Harper's Weekly* [Supplement], May 27, 1871, pp. 492–93. This MS has been bound into a handsome volume which was among the interesting items in the bookcases of the drawing room, formerly the office of Sir John Murray V.

partly intended to correct errors in the statement of Mr Bohn. They are for your private use and I trust no undue publicity will be given to them. It will not be in my power to come to England to give testimony in this matter, as has been suggested by your lawyer; but I am not disposed to enter into litigation on my own account and wish no legal measures to be taken on my behalf— above all I have no idea of compromising my character as a native born and thoroughly loyal American citizen in seeking to promote my pecuniary interest, though I am willing to take all proper steps to protect yours.

Memoranda

My father embarked at Falmouth to settle in America 25th May

Pasted to the opening page of the volume is a cutting, apparently from an American newspaper, and not unlikely sent by WI with this letter. The cutting states:

"The following is given in the *London Athenaeum* as a correct statement of the sums paid to Washington Irving by the Murrays, father and son, for copyrights:—

	£	s	d
Sketch Book,	467	10	0
Bracebridge Hall,	1,050	0	0
Traveller,	1,575	0	0
Columbus,	3,150	0	0
Companions of Columbus,	525	0	0
Grenada,	2,100	0	0
Tour on the Prairies,	400	0	0
Abbotsford and Newstead,	400	0	0
Legends of Spain,	100	0	0
	9,767	10	0

This statement is produced in reference to the recent interference with Mr. Murray's privileges. The remarks in a previous number of the *Athenaeum* on the defence of Mr. M. that Irving is not an alien in England, being the son of British parents, are made to take rather an unfair direction towards our distinguished countryman. The latter has not any 'desire in his old age to forswear the land of his birth and of his early devotion, &c.' The London affair is simply a contest of publishers, in which, as we understand it, Mr. Irving does not take any personal interest. He is willing in this respect to share the fate of his countrymen, and has not, that we are aware of, sought any English copyrights since the recent adverse decision. Least of all has he any desire to make himself a 'British subject' to receive this doubtful mess of pottage."

The listing of JMII's payments to WI is from *The Athenaeum*, Aug. 24, 1850, p. 899. This magazine took a lively interest, on JMIII's behalf, in the progress of the lawsuit. Previously (Aug. 3, p. 818; Aug. 10, p. 836; Aug. 17, p. 870) it had offered its readers weekly gossip on the subject.

1763 and arrived in New York 18th July following. He resided in New York until his death, with the exception of two years sojourn in a country town, during the war of the revolution. He was strongly devoted to the American cause throughout the war, and of course, on the return of peace took every step necessary to establish his character as an American citizen. He had been engaged in mercantile business for twenty years before my birth (April 3rd 1783) and continued in it until 1802 when he retired with a competency. He died Oct. 25th 1807. I was brought up and educated at his expense and not at that of my elder brothers as has erroneously been asserted, in the statement of Mr Bohn. I was destined for the bar; but, before I had completed my studies was sent to Europe for the benefit of my health. I embarked for Bordeaux on the 19th May 1804, remained nearly two years abroad, visiting Italy, Sicily, Switzerland, France, Belgium, Holland & England, and returned home in March 1806. Resuming the study of the law I was admitted to the bar November 21st 1806 but never practiced, having imbibed a taste for literary pursuits. In the indulgence of this I wrote some of the papers on Salmagundi and produced Knickerbocker's Hist N. York, which first appeared 6th Decr 1809. To enable me more completely to follow out my literary vein, two of my brothers in 1810 gave me a share in a mercantile concern which they were establishing in New York and Liverpool, requiring no attention to business on my part. I continued, therefore, my literary avocations.

The military service of which Mr Bohn makes mention took place during our last war with Great Britain, when the destruction of the Capitol at Washington in 1814 aroused every one to take some active part in the war. I then joined the military staff of the Governor of the State of New York as aid de camp, and continued as such until the return of peace.

On the 25th May 1815, I embarked for Liverpool on a second visit to Europe. The sudden and great reverses in business which took place on the return of peace overwhelmed the house in which my brothers had so kindly given me an interest, and involved me in its ruin.

I then determined to try my pen as a means of support and began the papers of the Sketch Book. While thus occupied I resided in London in furnished apartments, from July 1818 to August 1820. The MS. for the Sketch Book was transmitted piece meal to the United States to be published in numbers in New York. After several numbers had thus appeared I was induced to publish the work collectively in London. The first volume was published in Feby 1820. The second volume (partly printed from Manuscript) was published by Mr Murray 15th July. The seventh number of the American edition, comprising Westminster Abbey, Stratford on Avon, Little Britain and the Angler was not published in New York until Septr 13 1820 nearly two months after the publication of the Sketch Book in two volumes in London. The Sketch Book therefore, as a whole was first published in London. The copyright for the 7th number was taken out here 12th August, 1820.[44]

In Aug 1820 I removed to Paris where I remained until July 1821, when I returned to England with the rough manuscript of Bracebridge Hall which was not completed for publication until the following year. It was then published both in London and New York. The London edition appeared 23rd May 1822. The American May 21st. I observe that Mr Bohn alleges the New York edition to have been published by Mr Van Winkle on the 5th April of the above year. This is a mistake. I find by my correspondence with my brother that the MS of the 1st volume was sent from London Jany 29 1822 and of the 2d vol not until Feby 25th. The volumes were not published separately in New York and the second volume could not certainly have been received in time to publish it at the alleged date—five weeks from the time it was sent.

In 1822 I crossed to Holland and passed the summer, winter and following spring in Germany returning to Paris Aug 3d 1823. There I sketched out the Tales of a Traveller, but crossed to England in May 1824 before they were finished. The introduction of these tales is dated from the Hotel de Dormstadt Mayence, where I was actually detained by indisposition; but the tales in reality were written partly in Paris and partly in England. They were published collectively in London in two volumes August 25th 1824 but appeared in New York in four parts.

[44] See Appendix V for listing of dates on which JMII registered his copyrights for all these works in the Stationers' Hall Registry.

1st part published Aug 24th 1824
2d   "   "   Sept 7   "
3   "   "   "   25   "
4th   "   "   Octr 9   "

Three parts, therefore were published subsequent to the London publication.

I returned to Paris early in the autumn and in October made an excursion into Lorraine; for though Paris was my head quarters in France I made occasional excursions to various parts of the country, especially into Normandy.

The autumn of 1825 was passed among the vineyards of Medoc and the subsequent winter in Bordeaux until the latter part of February (1826) when I set out for Madrid, where I took up my residence for two years during which time I wrote the Life of Columbus and transmitted it in MS. to London and New York. It was published in London Feby 8th 1829 and in New York March 15th of the same year.

In March 1828 I set out on a tour of the South of Spain; visiting the scenes and localities of the campaign for the Conquest of Granada, having made a rough draught of a chronicle of that war. At Seville I prepared the chronicle for the press and transmitted it to London and New York for publication. It appeared in New York 20th April 1829 and in London 23d May of the same year.

Part of the summer of 1828 I passed at a country house in the neighbourhood of Port St Mary's opposite Cadiz, where I sketched out some of the voyages of the Companions of Columbus, from notes and memoranda taken in Madrid and Seville. The following winter was passed Seville.

In the spring of 1829 I made a second visit to Granada; where I passed three months in the Alhambra during which time I collected material for work since published under that name.

In July I set out for England being appointed Secretary to the American Legation in London. I remained in that city until the spring of 1832 during which time I completed and published the voyages of the Companions of Columbus (published in London 31st Decr 1830. In New York March 7th 1831).

In the spring of 1832 I returned to the United States where I arrived about the last of May.

Dates of Publication in US of my subsequent works
Alhambra June 11 1832
Crayon Miscellany No. 1 Containing

Tour on the Prairies	April 14/35
No 2 Abbotsford &c.	June 1 "
No 3 Legends of Spain	Octr 10 "

Astoria Octr 26 1836
Bonneville's Adv in Rocky Mountains June 20 1837

The foregoing memoranda are crudely thrown together, and some of them are probably superfluous.

Yours my dear Sir very truly
Washington Irving

After months of preparation, in May 1851, Murray commenced proceedings against Bohn in the Queen's Bench, only to drop them on the first day after Bohn's counsel appeared to be amenable to a compromise. The result was a moral victory, at least, for the House of Murray. On August 27, 1851, Bohn purchased the copyrights (which he had previously declared invalid) and printed stock of Irving's writings for the sum of two thousand guineas. The original British owner retained the right to reprint *The Sketch Book, Bracebridge Hall,* and *Tales of a Traveller* in inexpensive series.[45]

For Murray the issue was settled and he could turn to other important matters, but the litigation had stirred the embers of the smoldering resentment of British writers, such men as novelists E. L. Bulwer and G. P. R. James, who had to sit helplessly by and watch their writings reap huge financial rewards, in which they had little or no share, in the United States. Under no circumstances could a foreigner's writings be protected from pirate publishers by United States copyright laws. In July 1851 Bulwer went so far as to chair a public meeting in London at which the speakers deplored the fact that American writers (e.g., Irving) in Britain were not subjected to the same legal disdain as British writers in America.[46]

45 See Appendix V, item 16.
46 *The Athenaeum,* July 5, 1851, p. 721, reported and regretted this meeting,

When all of the aspects of the business transaction had been completed, John Murray wrote to Irving, explaining the outcome.

Albemarle Street, Sept. 19.

My dear Sir,

Having troubled you so often, and I fear seriously, on the subject of my lawsuit with Bohn, it is with peculiar satisfaction that I now write to tell you that it is at an end. Mr. Bohn has offered me terms which are satisfactory to me and not humiliating to him. He has destroyed for me all value in your works, and I make over to him the copyrights.

I regret to part with them, but it seemed to me the only way to get out of the squabble, which was becoming very serious, *my* law expenses alone having run up to £850.

One good, at least, has been elicited out of this contest—it has settled the right of foreigners to hold copyright in this country; for I am assured by my counsel, Sir Fitzroy Kelly, one of the soundest heads at our bar, that the recent decision of our judges on that head is not likely to be reversed by the House of Lords, or any other tribunal. Sir Fitzroy Kelly has studied the subject minutely, and made an admirable speech in the Queen's Bench, on my side. I hope, therefore, that the "Life of Washington," and other works to come from your pen, may yet bring advantage to their author from this country; but *priority of publication in England* is an indispensable condition, and must in all cases be guaranteed and carefully attested at the time of appearance.

No one can desire more than I do an international copyright arrangement with the Americans. In my desire, I am not surpassed by Mr. Bohn, nor Sir E. L. Bulwer; but I differ from them in the strong convinction which I feel, that it is not by pirating the American books that the object is to be attained.

I remain, my dear Sir, yours very sincerely,

John Murray[47]

Despite the optimistic outlook of Sir Fitzroy, the "recent decision of our judges"—apparently Boosey *versus* Jeffreys, in which

---

expressing much the same views as JMIII in his letter, quoted below, to WI. Bohn's full report was cited in n. 37, above.

[47] PMI, IV, 89–90.

aliens domiciled in England were assured of copyright privileges —was reversed by the House of Lords, in 1854, as Jeffreys *versus* Boosey. The whole proposition of alien copyright would blow hot and cold for several decades (until 1891) before the United States government assumed its civic responsibility in the world of letters by agreeing to accept international copyright laws. Perhaps Irving could have helped to settle the problem some fifty years earlier. Late in 1839, with a bill providing for an international copyright before the United States Congress, W. H. Prescott wrote Irving: "there is no doubt that you are one who, from your literary position in the country, should take a lead in it." [48] Irving, however, did nothing, except to write (after the failure of the bill had occasioned mutterings against him because he had declined to support the issue even with his signature on a petition) a confused letter to *The Knickerbocker* explaining that he had not signed the petition because he "did not relish the phraseology." [49] Compared with Washington Irving's contribution to the fight to get the United States under international copyright law, the author's efforts on behalf of Murray's contest in 1850–1851 seem prodigious.

As the 1850's moved along, Irving's correspondence with 50 Albemarle Street dwindled to isolated letters of introduction for visitors to London. Here, again, one suspects that he wrote more letters than have been preserved in the Murray Archives, for Irving had a wide circle of travel-minded friends.

65. *To John Murray III*

Sunnyside, Jan. 29th 1851.

My dear Mr Murray,

This letter will be handed to you by the Rev. Charles D. Cooper,[50] a gentleman of much worth and most amiable manners

---

[48] Quoted in STW, II, 215.

[49] PMI, III, 149. STW, II, 215, was at a loss to explain WI's attitude to the issue of international copyright.

[50] An Episcopal minister, Cooper was taking a European tour before settling down to be Rector of St. Philip's Church, Philadelphia. In 1868 Dr. Cooper moved to the Church of the Holy Apostles, which he served as Rector and

and a kind of connection of mine by marriage. Any attention you may find it convenient to pay him during his sojourn in London will be considered favors bestowed on myself.

I hope and trust the late decision in the matter of the copy right will prove efficient in protecting you against the pirates of the press.

Yours every very faithfully,
Washington Irving.

66. *To John Murray III*[51]

New York, Nov. 20th 1851.

My dear Sir,
This will be handed to you by my worthy and intelligent friend Thurlow Weed Esqr[52] who makes a short visit of curiosity to Europe. He of course is desirious of seeing something of the literary world of London and if you can contribute in any way towards gratifying this desire you will confer on me an especial favor. If Lockhart is in town, I wish you would make him acquainted with him.

With kindest remembrances to your family
Yours ever very faithfully,
Washington Irving.

67. *To John Murray III*

Sunnyside, Decr 8th 1852.

My dear Sir,
This will be handed to you by my friend Mr Henry T. Tucker-

Rector Emeritus until his death in 1902. John Curtin MacAfee, *The First Ninety Years of the Parish of the Holy Apostles, 1868–1958* (Philadelphia: privately printed, 1958), p. 4. Mrs. Cooper is highly complimented, but no factual information—other than her death in 1868—is given. Mrs. Wentworth Bacon, the wife of Sarah Paris Wentworth's grandson, is unable to suggest the "kind of connection" which Mrs. Cooper had with WI. Letter, Millbrook, New York, March 12, 1966.

51 Used by permission of the Manuscript Division, The New York Public Library, Astor, Lenox and Tilden Foundations. One wonders if this letter were ever at 50 Albemarle Street. In *Letters from Europe and the West Indies, 1843–1862* (Albany: Weed Parsons & Co., 1866), Weed gave an almost hour-by-hour account of his time in London (see letter of Dec. 9, 1851; June 15, 18, 1852, pp. 414–22, 629–51) without a single reference to JMIII.

52 Thurlow Weed (1797–1882), politician and journalist, had been the virtual dictator of the Whig party. As the party's defeat and dissolution became increasingly inevitable, Weed temporarily removed himself from the crisis scene by sailing for Europe. *DAB*, XIX, 598–600.

man,[53] who is probably already known to you by his writings, full of amenity and grace, which have stamped him one of our best critics and most classic essayists.

Recommending him as a gentleman worthy from his personal character and amiable manners of your kind civilities, I remain

Yours ever very truly,

Washington Irving.

Early in 1855 Putnam published *Wolfert's Roost and Other Papers*, mainly a selection of pieces lifted from *The Knicker-bocker*. Editions appeared almost immediately in London bearing the imprints of Bohn[54] and of Routledge and Sons, the latter hav-

[53] Henry Theodore Tuckerman (1813–1871), a bachelor of independent means, was a close friend of WI during his last years. After two years at Harvard, Tuckerman, for reasons of health, had toured Italy, publishing in 1835 his *Italian Sketch Book*. In 1852–1853 he made a brief visit to England.

On Dec. 6, 1852, Tuckerman had written to WI: "I expect to sail for England in the Baltic on Saturday next; and, although my stay will probably be quite brief, I am desirous of seeing Mr. Rogers. Will you give me a line to him, and any other friend in England whom it would be pleasant for me to see?" WI replied, sending a letter for Rogers (published in Clayden, *Rogers and His Contemporaries*, II, 427) and this letter for JMIII. In his letter to Tuckerman, WI wrote: "John Murray has succeeded to his father in the literary realm of Albemarle Street, which I used to find a favorite haunt of notorieties." PMI, IV, 91–92.

Tuckerman's published account of his visit to 50 Albemarle Street relates that, after a visit with Samuel Rogers, the traveler moved on to "Murray's office in Albemarle Street. I felt there, surrounded by the portraits of those, whose writings this famous publisher had first sent forth to charm the world, as if in the very sanctum of prosperous authorship . . . —the spirited face of Byron that here looks down on you, seemed innocent of all misanthropy; Scott appeared too healthy to worry about his estate, and Jeffrey too good natured even to provoke a challenge; Crabbe, one would swear, sat for his picture after the complete edition of his poems was paid for; Moore, (Sir Thomas Lawrence's last effort) looks as if he had just sung an encored song, and been smiled on by a countess, while Irving seems lapped in his happiest day-dreams; of the travellers, Sir John Franklin, Parry, and Barrow, have a look of stoicism, as if they had seen strange things, and overcome great obstacles.

"I recalled, as I descended the stairs, that proud day for Murray, when he saw the belligerent authors of 'Waverley' and 'Childe Harold' reconciled by him, in this very room, go out of it, arm in arm, limping affectionately together." *A Month in England* (London: Richard Bentley, 1854), pp. 47–48.

[54] Bohn's edition of *Wolfert's Roost* carried this amusing (in view of the publisher's earlier protests) announcement on its back cover: "The Works of Washington Irving, having for the most part been composed or published during his long residence in the Country, are, by the recent decision of the House of Lords, pronounced English copyright. The whole being, now, by arrangement with

ing previously published several "illegal" Irving titles. The collection was followed shortly by the first installment of Irving's long-anticipated multi-volume biography of George Washington. This was a work in which Irving believed strongly, and his enthusiasm breathed new vigor into his plans for publication. Surely the House of Murray would be interested in being the English publisher of a work of such universal importance. Hadn't John Murray written in a most favorable way in 1851 concerning this proposed work? So Irving addressed himself to 50 Albemarle Street; indeed, he sent advance sheets of the first volume of the *Life of Washington*. This letter is no longer known to exist, but clearly it invited Murray to be the "authorized" British publisher. With the advance sheets Murray could bring out his edition before the pirates had the opportunity of getting into print. To Irving, money was "no matter." He told John Murray III, "If my work be well received by the public, I shall be content, whatever be the pecuniary profits." [55]

The House of Murray was not interested in Irving's offer, but its head, perhaps remembering pleasant encounters at 50 Albemarle Street with the American in his younger day, took upon himself the task of acting as Irving's literary agent in London. The occasional fond remembrances of young John in Irving's early letters to John Murray II take on added meaning by this touching gesture. He sold the advance sheets to H. G. Bohn, after securing from him for Irving "a promise of £50, and a hope of something more if he [Bohn] can keep the field to himself." [56] This arrangement must have proved to be a satisfactory one, for Bohn published all five of the volumes of the *Life of Washington*,

---

Mr. Murray and Mr. Bentley, the property of Henry G. Bohn (at a cost of more than three thousand pounds), he is the only legal publisher of them, and will take the necessary measures against infringements of his rights."

[55] PMI, IV, 193.

[56] *Ibid.* JMIII went ahead to point out that there were some pages missing from the advance sheets. WI quickly forwarded JMIII's letter to Putnam, by way of PMI, to whom he wrote: "You will see that some negligence or omission in forwarding advance sheets to London may mar my interests in that quarter." *Ibid.*, 192–93.

carefully indicating with each volume that his was the "Authorized" British edition.

Irving's last letter to the familiar address was a letter of introduction for his nephew, the Reverend Mr. Pierre P. Irving, an Episcopal minister. It is easy to believe that the aging man, as he addressed the envelope (the only separate cover preserved in the Murray Archives), remembered aloud for the benefit of the younger man the times when the "King of the West" held court in his unmatched drawing room. The portraits were still to be seen—recent visitors had assured him of this fact—but the people he associated with the room were no longer to be found there. Carefully he dropped the sealing wax, and for the last time on a letter to 50 Albemarle Street, Irving pressed his fob into the red wax to make the familiar design.

68. *To John Murray III*[57]

New York, May 13th 1856.

My dear Mr Murray,

This will be handed to you by my nephew the Revd Pierre M. [P.] Irving who makes a short visit to England. Any civilities you may find it convenient to bestow upon him during his sojourn in London will be considered personal favors to

Yours ever very truly,
Washington Irving.

As *The Life of George Washington* ground to its fifth and final volume in 1859, the author's health was daily the concern of his nieces and his nephew Pierre M. Irving, who had been, since the late 1830's, his uncle's private secretary and finally his general manager. On March 15 Irving concluded the last page of the biography, thus putting a period at the end of his writing career.

When *The Eclectic Magazine* published Thomas Faed's "Scott and his Literary Contemporaries at Abbotsford," [58] Irving had the engraving framed and hung where he could easily see it on the

---

[57] In addition to the address, in WI's handwriting along the bottom of the envelope is "By the Revd P. P. Irving."
[58] XLIII (Jan. 1858), plate opposite 113.

parlor wall of Sunnyside; the outside of his home was already generously covered with climbing ivy grown from sprouts sent from Scott's home. To visitors he would say—his intonations "English . . . not American," [59] as Thackeray observed—"I knew every man of them but three," then add sadly, "and now they are all gone!" [60] This focal point of his parlor was an ideal starting point for reminiscing—Scott, Crabbe, Lockhart, Campbell, Moore, Wilkie, Wordsworth, even Jeffrey and Constable. There they were as Irving had known them in his prime. In actuality or in anecdotes, he had been with them all in Murray's drawing room, at Rogers' breakfast table, or in Lady Holland's dining room,[61] and his brain was teeming with stories, though his voice was breathless and weak.[62]

Other familiar figures from his past gathered in. Shortly after Leslie's death in May 1859, Irving experienced a strange dream-hallucination in which he saw his old friend.[63] News of the death of Leigh Hunt reminded him of the stories told by Mrs. Holloway, who had once had unpleasant financial dealings with the poet.[64] A reference to an English sixpence was enough to conjure up from his memory an entire London street scene.[65]

To quiet Irving's mind, Pierre and the nieces often read to him. Slidell's *A Year in Spain*, the John Murray edition, was his favorite selection. They "read it again and again. Its graphic pictures seemed to carry him back to pleasant scenes, and out of himself." [66] Books took on greater meaning in association with his

---

[59] *The Letters and Private Papers of William Makepeace Thackeray*, ed. Gordon N. Ray (London: Oxford University Press, 1946), II, 134.

[60] PMI, IV, 322. The engraving still hangs where WI originally had it placed. WI had not personally known Henry Mackenzie, John Wilson, or Robert Ferguson.

[61] See Lloyd Sanders, *The Holland House Circle* (London: Methuen, 1908), pp. 333–34.

[62] See N. P. Willis, "Visits to Sunnyside," and James Grant Wilson, "A Day with WI," in Evert A. Duyckinck, ed., *Irvingiana: A Memorial to WI* (New York: Charles B. Richardson, 1860), respectively pp. xlvii, lviii-lix.

[63] PMI, IV, 304.

[64] *Ibid.*, 308–309.

[65] *Ibid.*, 311.

[66] *Ibid.*, 312. This edition is still in the Sunnyside Library.

British acquaintances. Lord Dufferin's *Letters from High Latitudes* was more interesting when he discovered the author was related to Mrs. Norton, one of Murray's favorite poetesses whom Irving had first met in 1829.[67] On October 11, with the aged author growing weaker, Pierre recorded the last title he read to his uncle—*Reginald Dalton,* Lockhart's novel of 1823. Irving "relished the pictures of Oxford college life," [68] recalling perhaps Buckthorne's experiences and his own visits to the university town.

In his last interview for publication (November 7), Irving directed the attention of the newspaper reporter to the picture hanging over the piano.

"Are the portraits good?" the visitor asked.

"Scott's head is well drawn," Irving replied, "though the expression lacks something of Scott's force. Campbell's is tolerable. Lockhart's is the worst. Lockhart," he insisted, "was a man of very delicate organization, but he had a more manly look than in the picture."

To the suggestion that he should write his "reminiscences of those literary friends," Irving only exclaimed wearily, "Ah, it is too late now! I shall never take the pen again." [69]

In the late evening of November 27, 1859, Washington Irving died, taking with him, as had been said of John Murray II, at least "five hundred anecdotes of the great spirits of his time." Had the patriarch of American literature published his literary reminiscences in his last years, the resultant volume could hardly have avoided being, like his best work, more British than American. In this conjectural *Reminiscences*[70] there would have been

---

[67] *Ibid.,* 274, erroneously identified Lord Duffein as Mrs. Norton's son. He was her nephew. Described as "the Byron of modern poetesses," Caroline Sheridan Norton wrote a pleasant popular verse concerning Murray and his "hours of intellectual chat / O'er claret, venison, grouse, and pheasant." See Smiles, II, 416.

[68] PMI, IV, 314. See above, p. 61, fn. 17.

[69] *Ibid.,* 322.

[70] That WI may have considered writing such a book as early as 1821 is indicated by his reply to Brevoort's request for "more particulars of the interesting characters he was meeting." See p. 25.

a prominent figure who moved in and out of the pages introducing impressionable Irving about his superbly outfitted drawing room, trying to direct his pen into original channels, negotiating with him over future works, or pouring more claret into his glass and another choice anecdote into his ear. This would have been John Murray II. Over the years Irving called him a variety of names, but even in a moment of extreme anger, as when on October 22, 1831, he threatened to take his work to "some other bookseller who is a *mere man of business*," [71] the American's effort at sarcasm showed that he had valued the publisher beyond financial considerations. In the end as at the beginning, Washington Irving acknowledged John Murray II as the aristocrat of publishers, and his hypothetical *Reminiscences* would have revealed, like the pieces of his correspondences held together by the covers of this book, the tremendous impact Murray had on Irving's life and literary career.

[71] Italics mine. See p. 158.

APPENDICES

I. Lost Letters: Washington Irving to the John Murrays

In spite of the careful filing system at 50 Albemarle Street, it was inevitable that during a period of 150 years some letters would be lost. Perhaps, in those days of less dependable international postal service, some letters did not even arrive safely at that address.

It seems likely that WI would have written many more letters of introduction to the Murrays than those represented in this collection. That they would not have found their way automatically into the official business file would have been only natural since they were of a purely personal nature.

A study of the various published journals and similar sources indicates that WI addressed himself to 50 Albemarle Street on the days mentioned below, but the Murray Archives offers no correspondence on or near these dates.[1]

Oct. ?, 1819	*The Sketch Book*, AREd., "Preface."
Dec. 22, 1823	STW, *Journal (1823–1824)*, p. 91.
Jan. 28, 1824 [2]	STW, *Journal (1823–1824)*, p. 115.
July 9, 1824 [3]	STW, *Journal (1823–1824)*, p. 221.
July 13, 1824 [3]	STW, *Journal (1823–1824)*, p. 226.
March 3, 1825	Trent & Hellman, II, 98.
Jan. ?, 1832	PMI, II, 474.
April ?, 1855	PMI, IV, 192–93.

II. The John Murrays to Washington Irving:
A Survey of Epistolary Remains

Washington Irving never let pass an opportunity to accuse JMII of neglecting his correspondence with him, and truly WI

[1] WI's journal notations regarding the dates on which he wrote certain letters do not always agree with the date lines on the actual letters received by JM. It was not at all unusual for WI to backdate (if we accept his private journals as our authority) a letter as much as three days, an insignificant length of time when communication was so slow.

[2] This notation may record the arrival of a letter from JMII; a more likely reading, however, is that WI wrote to JMII on this date.

[3] On these dates WI may have dispatched packets of MSS only, perhaps not even enclosing a cover letter.

seems to have treasured each letter from his publisher. At any rate, when PMI set about writing his uncle's biography, he obviously had an extensive file of JMII letters from which to draw. Unfortunately, most of these letters have been lost.

A careful survey of manuscript repositories in the United States located only a few items. Fragments and occasionally whole letters, however, can be found in the work by PMI.

JMII to WI, Oct. 27, 1819	MS in Berg Collection, New York Public Library.
JMII to WI, Oct. 26, 1820	Short excerpt quoted in PMI, II, 24–26
JMII to WI, June 29, 1821	Quoted in full in PMI, II, 48.
JMII to WI, Nov. 8, 1823	Quoted, perhaps in full, in PMI, II, 177.
JMII to WI, before July 20, 1825 [1]	A few words quoted in PMI, II, 238; referred to in Trent & Hellman, II, 140.
JMII to WI, July [?], 1826 [1]	A few words quoted in PMI, II, 249.
JMII to WI, Oct. 25, 1831	MS copy in Murray Archives.
JMIII to WI, Jan. 30, 1832	MS in Yale University Library.
JMIII to WI, Sept. 10, 1851	Quoted in full in PMI, IV, 89–90.
JMIII to WI, before May 22, 1855	A few words quoted in PMI, IV, 192–93.

III. OFFICIAL DOCUMENTS AT 50 ALBEMARLE STREET CONCERNING WASHINGTON IRVING'S WRITINGS

These documents culled from the Murray Archives cover the entire period of this publishing house's relationship with Irving and

---

[1] Lacking an actual date line from JMII, it is difficult to designate a specific date for some of these letters.

in themselves provide a quick look at this important phase of Irving's career as a writer.

1. Promissory note, London, Aug. 16, 1820, from JMII for 250 guineas for copyright of *The Sketch Book*. At Messrs. Brooks, Son & Dixon, Bankers, Chancery Lane. Endorsed on back by WI to Henry Van Wart.

2. Receipt, London, Aug. 16, 1820, for above item, signed by WI.

3. Receipt, London, March 12, 1822, for 1,000 guineas from JMII for copyright of *Bracebridge Hall*. Signed by WI.

4. Receipt, London, Aug. 13, 1824, for 1,500 guineas from JMII for *Tales of a Traveller*. Signed by WI.

5. Receipt, London, Sept. 24, 1827, for 300 guineas from JMII "in part payment of Three thousand guineas for the copyright of 'Washington Irvings History of the Life and Voyages of Christopher Columbus.' " Signed by Thomas Aspinwall. Attached to this are seven promissory notes, dated London, Jan. 1, 1828, and paid in amounts and on dates as follow: at 6 months, £400 on July 4; at 9 months, £500 on Oct. 4; at 12 months, £400 on Jan. 4, 1829; at 15 months, £400 on April 4; at 18 months, £400 on July 4; at 21 months, £400 on Oct. 4; at 24 months, £400 on Jan. 4, 1830. Drawn at Messrs. Dixon, Langdale & Co., Bankers, Chancery Lane.

6. Contract, May 7, 1828, for *Life of Columbus*, £3,150.

7. Five promissory notes, London, Jan. 10, 1829, from JMII covering the copyright of *The Conquest of Granada*; due at 8 months, £400 paid on Sept. 13; due at 12 months, £400 paid on Jan. 13, 1830; due at 16 months, £400 paid on May 13; due at 20 months, £400 paid on Sept. 13; due at 24 months, £500 paid on Jan. 13, 1831. The first and last notes were endorsed by WI to Henry Van Wart; the others WI signed over to Thomas Aspinwall.

8. Parchment contract, 3 x 3 feet, the Alhambra, July 4, 1829, assigning copyright of *The Conquest of Granada* to JMII under conditions listed under 7, above. Signed by WI.

9. Three promissory notes, London, Dec. 17, 1830, from JMII covering the copyright of *Companions of Columbus;* due at 6 months, £175 paid on June 20; due at 9 months, £175 paid on Sept. 20; due at 12 months, £175 paid on Dec. 20. All endorsed to Henry Van Wart by WI.

10. *Unsigned* contract, London, Feb. 5, 1835, for publishing *Tour on the Prairies.* JMII would take entire risk and after deducting from sales all expenses, the profit would be divided into three parts, two-thirds to be paid to WI, one-third to JMII.

11. Promissory note, London, March 2, 1835, from JMII for copyright of *Tour on the Prairies* for £400, due 4 months from date. Paid in full on July 5.

12. Promissory notes, London, May 4, 1835, from JMII covering copyright of *Abbotsford, and Newstead Abbey;* due at 6 months, £200 paid on Nov. 7; due at 9 months, £200 paid on Feb. 7, 1836.

13. Indenture acknowledging ownership by JMIII of copyrights, noted as purchases of JMII, above, Sunnyside, Aug. 19, 1850. Signed by WI and witnessed by Saunders Irving and PMI. Stamped at Her Britannick Majesty's Consulate in New York.

14. Power of Attorney to JMIII, Sunnyside, Aug. 21, 1850, for use in court fight with publisher Henry G. Bohn over copyrights of WI's works. Signed by WI. Stamped at Her Britannick Majesty's Consulate in New York.

15. Affidavit, New York, Sept. 27, 1850, from Ebenezer Irving concerning publication dates of American editions of WI's works. Stamped at Her Britannick Majesty's Consulate in New York.

16. Contract between JMIII and Henry G. Bohn, London, Aug. 27, 1851, ending court fight over the copyrights of *The Sketch Book, Bracebridge Hall, Tales of a Traveller, Life of Columbus, Tour on the Prairies,* and *Abbotsford, and Newstead Abbey.* JMIII was to be allowed to reprint *Tales of a Traveller* and *Bracebridge Hall* in his Colonial Library and *The Sketch Book* in his Family Library. Regarding the expenses of the lawsuit, "each party shall pay his own costs both at Equity and Common Law."

216

IV. Washington Irving's Notes Used in the Preparation of Letter 64

In August 1850 JMIII sent WI a list of twelve questions to which he needed answers concerning each of the titles that WI had sold to JMII. In a not very systematic fashion WI attempted to answer all the questions in Letter 64. That letter was based on notes which he had made, with PMI's research assistance, in a small notebook, portions of which are among the WI Papers in the Yale University Library.

From these fragments, quoted below,[1] it is easy to see the nature of each of JMIII's questions.

Tales of a Traveller   [pp. 12–13]

1. Commenced in Paris in the winter of 1823–4. Finished in England early in the summer of the same year.

2. Revised in the United States in 1850.

3. Treated with Mr. Murray for the work by letter from Paris dated March 18, 1824. Bargain completed in London shortly afterwards.

4. I agreed to sell it to him for 1500 guineas. The agreement was verbal.

5. I delivered the MSS. to him in London in the course of the spring and summer of 1824 and in pursuance of the agreement.

6. I received in payt his notes for 1500 gns. and gave him a receipt stating that it was for the copy right and that I would make a complete assignment of the same when required Receipt dated London Aug 13th 1824.

7. I sent the MS. to my Brother in US in portions. It was published in New York in 4 parts 1st part Aug 24th 1824, 2d Sept 9th 1824, 3d Sept 25th, 4th Oct 9th 1824.

8. Published in America by Carey Lea & Blanchard Philadelphia, dates as above.

1 Used by permission of the Yale University Library, New Haven, Conn.

9. First published in England by Mr. Murray 2 vols Aug 24th 1824.

10. I intended the first part to be published in America simultaneously with the volume in England.

11. Published by Mr. Murray on his own account.

12. I resided in England at the time of its publication there.

Companions of Columbus   [pp. 20–21]

1. Sketched out in Spain in 1827. & Finished in England 1830.

2. The revised edition corrected & completed in the United States in 1848. I residing there at the time.

3. Treated with Mr. Murray for the sale of work latter part of 1830.

4. Verbal agreement to sell it to him for 500 guineas. recd payt in notes.

5. Delivered MS. to Murray in London 1830 in pursuance of agreet.

6. I recd 500 guineas, in notes. do not recollect about a receipt.

7. Sent in sheets to E I in America [printers?] to print an edition sold by him to Messrs Carey & Lea Philadelphia.

8. First published in Am. by Carey & Lea Phila March 7 1831.

9. First publd in England Decr. 1830 by Mr. Murray.

10. Simultaneous publication intended in Engd and America.

11. Publication by Murray was on his own account.

12. I was residing in Engd at the time of its first publication there.

Tour on the Prairies   [pp. 22–23]

1. Composed in N York 1834.

2. Corrected for the last revised edition 1849 in the State of New York where I was then residing.

3. I first treated with Mr. Murray for the work in the spring of 1833.

4. I agreed to sell it to him for 400 £ sterling Col. Aspinwall, my agent, gave a receipt for the same, dated March 3d 1835, stipulating in my name to execute any final instrument of sale that might be necessary.

5. The MS. delivered to Mr. Murray by my agent in 1835—pursuant to agreement.

6. I received four hundred pounds in promissory notes for which my agent gave a receipt.

7. I made an arrangt for the publication in American with Messrs Carey Lea & Blanchard of Phila.

8. It was first published by them April 11th or 14 1835.

9. First published in England by Mr Murray March 2d 1835.

10. Publication in Engd & America intended to be simultaneous.

11. Published by Mr. Murray on his own account.

12. I was residing in N York at the time the work was first published in England.

Abbotsford   [pp. 24–25]

1. Composed in N York 1834.

2. Revised for the last complete edition of my works in 1848 or 9.

3. First treated with Mr. Murray for the sale early in 1835.

4. An agreement was made with him through my agent Col Aspinwall. I do not recollect the price.

5. The MS. was delivered to him by my agent pursuant to agreement.

6. I do not recollect the [same?]. I presume a receipt was given by my agent.

7. I made an agreement with Messrs Carey Lea & Blanchard Phila. The work was published under my supervision.

8. It was first published by Carey Lea & Blanchard Philadelphia June 1, 1835.

9. First published by Murray in London, May 1, 1835.

10. I intended the publication in both countries to be simultaneous.

11. Published by Mr. Murray on his own account.

12. I resided in New York at the time the work was first published in England.

V. OFFICIAL COPYRIGHT REGISTRY DATES OF IRVING TITLES PUBLISHED BY JOHN MURRAY II

Perhaps the most unfrequented record repository in London is the vault of Stationers' Hall, which contains all of the official copyright registrations prior to 1840.

On the dates indicated, the official registry shows that JMII deposited eleven copies of the title, each entry being properly noted by the registrar.

Registry Book	Title	Date of Registration
Feb.–Sept. 1820, p. 551.	*The Sketch Book* Identified as by Geoffrey Crayon	Aug. 10, 1820
May 1822–Sept. 1823, p. 7	*Bracebridge Hall* Identified as by Geoffrey Crayon	May 17, 1822
Oct. 1823–April 1825, p. 332.	*Tales of a Traveller* Identified as by Geoffrey Crayon	Sept. 7, 1824
Oct. 1826–April 1828, p. 523	*Life and Voyages of Columbus* WI identified as author	March 17, 1828

May 1828–Jan. 1830, p. 308	*Chronicle of the Conquest of Granada* WI identified as author	March 5, 1829
Jan. 1830–July 1831, p. 434	*Companions of Columbus* Registered as No. 18 of Family Library; no author named	March 8, 1830
Jan. 1835–Aug. 1836, p. 31	*Tour on the Prairies*	March 2, 1835
	Abbotsford, and Newstead Abbey	May 4, 1835
p. 93	*Legends of Spain* All identified as by the author of *The Sketch Book*	Dec. 15, 1835

I. Washington Irving's Works

Two published bibliographies cover Washington Irving's published writings: William R. Langfeld and Philip C. Blackburn, *Washington Irving: A Bibliography* (New York: New York Public Library, 1933); Stanley T. Williams and Mary E. Edge, *A Bibliography of the Writings of Washington Irving: A Check List* (New York: Oxford University Press, 1936).

The titles listed below (with British Museum call numbers) are the copies that were used in the preparation of this study.

A. *Published by Murray*

A Humorous History of New York, 1820.	838.f.8.
The Sketch Book [1st ed. of Vol. II], 1820.	12360.ccc.21.
The Sketch Book, 2 vols., 1820.	838.5.3.
A History of New York, 2 vols., 1821.	10414.aa.25.
The Sketch Book, 2 vols., 1821.	12356.e.33.
Bracebridge Hall, 2 vols., 1822.	838.f.4,5.
Tales of a Traveller, 2 vols., 1824.	838.f.7.
A History of the Life and Voyages of Christopher Columbus, 4 vols., 1828.	615.g.4.
A Chronicle of the Conquest of Granada, 2 vols., 1829.	1196.g.16.
The Life and Voyages of Christopher Columbus	

[abridged as Family Library, No. 11], 1830.[1]   12200.gg.8(1).

Voyages and Discoveries of the Companions of Columbus [Family Library, No. 18], 1831.   12200.gg.8(2).

The Life and Voyages of Christopher Columbus, 1831.   010632.a.9.

A Tour on the Prairies, 1835.   1208.h.12.

Abbotsford, and Newstead Abbey, 1835.   1208.h.13.

Legends of the Conquest of Spain, 1835.   1208.h.14.

Bracebridge Hall [Home and Colonial Library, No. 11], 1845.   1155.b.6(2).

Tales of a Traveller [Home and Colonial Library], 1848.   1155.b.17(3).

The Life and Voyages of Christopher Columbus, Together with His Companions, 3 vols., 1849.   1448.4.25.

Oliver Goldsmith: A Biography [Home and Colonial Library], 1849.   1155.c.2(2).

Oliver Goldsmith: A Biography, 1849.   12295.e.4.

The Sketch Book, 1849.   12295.e.5.

Tales of a Traveller, 1850.   12295.e.2.

Lives of Mahomet and His Successors, 2 vols., 1850.   9055.dd.23.

B. *Published by Other British Publishers*

The Sketch Book [Vol. I, issued at WI's expense]. London: John Miller, 1820.   837.h.66.1.

A History of New York. London: W. Wright, 1820.   12705.g.31.

Letters of Jonathan Oldstyle, Gent. London: Effingham Wilson, 1824.   838.h.37.

The Alhambra. 2 vols. London: Colburn and Bentley, 1832.   838.f.6.

---

1 The New York Public Library has a copy of this abridgment with JMII's imprint, dated 1831, and labeled "Murray's Family Library, vol. 34" (Call number NYPL: HAM).

Poems, by W. C. Bryant. Ed. WI. London: John
  Andrews, 1832.   994.i.6.
Astoria: or, Enterprise beyond the Rocky Moun-
  tains. 3 vols. London: Richard Bentley, 1836.   1050.1.7.
Adventures of Captain Bonneville, or Scenes be-
  yond the Rocky Mountains of the Far West.
  3 vols. London: Richard Bentley, 1837.   1050.1.8.
Life of Mahomet. London: H. G. Bohn, 1852.   12296.d.16
The Works of WI. 10 vols. London: H. G. Bohn,
  1853.   12295.bb.7.
Wolfert's Roost and Other Tales. London:
  H. G. Bohn, 1855.   12296.d.2.
Life of George Washington. 5 vols. London:
  H. G. Bohn, 1855–1859.   12296.d.1.

C. *Published in the United States*

Bracebridge Hall, 2 vols. New York: C. S. Van
  Winkle, 1822.   012703.f.16.
Tales of a Traveller. 2 vols. Philadelphia: H. C.
  Carey & Lea, 1824.   12703.g.20.
A History of the Life and Voyages of Christopher
  Columbus. 2 vols. New York: G. C. H. Carvill,
  1831.   10631.d.24.
A Tour on the Prairies. Philadelphia: Carey, Lea
  & Blanchard, 1835.   1457.c.2.
The Works of WI [Author's Revised Edition].
  15 vols. New York: G. P. Putnam, 1857.   012296.aa.4.

II. WASHINGTON IRVING

A. *Manuscript Materials*

The Langfeld-Blackburn bibliography provides a remarkably
complete survey of extant Irving manuscripts, but during the
thirty years since its appearance, many of the items have changed
hands—mostly moving into the collections of the larger libraries

in the United States. Two recent publications have brought this up-to-date: Modern Language Association's *American Literary Manuscripts* (Austin: University of Texas Press, 1960); Herbert L. Kleinfield, "A Census of Washington Irving Manuscripts," *Bulletin of the New York Public Library*, LXVIII (Jan. 1964), 13–32. These bibliographies, however, deal only with the United States. *A Guide to Manuscripts Relating to America in Great Britain and Ireland*, ed. B. R. Crick and Miriam Alman (London: Oxford University Press, 1961), lists some Irving manuscripts in the United Kingdom, but it includes none of the items from the Murray Archives.

The repositories listed below have generously allowed me to use unpublished Irving and Thomas Aspinwall letters in their collections.

Columbia University Library, New York City.
Harvard University Library, Cambridge, Mass.
Henry E. Huntington Library, San Marino, Cal.
John Rylands Library, Manchester.
National Library of Scotland, Edinburgh.
New York Historical Society, New York City.
New York Public Library, New York City.
Historical Society of Pennsylvania, Philadelphia.
Pierpont Morgan Library, New York City.
Princeton University Library, Princeton, N. J.
University of Rochester Library, Rochester, N. Y.
Scripps College Library, Claremont, Cal.
Sunnyside, The Sleepy Hollow Restorations, Inc., Tarrytown, N. Y.
University of Virginia Library, Charlottesville.
Yale University Library, New Haven, Conn.

B. *Published Items*

The Williams-Edge bibliography is complete to its date of publication. A full listing of books and articles relating to Irving since that time could be compiled from the periodic bibliographies of

American Literature and the *PMLA*. A readily available list of articles prior to 1950 is in Lewis Leary's *Articles on American Literature, 1900–1950* (Durham, N. C.: Duke University Press, 1954), pp. 151–54.

1. Journals and Letters (generally in order of composition)

Journal of Washington Irving, 1803, ed. Stanley T. Williams. New York: Oxford University Press, 1934.

Washington Irving: Notes and Journals of Travel in Europe, 1804–1805, ed. William P. Trent. 3 vols. New York: Grolier Club, 1921.

The Letters of Washington Irving to Henry Brevoort, ed. George S. Hellman. 2 vols. New York: G. P. Putnam's Sons, 1915.

The Journals of Washington Irving, 1815–1842, ed. William P. Trent and George S. Hellman. 3 vols. Boston: Bibliophile Society, 1919.

Notes While Preparing Sketch Book &c. 1817, ed. Stanley T. Williams. New Haven: Yale University Press, 1927.

Tour of Scotland 1817, ed. Stanley T. Williams. New Haven: Yale University Press, 1927.

"Washington Irving to Walter Scott: Two Unpublished Letters," ed. Ben Harris McClary. *Studies in Scottish Literature*, III (Oct. 1965), 114–18.

Washington Irving and the Storrows: Letters from England and the Continent, 1821–1828, ed. Stanley T. Williams. Cambridge: Harvard University Press, 1933.

"Correspondence of Washington Irving and John Howard Payne," ed. Thatcher T. Payne Luquer. *Scribner's Magazine*, XLVIII (Oct.-Nov. 1910), 461–82, 597–616.

"Irving and Moore Again," ed. David Bonnell Green. *Notes and Queries*, CCIV (Aug. 1959), 288–89.

Journal of Washington Irving (1823–1824), ed. Stanley T. Williams. Cambridge: Harvard University Press, 1931.

"Washington Irving's Madrid Journal, 1827–1828 and Related Letters," ed. Andrew Breen Myers. *Bulletin of the New York*

Public Library, LXII (May 1958), 217–27; (June 1958), 300–11; (July 1958), 407–19; (Aug. 1958), 463–71.

Journal of Washington Irving: 1828, ed. Stanley T. Williams. New York: American Book Company, 1937.

Washington Irving Diary, Spain, 1828–1829, ed. Clara Louisa Penney. New York: Hispanic Society of America, 1930.

"Washington Irving's Literary Midwifery: Five Unpublished Letters from British Repositories," ed. Ben Harris McClary. *Philological Quarterly*, XLVI (April 1967), 277–83.

"Washington Irving's Amiable Scotch Friends: Three Unpublished Letters to the John Gibson Lockharts," ed. Ben Harris McClary. *Studies in Scottish Literature*, IV (Oct. 1966), 101–104.

The Western Journals of Washington Irving, ed. John Francis McDermott. Norman: University of Oklahoma Press, 1944.

Washington Irving to Thomas Aspinwall, April 12, 1847, in *Carroll A. Wilson: Thirteen Author Collection of the Nineteenth Century and Five Centuries of Familiar Quotations*, ed. Jean C. S. Wilson and David A. Randall. New York: Charles Scribner's Sons, 1950.

2. Biographical and Critical Studies

Anon. [Printed Letter concerning Irving's use of Sir James Prior's *Life of Oliver Goldsmith*.] N.p., 1849. [B. Mus. 1414.1.1.(8)].

Aspinwall, Thomas. "Remarks on Washington Irving," *Proceedings of the Massachusetts Historical Society*, IV (Dec. 1859), 404–408.

Beach, Leonard. "Washington Irving: The Artist in a Changing World," *University City Review*, XIV (Summer 1948), 259–66.

Bowers, Claude. *The Spanish Adventures of Washington Irving*. Boston: Houghton Mifflin, 1940.

Brooks, Van Wyck. *The World of Washington Irving*. London: J. M. Dent & Sons, Ltd., 1945.

Butler, Joseph T. *Sunnyside: Washington Irving's Home.* Tarrytown, N. Y.: Sleepy Hollow Restorations, Inc., 1962.

Davis, R. B. "Washington Irving and Joseph C. Cabell," *English Studies in Honor of James Southall Wilson.* Charlottesville: University of Virginia Press, 1950.

Dawson, Flora. *Princes, Public Men, and Pretty Women.* London: Richard Bentley, 1864.

Duyckinck, Evert A., ed. *Irvingiana: A Memorial to Washington Irving.* New York: Charles B. Richardson, 1860.

Griswold, Rufus Wilmot. [Review] *Graham's Lady's and Gentleman's Magazine,* XVI (Oct. 1842), 219; (Dec. 1842), 344.

Hedges, William L. *Washington Irving: An American Study, 1802–1832.* Baltimore: The Johns Hopkins Press, 1965.

Hellman, George S. *Washington Irving Esquire, Ambassador at Large from the New World to the Old.* New York: Alfred A. Knopf, 1925.

Irving, Pierre M. *The Life and Letters of Washington Irving.* 4 vols. New York: G. P. Putnam, 1864.

Kirby, Thomas A. "Irving and Moore: A Note on Anglo-American Literary Relations," *Modern Languages Notes,* LXII (April 1947), 251–55.

Leary, Lewis. *Washington Irving.* (Pamphlets on American Writers, No. 25.) Minneapolis: University of Minnesota Press, 1963.

McClary, Ben Harris. "Two of Washington Irving's Friends Identified," *American Literature,* XXXVII (Jan. 1966), 471–73.

———. "Washington Irving in Brighton, 1824," *Sussex Life,* II (July 1966), 35–36.

Pochmann, Henry A., ed. *Washington Irving: Representative Selections.* New York: American Book Co., 1934.

Putnam, George Haven. *Washington Irving: His Life and Work.* New York: G. P. Putnam's, 1903.

Putnam, George P. "Memories of Distinguished Author: Washington Irving," *Harper's Weekly* [Supplement], May 27, 1871, p. 495.

Reichart, Walter A. *Washington Irving and Germany.* Ann Arbor: University of Michigan Press, 1957.

Snell, George. "Washington Irving: A Revaluation," *Modern Language Quarterly,* VII (Sept. 1946), 303–10.

Wagenknecht, Edward. *Washington Irving: Moderation Displayed.* New York: Oxford University Press, 1962.

Webster, C. M. "Washington Irving's Expurgation of 1809 *History of New York," American Literature,* IV (Nov. 1932), 293–95.

Williams, Stanley T. "The First Version of the Writings of Washington Irving in Spanish," *Modern Philology,* XXVIII (Nov. 1930), 185–201.

————. *The Life of Washington Irving.* 2 vols. New York: Oxford University Press, 1935.

————. "Washington Irving's First Stay in Paris," *American Literature,* II (March 1930), 15–20.

Wilson, J. L. "Washington Irving's 'Celebrated English Poet,'" *American Literature,* XVIII (Nov. 1946), 247–49.

III. The House of Murray

A. *Manuscript Materials*

While writing the study of JMII, Samuel Smiles sifted through the vast store of manuscript letters at 50 Albemarle Street. Since that time, numerous scholars have nibbled at smaller projects, but the Murray collection remains largely unviolated. The official books covering the earlier years have been in storage and unavailable for some time. Sir John planned to set up an Archives Section through which these records could be made accessible to interested scholars, and Mr. John Murray informs me that the firm still is moving in this direction. It is difficult to prophesy, however, when this will be a reality.

As recorded in appropriately placed footnotes, I have had access to several manuscript items from the Murray Archives which—though not directly related to WI—have contributed to a clearer understanding of my subject.

B. *Published Items*

Anon. *Report of the Trial of Mr. John Murray, in the Court of King's Bench, at Westminster-Hall, the 19th December 1829, on an Indictment of Libel on Messrs. Lecesne and Escoffery, of Jamaica.* London: Bagster and Thomas, 1830.

Bennett, Scott. "The Family Library, 1825–1835: The Uses of Literary in a Revolutionary Age." Ph.D. thesis: Indiana University, 1967.

Espinasse, F. "The House of Murray," *Harper's Monthly Magazine* [European Edition], X (Sept. 1885), 503–22.

Grant, James. *Portraits of Public Characters.* 2 vols. London: Saunders and Otley, 1841.

Murray, John, I. "A Letter to W. Mason, A.M., Precentor of York, Concerning his Edition of Gray's Poems, and the Practice of Booksellers." London: JM, 1777.

Murray, John, IV. *John Murray III, 1808-1892: A Brief Memoir.* New York: Alfred A. Knopf, 1920.

Paston, George [Emily Morse Symonds]. "At John Murray's," *Cornhill Magazine*, N.S. LXIX (Aug.-Oct. 1930), 129–46, 280-97, 436-51.

———. *At John Murray's: Records of a Literary Circle, 1843–1892.* London: JM, 1932.

Smiles, Samuel. *A Publisher and his Friends: Memoir and Correspondence of the Late John Murray, with an Account of the Origin and Progress of the House, 1768-1843.* 2 vols. London: JM, 1891.

IV. The Book Trade

Anon. *A Famous Bookstore* [Galignani's]. Paris: The Galignani Library, 1920.

Anon. *The London Catalogue of Books, 1816-1851.* London: Thomas Hodgson, 1851.

Barber, Giles. "Galignani's and the Publication of English Books in France from 1800 to 1852," *The Library*, 5th Ser., XVI (Dec. 1961), 267–86.

Barnes, James J. *Free Trade in Books: A Study of the London Book Trade since 1800.* Oxford: The Clarendon Press, 1964.

Blunden, Edmund. *Keats's Publisher: A Memoir of John Taylor.* London: Jonathan Cape, 1936.

Bohn, H. G., ed. *The Question of Unreciprocated Foreign Copyright in Great Britain: A Report on the Speeches and Proceedings at a Public Meeting held . . . July 1, 1851.* London: H. G. Bohn, 1851.

Campbell, R. *The London Tradesmen.* London: T. Gardner, 1759.

Collins, A. S. *The Profession of Letters: A Study of the Relation of Author to Patron, Publisher, and Public, 1780-1832.* London: George Routledge & Sons, 1928.

Constable, Thomas. *Archibald Constable and his Literary Correspondents.* 3 vols. Edinburgh: Edmonston and Douglas, 1873.

Cordasco, F. G. M. *The Bohn Libraries.* New York: Burt Franklin, 1951.

Curwen, Henry. *A History of Booksellers: The Old and the New.* London: Chatto & Windus, 1873.

Dibdin, Thomas Frognall. *Bibliophobia.* London: H. G. Bohn, 1832.

Exman, Eugene. *The Brothers Harper.* New York: Harper & Row, 1965.

Gettmann, Royal A. *A Victorian Publisher: A Study of the Bentley Papers.* Cambridge: Cambridge University Press, 1960.

Gohdes, Clarence. *American Literature in Nineteenth-Century England.* Carbondale: Southern Illinois University Press, 1944.

Growell, Adolph. *Book-Trade Bibliography in the United States in the Nineteenth Century.* New York: The Dibdin Club, 1898.

Kaser, David. *Messrs. Carey & Lea of Philadelphia: A Study in the History of the Booktrade.* Philadelphia: University of Pennsylvania Press, 1957.

Knight, Charles. *Passages of a Working Life.* 3 vols. London: Bradbury & Evans, 1864.

Ladas, Stephen P. *The International Protection of Literary and Artistic Poetry.* 2 vols. New York; The Macmillan Co., 1938.

MacFarlane, Charles. *Reminiscences of a Literary Life.* London: JM, 1917.

Mumby, Frank Arthur. *Publishing and Bookselling: A History from the Earliest Times to the Present Day.* London: Jonathan Cape, 1930.

Neal, John. *Wandering Recollections of a Somewhat Busy Life.* Boston: Roberts Brothers, 1869.

Plant, Marjorie. *The English Book Trade.* London: George Allen & Unwin, Ltd., 1965.

Putnam, George Haven. *Memories of a Publisher, 1865–1915.* London: G. P. Putnam's Sons, 1915.

Rich, Obadiah. *Bibliotheca Americana Nova.* 2 vols. London: O. Rich, 1835.

————. *Catalogue of Books Relating to America.* London: O. Rich, 1832.

————. *A Catalogue of a Collection of Manuscripts Principally in Spanish, Relating to America.* London: O. Rich, 1848.

Spiller, Robert E., and Philip C. Blackburn. *A Descriptive Bibliography of the Writings of James Fenimore Cooper.* New York: R. R. Bowker Co., 1934.

Timperley, C. H., comp. *Dictionary of Printers and Printing.* London: H. Johnson, 1839.

V. RELATED PUBLISHED SOURCES

A. *Contemporary Periodicals*

1. Newspapers

With the exception of the Philadelphia newspaper, all titles listed below are represented by a more or less complete file in the Colindale Newspaper Library of the British Museum. Publication place was London unless otherwise indicated.

The Age	*The Herald*
Bell's Weekly Messenger	*The London Gazette*

The Courier	*The Morning Chronicle*
Evening Bulletin (Philadelphia)	*The Morning Post*
Galignani's Messenger (Paris)	*The Representative*
Hampshire Advertiser (Southampton)	*The Times*

2. Reviews and Magazines

One can glean from Williams' *Life of Washington Irving* an extended collection of references to reviews of Irving's writings in British periodicals. More than likely, Williams used the periodicals of the British Museum in making his original notes. Tragically, a large number of those titles are no longer available there; slip after slip was returned to me marked "Destroyed by bombing in the war." The major periodicals however, as discussed by Walter James Graham, *English Literary Periodicals* (New York: Thomas Nelson & Sons, 1930), are available. Publication place was London unless otherwise noted.

The Athenaeum
Blackwood's Edinburgh Magazine
The Eclectic Magazine of Foreign Literature (New York)
The Edinburgh Review
The European Magazine, and London Review (London and Paris)
Fraser's Magazine
Gentleman's Magazine
The Kaleidoscope (Liverpool)
The Literary Gazette
The London Magazine
The Monthly Review, or, Literary Journal
The New Monthly Magazine and Literary Journal
Quarterly Journal of Literature, Science, and the Arts
Quarterly Review
Westminster Review

B. *Autobiographies, Journals, and Letters*

Bancroft, George. *The Life and Letters of George Bancroft,* ed.

M. A. DeWolfe Howe. 2 vols. London: Hodder & Stoughton, 1908.

Barrow, John. *An Auto-biographical Memoir of Sir John Barrow, Bart., Late of the Admiralty.* London: JM, 1847.

Bristed, Charles Astor. *Five Years in an English University.* New York: G. P. Putnam, 1852.

Constable, John. *The Letters of John Constable, R. A. to C. R. Leslie, R. A. 1826–1827,* ed. Peter Leslie. London: Constable & Co., 1931.

Cooper, James Fenimore. *Correspondence of James Fenimore Cooper,* ed. James Fenimore Cooper. 2 vols. New Haven: Yale University Press, 1922.

Crabbe, George. *The Poetical Works, with his Letters and Journals, and his Life, by his Son.* George Crabbe, Jr., ed. 8 vols. London: JM, 1847.

Disraeli, Benjamin. *Lord Beaconsfield's Correspondence with his Sister, 1832–1852.* London: JM, 1886.

Foster, Emily. *The Journal of Emily Foster,* ed. Stanley T. Williams and Leonard B. Beach. New York: Oxford University Press, 1938.

Griffin, Edmund D. *Remains of the Rev. Edmund D. Griffin,* comp. Francis Griffin. 2 vols. New York: G. & C. Carvell, 1831.

Goodrich, S. G. *Recollections of a Lifetime.* 2 vols. New York: Miller, Orton and Milligan, 1857.

Haydon, Benjamin R. *Autobiography of Benjamin R. Haydon,* ed. Tom Taylor, 2 vols. London: Peter Davis, 1926.

Kemble, Frances Ann. *Record of a Girlhood.* 3 vols. London: Richard Bentley and Son, 1878.

Leslie, C. R. *Autobiographical Recollections,* ed. Tom Taylor. 2 vols. London: JM, 1860.

Moore, Thomas. "Another Moore Letter," ed. Ben Harris McClary. *Notes and Queries,* N.S. XIV (Jan. 1967), 24–25.

_____. *Catalogue of the Loan Collection of Relics of Thomas Moore* [Moore Centenary Celebration in Dublin, May 28, 1870]. Dublin: Joseph Dollard, 1879.

———. *Memoirs, Journal, and Correspondence of Thomas Moore*, ed. Lord John Russell. 8 vols. London: Longman, Brown, Green and Longmans, 1853.

Prescott, William Hickling. *The Correspondence of William Hickling Prescott*, ed. Roger Wolcott. Boston: Houghton Mifflin Co., 1925.

Scott, Walter. *The Letters of Sir Walter Scott* [Centenary Edition], ed. H. J. G. Grierson. 12 vols. London: Constable & Co., Ltd., 1934.

Southey, Robert. *The Life and Correspondence of the Late Robert Southey*, ed. Charles Cuthbert Southey. 6 vols. London: Longman, Brown, Green and Longmans, 1850.

———. *Selections from the Letters of Robert Southey*, ed. John Wood Warter. London: Longman, Brown, Green, Longman, & Roberts, 1856.

Thackeray, William Makepeace. *The Letters and Private Papers of William Makepeace Thackeray*, ed. Gordon N. Ray. 4 vols. London: Oxford University Press, 1946.

Ticknor, George. *Life, Letters, and Journals of George Ticknor*, ed. G. S. Hillard. 2 vols. London: Sampson Low & Co., 1876.

Tuckerman, Henry Theodore. *A Month in England*. London: Richard Bentley, 1854.

Weed, Thurlow. *Letters from Europe and the West Indies, 1843–1862*. Albany: Weed, Parson & Co., 1866.

C. *City Directories and Guides*

Johnstone's London Commercial Guide and Street Directory . . . Corrected to August 31, 1817. London: Barnard and Farley, 1817.

Galignani's New Paris Guide. [13th ed.] Paris: Galignani's, 1825.

Gore's Directory of Liverpool . . . for 1818. Liverpool: J. Gore, 1817.

Robson's Improved Directory, Street-Guide, and Carrier's List [appearing under slightly varying titles]. London: W. Robson, 1820, 1826, 1829, 1832, 1842.

The Royal Blue Book and Fashionable Directory . . . *for 1822*. London: T. Gardiner, 1822.

Pigot and Co.'s Metropolitan New Alphabetical Directory [appearing under varying titles]. London: Pigot and Co., 1828, 1833.

Clayton's Court Guide . . . *corrected for January 1830*. London: Clayton, 1830.

History and General Directory of the Borough of Sheffield, comp. William White. Sheffield: Robert Leader, 1833.

The Directory of Birmingham. Birmingham: Wrightson & Webb, 1835.

Watkins's Commercial and General London Directory. London: F. W. Watkins, 1851.

Hodson's Booksellers, Publishers and Stationers' Directory for London. London: W. H. Hodson, 1855.

VI. RELATED MANUSCRIPT RECORDS AND SCRAPBOOKS

Newspaper Clippings: Local History Scrapbook in Birmingham Public Library.

Rate Book of 1819: Archives Department, City of Westminster Libraries, London.

Printer's Records: A. & R. Spottiswoode (MSS. 48819, ff. 101, 102–103, 106) in British Museum.

Weather Records: Royal Meteorological Society. London.

Court (14/1162/105) and Foreign Office (5/256, 263; 72/240, 300, 301, 329) Records: Public Record Office, London.